THE INSIDER'S GUIDE TO

EASTERN

CANADA

THE INSIDER'S GUIDES

AUSTRALIA • BALI • CALIFORNIA • CANADA • CHINA • EASTERN CANADA • FLORIDA • HAWAII • HONG KONG • INDIA • INDOCHINA • INDONESIA • JAPAN • KENYA • KOREA • NEPAL • NEW ENGLAND • NEW ZEALAND • MALAYSIA AND SINGAPORE • MEXICO • PORTUGAL • RUSSIA • SPAIN • THAILAND • TURKEY • WESTERN CANADA

The Insider's Guide to Eastern Canada
First Published 1993
Moorland Publishing Co Ltd
Moor Farm Road, Airfield Estate, Ashbourne, DE61HD, England
by arrangement with Novo Editions, S.A.
53 rue Beaudouin, 27700 Les Andelys, France
Telefax: (33) 32 54 54 50

© 1993 Novo Editions, S.A.

ISBN: 0 86190 395 1

Created, edited and produced by Novo Editions, S.A.
Editor in Chief: Allan Amsel
Original design concept: Hon Bing-wah
Picture editor and designer: Gaia Text, Munich
Text and artwork composed and information updated
using Ventura Publisher software

PHOTO CREDITS
The Ontario Ministry of Tourism and Recreation — pages 207, 208, 211, 215 and 216–217.

Printed by Samhwa Printing Company Limited, Seoul, Korea

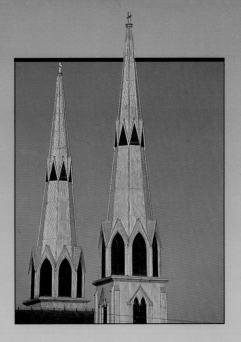

THE INSIDER'S GUIDE TO

EASTERN

CANADA

By Donald Carroll

Photographed by
Nik Wheeler and Robert Holmes

MPC

Contents

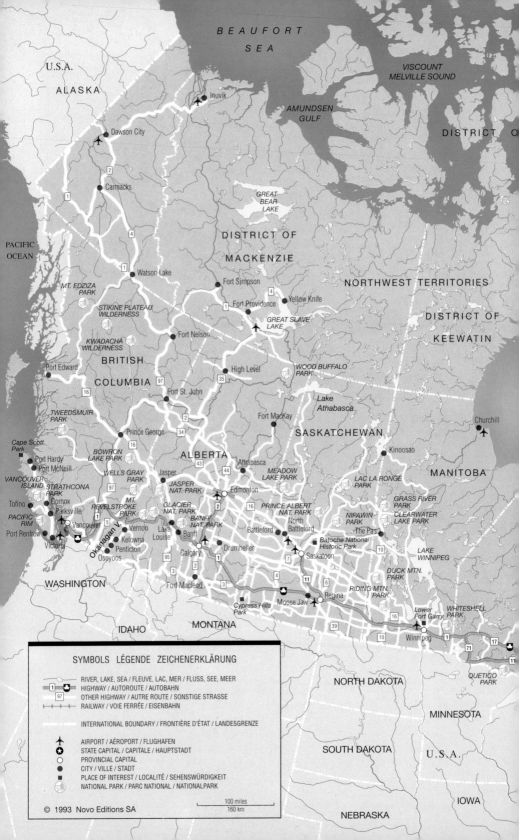

DENMARK
GREENLAND

INSIDER'S GUIDE
CANADA

LANCASTER SOUND

BAFFIN BAY

FRANKLIN

ATLANTIC OCEAN

FOXE BASIN

HUDSON STRAIT

HUDSON BAY

Hebron

Nain

Cartwright

NEWFOUNDLAND

Happy Valley-Goose Bay

Smallwood Reservoir

LABRADOR

L'Anse aux Meadows

Churchill Falls

Lourdes-de-Blanc-Sablon

Labrador City

Springdale
Trinity
Bonavista
Gander
Clarenville
St. John's
Deer Lake
Grand Falls
Whitbourne
CAPE SPEAR
Corner Brook
Marystown
AVALON PEN.
Grand Bank

GROS MORNE NAT. PARK

Long Range Mtn.

Wabush

QUEBEC

POLAR BEAR PARK

WINISK WILD RIVER PARK

JAMES BAY

GULF OF ST. LAWRENCE

Port aux Basques

PARC DE LA GASPESIE

Sainte-Anne-des-Monts
Cap Chat
Gaspé
Gaspé Peninsula
138
Matane
Chéticamp
Ingonosh

ONTARIO

20

NEW BRUNSWICK
Grand Falls

PR. EDWARD ISL.
Louisbourg
105

Quebec
11
Charlottetown

Fredericton
2
Grand Pré
NOVA SCOTIA
40
112

11
Saint John
Windsor
Halifax
Chester
MISSINAIBI LAKE PARK
Annapolis Royal
Lunenberg
PUKASKWA PARK
Digby
11
117
Grand Falls
MAINE
Yarmouth
Shelburne

SUPERIOR PARK
Sudbury
10
LAKE SUPERIOR
Thunder Bay
17
ALGONQUIN PARK
Montreal
69
Ottawa
Cornwall
Sault Ste. Marie
7
401

VERMONT

LAKE HURON
Kingston
LAKE ONTARIO
Waterloo
Kitchener
Toronto
Stratford
St. Catherines
Niagara Falls
NEW HAMPSHIRE
London
Niagara Falls
NEW YORK

MICHIGAN
Windsor
401
LAKE ERIE

LAKE MICHIGAN

ATLANTIC OCEAN

PENNSYLVANIA

Welcome to Canada

TRUE OR FALSE? Canada is an unexciting country with no authentic voice or national identity of its own.

Answer: true.

True, that is, if you consider it exciting to walk along rubbish-strewn streets in constant danger of being mugged, or if you measure a voice's authenticity in decibels, or if you think periodic convulsions of flag-clutching jingoism are symptoms of a healthy national identity. By all of these criteria Canada will be found wanting, but if you like the idea of a gigantic country that

majority of the population is concentrated in a narrow band along the long border with the U.S.

From a strictly demographic point of view, the two most striking things about this population are that it is overwhelmingly urban — over 75 percent of Canadians live in the cities — and surprisingly heterogeneous. Unlike their American counterparts, who have historically been quick to jettison their cultural baggage in the rush to become assimilated, immigrants to Canada have tended to cherish and safe-

can be enjoyed without a gigantic wallet, a New World nation that has taken care not to squander its Old World inheritance, a place where the dazzle of the landscape is matched by the kaleidoscopic mix of peoples who inhabit it, then you will like Canada. A lot.

And there is a lot of it to like. Covering almost 10 million sq km (3.9 million sq miles), it is the third largest country in the world, after Russia and China. Unlike Russia and China, however, or its next-door neighbor to the south, Canada has only 27 million inhabitants — fewer than California. And while the land is divided up into 10 provinces and two immense territories extending well into the Arctic Circle, the vast

guard their distinctive traditions, preserving the old in order to civilize the new. Thus it is not uncommon to see signs in Finnish by Lake Superior or to hear Ukrainian spoken on the Manitoban prairies. Likewise, members of various other nationalities and ethnic groups in Canada have discovered that you can create cheery enclaves without creating dreary ghettos.

It's a pity that President Kennedy appropriated the phrase "a nation of immigrants" to describe the United States, because it actually applies more accurately to Canada (as indeed does another presidential coinage, of more recent vintage, Mr. Bush's "kinder, gentler nation"). Whereas the U.S. may have been *founded* by immigrants, and substantially populated by them for a century or more, Canada is still being shaped by immigration. At the turn of the century the country had a population of barely five million; since then two tidal waves of immigrants — the first before World War I and the second following World War II — have washed up on Canada's shores, helping to boost the population to its present level and helping to determine what kind of nation will enter the 21st century.

Unhappily, it appears at this writing that it will be a nation whose greatest triumph

things, that most Canadians are within reach of American radio and television stations. This has been a major concern of Canadian intellectuals for the better part of this century. It first surfaced as a worry in the twenties, when Canada was absorbed into the American radio system at a time when the U.S. was beginning to flex its imperial muscles. Then, after the end of World War II, when America was at the zenith of its power and influence, there came the new threat of cultural annexation by television.

— the achievement of a multicultural, bilingual state — will be unraveling as the frictions between the two predominant cultures, the British and French, prompt Quebec to tear itself away from the Confederation. But of this more later. Happily, Canada's other great achievement, which is to have shared a continent with America without becoming totally Americanized, looks like it will continue to be a distinguishing feature of the Canadian way of life.

But it won't come easy. It never has. For one thing, most Canadians live close to the U.S. border, which at 6,379 km (3,964 miles) is the longest unguarded national boundary in the world. This means, among other

So seriously was this threat viewed that no fewer than three royal commissions were set up between 1949 and 1961 to address "the problem of American culture in Canada", and specifically to seek ways of organizing "resistance to the absorption of Canada into the general cultural pattern of the United States." There was little the commissioners could do, however, apart from encouraging the Canadian Broadcasting Corporation in its policy of featuring homegrown material. And even this rearguard

OPPOSITE: The town that always stays up to welcome its guests; Niagara Falls gives tourists a sign or two. ABOVE: The town that stays up all summer; Inuvik, in the Northwest Territories, is backlit by the midnight sun.

Even Canadian sport has not escaped American colonization. All of the top teams in the one sport about which Canadians are passionate — ice hockey — play in America's National Hockey League. And having been (quite rightly) converted to the glories of baseball, Canadians see their top baseball teams competing in the American major leagues. Not even their individual sporting heroes seem able to resist the

action, faithfully pursued by the CBC since its creation in 1936, has never received whole-hearted government support. And today that support is decidedly half-hearted: during the time I spent in Canada 11 CBC television stations had to close down because of cuts in government funding. And Radio Canada International — the Canadian equivalent of the BBC World Service — is facing almost certain extinction because of lack of government support. Meanwhile, the most recent surveys show that 80 percent of total television viewing in the big metropolitan areas near the border is of American programs; even in Edmonton, which receives only Canadian stations, the figure is 66 percent.

Nor is the cross-border invasion limited to the airwaves. American films occupy most of the cinema screens, while American magazines dominate the newsagents' shelves. And of the 40 books on the national bestseller lists when I was there — fiction and non-fiction, hardcover and paperback — only six were by Canadian authors, and only three of those were published by Canadian firms!

Americans: within the past few years, Wayne Gretzky, "The Great One", ice hockey's all-time superstar, abandoned Edmonton for Los Angeles, and Ben Johnson, Canada's greatest-ever sprinter, was stripped of his Olympic gold medal after failing a drugs test, and then had to watch while the medal was awarded to his arch-rival, the American Carl Lewis. Perhaps the only sport in which Canadians have managed to remain somewhat aloof is American football, but that is only because they enthusiastically embraced the game, made a few minor adjustments here and there, and then renamed it Canadian football. I have watched it (with more enthusiasm, it must be said, than most Canadians) and I have to say that one needs a real aficionado, or perhaps a theologian, to explain how it differs from the original.

ABOVE TO BOTTOM RIGHT: Some of the faces reflecting Canada's ethnic and cultural diversity.

It is tempting to say — no, it is true to say, so I will say it: Canadian football is symbolic of Canadian society insofar as it presents the outsider with difficulties in distinguishing it from its more familiar American counterpart. And this, not surprisingly, fills Canadians with an overwhelming sense of frustration. So much so, in fact, that when I told a prominent Canadian businessman over lunch (truthfully) that I had never met a Canadian I didn't like, he reacted with exasperation bordering on disgust. "That's precisely our problem", he said. "*Nobody* dislikes us, because nobody knows us. To the rest of the world we're just nicer, quieter Americans." Although I felt constrained to insist that this was not a bad thing to be, I could see his point: it must be maddening to be forever treated like the Canadian dollar is treated,

quip, told Americans on a visit to Washington in 1969: "Living next to you is in some ways like sleeping with an elephant. No matter how friendly and even-tempered the beast, one is affected by every twitch and grunt."

John Bierman, the distinguished English biographer and author of *Dark Safari* who now lives in Toronto, puts it this way: "If you could perforate along the 49th parallel, tear along the dotted line and push Canada out into the Pacific or Atlantic, I'm sure they'd be a totally different people. But the identity crisis is perpetual."

To deal with this "crisis" many Canadians have chosen to reach back, sometimes way back, into their colonial past for a suitable identity. Thus there are parts of the country where stylized versions of the British and French ways of life have been lovingly, not to say fanatically, preserved. This understandably leads outsiders to the frequent conclusion that Canadians have a neurotic preoccupation with being seen as Not-Americans. And indeed in some cases they have. But in my travels around the country I have found that for all the agonizing over their soft-focus national profile, the great majority of Canadians sensibly realize that they quite

as a slightly discounted version of the real thing.

Equally maddening, if not more so, is the fact that most *Americans* regard Canadians as nicer, quieter versions of themselves. No wonder, then, that Canadians are forever worrying about their national identitiy being obliterated by the long shadows cast by the colossus to the south. As former Prime Mininster Pierre Trudeau, in a celebrated

probably live in the best of all possible worlds.

After all, their country is situated in a neighborhood where there is only one neighbor — and that one is so friendly that neither of them has ever bothered to put up a fence. They have the luxury of living in cities that are not only handsome and comfortable but come equipped with the world's largest backyard, in the form of wilderness areas of awe-inspiring beauty. Their society has the civilizing patina of history while enjoying all the benefits of modern technology. In short, as a member of the Commonwealth of Nations with a large Francophone population, Canada is in the privileged position of being able to boast of a British monarch but American telephones, French cooking but American plumbing.

In the great tradition of ignoramuses who often say prescient things by accident, Al Capone once said, "I don't even know what street Canada is on." Everyone laughed, but old Scarface had put his chubby finger on one of Canada's most pressing needs. Nor could he have known that after his death Canada *would* come to live on one principal street, the Trans-Canada Highway. Over 90 percent of all Canadians now live within 80 km (50 miles) of this one road. What's more, the great preponderance of major tourist attractions are within easy reach of the TCH. Nearly 8,000 km (5,000 miles) long, with a water jump at each end, the highway runs all the way from St. John's, Newfoundland to Victoria, British Columbia, at the tip of Vancouver Island. In this book we will follow it as far as Thunder Bay, Ontario, on the northwest shore of Lake Superior, pausing en route to explore the byways and unbeaten paths that lead to towns and cities of unusual charm as well as to scenic areas of exceptional loveliness, both rugged and gentle.

Now, before we begin our journey, a word about prices. With a few exceptions, I have deliberately avoided giving exact prices. This is because I have learned that the only thing you can absolutely depend on in this business is that the prices will have changed before the ink is dry (some-

times, surprisingly, for the better — as special offers and new types of discounts are introduced). I have therefore confined myself to price *categories* where hotels and restaurants are concerned. HOTELS in the **Luxury** category, for example, will charge over $150 a night for a double room; **Mid-range** hotels will charge between $75 and $150; **Inexpensive** hotels will charge less, sometimes much less. At RESTAURANTS listed as **Expensive** you can expect to pay more than $50 per person for a meal, excluding wine; **Moderate** restaurants will charge between $25 and $50; **Inexpensive** ones will cost you less — sometimes, again, much less. When hotels or restaurants fall at either of the two extremes — *very* expensive or inexpensive — I have so indicated.

Welcome to Canada

Another word about prices. All the prices given in this book, and the categories outlined above, are in Canadian dollars. Now, most travel writers I have read will tell you to remember that the Canadian dollar is worth about 20 percent less than the American dollar. My advice is precisely the opposite: *Forget* that the Canadian dollar is worth less. Don't translate; think in American dollars. This is because all the prices quoted in Canada are exclusive of the layers of taxes that are added later — sales taxes, goods and services taxes, even "taxes on taxes", as one hotelier wanly pointed out to me. So by the time your bill is added in Canadian dollars, it will come to almost exactly the original, untaxed figure in American dollars. If you keep in mind this one simple trick, you will know a real bargain when you see one.

And when you see Canada, you will rapidly begin to suspect that when it comes to shopping for countries, Canadians may have found the best bargain of all.

As the country's Chinatowns attest, Canadians have managed to create cheery enclaves without creating dreary ghettoes.

The Country and Its People

THE HISTORICAL BACKGROUND

Just when the first immigrants arrived in Canada is a matter of considerable debate among the experts — some say it could have been up to 40,000 years ago, while others insist that it was no more than 11,000 years ago — but there is no argument over who they were or where they came from. They were nomadic tribes from Asia, principally Siberia and Mongolia, who crossed into North America across a land bridge which

around 1000 AD. Arriving at the northwestern tip of Newfoundland, which they named Vinland ("land of grapevines"), they established a settlement at the site of present-day L'Anse aux Meadows. Unfortunately, the archaeological remains don't tell us how long the settlement survived or what finished it off, but it is generally assumed that a combination of the harsh winters and harsh Indians drove the settlers away before they had a chance to establish a viable colony.

The next proven landing in Canada was not for another five centuries, when in

appeared over the Bering Strait during successive Ice Ages. They and their descendants then fanned out across the continent, establishing different Amerindian societies and civilizations which in some cases became highly developed as early as the eighth millenium BC.

THE FIRST EUROPEANS

There is evidence, although inconclusive, to suggest that the first European to set foot in North America was a sixth-century Irish monk, St. Brendan, who according to legend landed briefly on the coast of Newfoundland. But the earliest verified landing was made by Vikings sailing from Greenland

1497 the Venetian John Cabot (*né* Giovanni Caboto) arrived in Newfoundland, and then Nova Scotia, to claim these new-found lands for England and Henry VII. (For all practical — i.e., fishing — purposes the nearby sea had already been claimed by the Portuguese, Basque, and Breton fishermen who in the previous century had discovered the Grand Banks fishing grounds off the coast of Newfoundland to be among the richest in the world.) The next claimant to what was already shaping up as another stage for the worldwide Anglo-French rivalry was the Breton Jacques Cartier, who in 1534 sailed into the Gulf of St. Lawrence, touching land at Prince Edward Island, which he named Ile St. Jean, and the Gaspé

Peninsula before sailing down the St. Lawrence as far as an Indian village in the shadow of an impressive hill, which he named Mont Réal. He claimed the entire area for France, referrring to it by the Algonquin Indians' word for "settlement": Kannata.

NEW FRANCE

Since Cartier didn't return to France laden with the hoped-for gold and gems, French interest in Canada quickly waned, only to be revived at the start of the seventeenth century by, of all things, the demands of *haute couture*. In a word, furs. Thus in 1605 the French explorer Samuel de Champlain established the first permanent European settlement in Canada at Port Royal, Nova Scotia, on the Bay of Fundy, in hopes of trading with the Indians for their beaver pelts. Three years later Champlain founded another settlement on a plateau overlooking the St. Lawrence River at the bend where the river suddenly narrows. He named the village Quebec, and as the center of the fur trade it rapidly grew into the most important city in New France.

Following in the footsteps of the explorers and the fur traders, the Jesuits swiftly began the spiritual and intellectual colonization of the region. Their more contemplative lay counterparts, the Société de Notre Dame, moved in on Cartier's "royal mountain" and founded the settlement of Montreal in 1642. Before long it had supplanted Quebec as the center of the fur trade in New France.

The two decades spanning the middle of the seventeenth century were difficult ones for the French settlers, as they became inexorably drawn into the bitter tribal conflicts between the Hurons, their principal trading partners, and the warlike Iroquois. But the real threat to their colonial supremacy came, as always, from the British. Although the British had watched uneasily as New France expanded, their primary concerns had remained the settling and securing of their American colonies and the exploitation of the fertile fishing grounds off the Canadian coast. Canada itself was of interest only insofar as somewhere within its precincts there had to be the long-sought Northwest

Passage to the Orient. Gradually, however, it began to dawn that Canada, or New France, was part of a continent that was itself a treasure trove of riches — and Britain had the key to the back door.

In 1610 the English navigator Henry Hudson sailed into the giant bay that now bears his name. Sixty years later Hudson Bay in turn gave its name to a commercial enterprise, the Hudson's Bay Company, which was to leave an indelible mark on the history of Canada. Formed by British fur merchants to provide an alternative to

Quebec as an outlet for the fur trade, it was granted by Charles II right to all the lands drained by rivers flowing into Hudson Bay. Thus backed by a solicitous sovereign and a powerful navy, it was to become the largest fur trading company in North America, and is still today a force to be reckoned with in Canadian retailing.

Although British military activity in Canada was minimal during the War of the Spanish Succession (1701–1713), under the Treaty of Utrecht France was forced to relinquish all claims to Hudson Bay and

OPPOSITE: A bridal party of Kwakiutl Indians, photographed by Edward Curtis in 1914, arrives at the groom's village. ABOVE: Another early way of arriving at villages.

Newfoundland, and to give up Acadia, which the British promptly renamed Nova Scotia ("New Scotland"). There was a period of relative peace and tranquility for the next 40 years, broken only in 1744 by the British seizure of the French fortress of Louisbourg on Cape Breton Island. It was handed back four years later under the Peace of Aix-la-Chapelle.

The Seven Years' War, known in America as the French and Indian War, was to be the decisive turning point in Canadian history. The war began well for the French and their

Indian allies, as the British forces in battle after battle showed themselves to be tactically unprepared for what amounted to quasi-guerrilla warfare. But the tide began to turn in 1758 with the arrival of British land and naval reinforcements. A successful siege of the fortress at Louisbourg led to its recapture, giving the British control of the entrance to the Gulf of St. Lawrence, while at the Lake Ontario end of the St. Lawrence River the British took the vital Fort Frontenac. Then, in the summer of 1759, an assault force under the command of 32-year-old General James Wolfe, the youngest general in the British army, sailed from the Atlantic down the St. Lawrence to Quebec. All summer long Wolfe's artillery pounded the city, reducing it to rubble but without budging the French forces under the Marquis de Montcalm in their citadel atop the steep cliffs above the town. Then, on the night of September 12, Wolfe tried a daring maneuver. He led a force of 5,000 infantrymen in boats to a point behind the city, where they silently scaled the cliffs and assembled on

the Plains of Abraham. The next morning, the startled French forces, flushed out of their fortified redoubt, were slaughtered. Quebec had fallen. Both Wolfe and Montcalm were killed. The battle had lasted 15 minutes.

Although it was one of the shortest battles on record, its consequences ultimately reverberated around the world. The fall of Quebec effectively marked the fall of New France, and when the French handed over all of Canada under the terms of the Treaty of Paris in 1763, the British were left as undisputed masters of the entire North American continent. Some historians argue, however, that it was a Pyrrhic victory in that the British were also left over-confident and over-stretched, not to mention out-of-pocket, while the many American colonists who fought on the British side, including one George Washington, had gained wartime experience as well as insights into British military strategy that would prove invaluable a few years later when the Americans launched their War of Independence.

BRITISH CANADA

The conquest of Canada brought another problem for Britain: what to do about the predominantly French population in the new territory over which they now ruled. In the end, they did the decent thing — and paid dearly for it. By passing the Quebec Act of 1774, the British gave the French Canadians the right to continue using their own language, the secure ownership of their property, the primacy of French civil law, and the freedom to practice the Roman Catholic religion (including the Church's right to collect tithes). This did not go down at all well with the overwhelmingly Protestant population in the 13 American colonies, who were already incensed over what they considered unjust taxes imposed by Britain to help pay for the war against France. And when the boundaries of the province of Quebec were extended to protect the French Canadian fur traders operating in the Ohio and Mississippi River valleys, the American colonists decided that they had had enough.

The colonial rebellion became the American Revolution late in 1775 with attacks on Montreal and Quebec City which, had they been successful, would almost certainly have heralded a fairly swift victory for the Americans. In fact, the attack on Montreal was successful, but so brutish was the behavior of the "liberators" that most French Canadians decided they would prefer not to be thus liberated and went on to fight fiercely alongside the British, thus denying the Americans an early knockout.

By the time the war ended in 1783, Canadians had a new neighbor, the United States of America, and also a lot of new Canadians, for about 50,000 Americans who remained loyal to the British Crown had fled northwards. Most of them settled in Nova Scotia and what is now New Brunswick, although about 7,000 made their way to present-day Ontario. More still arrived at the end of the war claiming to be Loyalists, but their devotion to George III might possibly have been influenced by the offer of free land to Loyalist immigrants. In any case, as a result of the American Revolution, Canada received a large transfusion of English-speaking immigrants, many of whom were well-educated and had occupied positions of responsibility and influence under the old colonial regime. Thus did the balance of power in Canada begin to shift away from the French Canadians.

In the years following the war Canada became transformed both politically and territorially. In 1791 the province of Quebec was divided into Upper Canada (mainly English-speaking, now Ontario) and Lower Canada (mainly French-speaking, now Quebec), each with its own lieutenant governor and parliament. Meanwhile, the vast and hitherto neglected lands to the west were gradually being opened up in the wake of the pioneering explorations of Alexander Mackenzie, who in 1793 became the first white man to cross Canada all the way to the Pacific coast, and Simon Fraser and David Thompson, who were the first to map the great mountains and rivers from the Rockies to the Pacific.

The War of 1812 was the last neighborhood brawl before the United States and Canada settled down to live together more or less happily ever after. The war had a number of causes: border disputes, British interference with American shipping, fierce rivalry in the lucrative fur trade, American

claims that the British were behind Indian raids on American border settlements, British claims that Americans were trying to export republicanism to Canada, and so forth. Whatever the justice of any of these claims, they added up to war. Although both sides got in some telling blows—the Americans captured Toronto (or York, as it then was) and burnt it to the ground, whereupon the British retaliated by capturing Washington and burning the White House—neither side really seemed to have much appetite for the fight. The Americans wanted to get on

with nation-building and the British wanted to get on with countering the Napoleonic threat at home, while the Canadians wanted to be left in peace. So in 1814 they got together and declared the war over.

Not surprisingly, considering the enormous size of the two countries, the border issue was not immediately resolved. The first major step was taken in 1818 when they agreed on the 49th parallel as their mutual border from the Great Lakes to the Rockies, but it was not until 1842, after much haggling and a little skirmishing, that the Canadian border with the New England states was established. The last link, the border with the Oregon Territory west of the Rockies, was established along the 49th parallel in 1846.

As increased immigration swelled the population, French Canadians became convinced that the British were deliberately trying to dilute their power by swamping them with English-speaking newcomers.

ABOVE: The opening ceremony at Expo 86 in Vancouver, British Columbia. OPPOSITE: The view from Fort Anne in Annapolis Royal, Nova Scotia.

As a result, in 1837 French Canadians under the leadership of Louis-Joseph Papineau demanded automony for Lower Canada (Quebec) so that they could establish an independent republic. When the British refused, a violent rebellion broke out which was not finally defeated until 1838. It was the first time that the call for an independent Quebec had been heard. It would not be the last.

Nor were the French Canadians the only ones growing impatient with British rule around this time. In Upper Canada (Ontario) a rough and ready coalition of economic have-nots led by newspaper editor William Lyon Mackenzie rose up against the oligarchic Tory establishment and demanded that the government be remodeled along American lines. When these demands, predictably, were not met, Mackenzie too resorted to armed rebellion with even less success than Papineau, whom he soon joined in exile in the U.S.

Although both insurrections had been easily put down, they succeeded in lighting an anti-colonialist fuse that would prove unquenchable.

Nevertheless, Canada at mid-century was a picture of expansion and growth. New waves of immigrants boosted the population of the Maritime Provinces, which were beginning to prosper as a result of their flourishing lumber, fishing, and shipbuilding industries. The population explosion also led to the creation of settlements further westward, in addition to providing the labor needed to build the canals, roads, and railways that made the westward expansion possible. In less than 20 years, over 3,000 km or 2,000 miles of railroad tracks were laid. All that was needed for Canada to become a truly coast-to coast country was for some sort of tug to be exerted from the other side of the Rockies. That tug, when it came, turned out to be a powerful yank: in 1858 gold was discovered in the Fraser River Valley.

The Gold Rush that followed was so frenetic, and so dominated by Americans rushing northwards to stake their claims, that Britain quickly proclaimed a new Crown colony, British Columbia, to control the stampede into the territory.

The entrance to Ottawa's Confederation Building.

British colonies now straddled the continent from the Atlantic to the Pacific.

THE DOMINION OF CANADA

With the old Anglo-French strains still causing problems, and with the turmoil to the south caused by the American Civil War, not to mention the ordinary growing pains brought on by rapid population growth and territorial expansion, it was widely felt that the colonies should come together and forge a stronger union among themselves. So in 1864 delegates from the various colonies convened in Charlottetown, Prince Edward Island, to begin laying the groundwork for a new confederation. Three years later, the British North America Act of 1867 created

the Dominion of Canada, in which the colonies of Nova Scotia, New Brunswick, Ontario, and Quebec became provinces in a confederated union with self-rule under a parliamentary system of government. Manitoba joined the Confederation in 1870, British Columbia in 1871, and Prince Edward Island in 1873. Alberta and Saskatchewan joined in 1905; Newfoundland, typically, held out until 1949, when it finally became Canada's tenth province.

As important as this political union was to Canada's development, it was more symbolic than real so long as there was no corresponding physical link between the provinces. In fact, three of the provinces — Nova Scotia, Prince Edward Island, and British Columbia — only agreed to join the Confederation on condition that a transcontinental railway was built to tie the new nation together. Work on this mammoth project began in 1881 and, incredibly, was completed in only four years. In 1885, at Rogers Pass in the Selkirk Mountains, the last spike was driven: the Canadian Pacific Railway was in business.

As was to be expected, however, this mighty triumph of engineering was not achieved without casualties. The coming of the Iron Horse meant the virtual disappearance of the buffalo, the driving of Indians from their ancestral homelands, and the deaths of hundreds of (mostly Chinese) laborers on the railroad itself. It also precipitated a bloody uprising in 1885 on the part of the Matis, who were the descendants of

French trappers and Indian women, aided and abetted by several tribes of Plains Indians, all of whom felt threatened by the armies of new settlers swarming over their land. Already driven out of Manitoba as far west as the southern banks of the Saskatchewan River, the Matis and their Indian allies, under the leadership of Louis Riel, overwhelmed the Mounted Police post at Duck Lake, attacked the town of Battleford, and captured and burned Fort Pitt. But their successes were short-lived. Before long they were subdued by the superior firepower of

Prairie Provinces became one of the great grain-producing areas of the world. And, for icing on the national cake, in 1896 gold was discovered in the Klondike, setting off the biggest gold rush in history as 100,000 fortune-seekers poured into the Yukon. These were heady times.

Thus Canada entered the twentieth century in a buoyant mood. It was also blessed during the years 1896–1911 with one of its greatest prime ministers, Sir Wilfrid Laurier, a French Canadian and Roman Catholic who set himself the Herculean task of end-

the Canadian forces, and Riel was hanged. His execution became another source of resentment among French Canadians, who felt that he would not have been treated so harshly had he not been a Roman Catholic of French ancestry.

With the country now linked literally and politically from sea to sea, the final years of the nineteenth century saw Canada blossom dramatically as a nation. As thousands upon thousands of new immigrants arrived, new lands were settled and cultivated, hydroelectric projects were initiated, new manufacturing industries were started up alongside the already-thriving industries of lumbering, fishing, mining, pulp and paper. Above all, agriculture boomed as the

ing the antagonism and suspicion between Canada's Anglo and French communities. But World War I came along and deepened the rift: French Canadians violently objected to military conscription, which was introduced in 1917 after the Canadian volunteer forces fighting alongside the British in the trenches had suffered such appalling losses that there were no volunteers left to fight. The French Canadian point of view — that the war had nothing to do with them, and therefore they shouldn't be drafted to fight in it — left much residual bitterness on both sides after the war was over.

A happier legacy of the war was an economy enriched by a vastly increased manufacturing capacity, streamlined industrial development, expanded mining activity, and burgeoning exports of wheat. Along with Canada's post-war prosperity came growing independence from Britain, acknowledged by the British at the Imperial Conference of 1926 when Canada was granted the right to conduct its own international affairs without reference to London, and sealed by the Statute of Westminster in 1931 which made Canada an independent nation.

Then came the Depression, which was even worse in Canada than in the U. S. Suddenly the Promised Land was a ravaged land, as drought erased the wheat fields and unemployment stalked the cities. The misery of the "Dirty Thirties", as the Canadians called the decade, lasted until September 1939 when Hitler marched to the rescue by marching into Poland. Canada, following Britain's lead, immediately declared war on Germany, whereupon the economy coughed, spluttered, then roared back to life.

Also revived, sadly, was the bitter Anglo-French debate over military conscription, which once again split the country. And, again, Canada suffered battlefield losses out of all proportion to its population. On the other side of the ledger, the Canadian economy prospered out of all proportion to its pre-war capacity as almost 10 percent of the population were engaged in war-related industries. Thanks to the war, Canada became one of the world's major industrial nations as well as an important military power, a co-founder of the United Nations, and a member of NATO.

Peace was as good to Canada as the war had been. A huge oil field was discovered near Edmonton, Alberta, in 1947; giant uranium deposits were discovered in Ontario and Saskatchewan; its extraordinary mineral riches made Canada the world's leading producer of nickel, zinc, lead, copper, gold, and silver; its inexhaustible water resources made possible countless hydroelectric projects, including the world's biggest; its forests made it the world's foremost exporter of newsprint, while its oceans made it the world's foremost exporter of fish. And as if that weren't enough, Canada was fortunate in having the world's best customer for raw materials right on its doorstep.

Another milestone in Canada's rise among the world's top industrial nations was the opening in 1959 of the St. Lawrence Seaway, a joint U.S.–Canadian project that made possible shipping from the Great Lakes to the Atlantic. Three years later the Trans-Canada Highway was completed, a concrete link spanning all 10 provinces.

In 1967 Canada celebrated its hundredth birthday by throwing itself a big party in the form of a World's Fair — Expo '67 — in Montreal. And Canadians had much to celebrate: a vigorous and rapidly expanding

economy, one of the highest standards of living in the world, advanced social welfare programs providing health care and other benefits for all citizens, virtually unlimited natural resources, and a history of international conduct such that Canada had managed to join the front rank of the world's nations without making any enemies. What better reasons for having a party?

CANADA TODAY

Alas, there was a ghost at the birthday party. The old specter of separatism which had haunted the Confederation during the entire century of its existence was suddenly summoned up in a speech by visiting President de Gaulle. Speaking to a large throng outside the Montreal City Hall, he declared, *"Vive le Québec libre!"* Considering that he was present in Canada as a guest of a nation

OPPOSITE: Similar headgear, but worlds apart: faces from the Northwest Territories (left) and the southern prairies. ABOVE: The Prince and Princess of Wales at the opening of Vancouver's Expo 86.

celebrating its "unity through diversity", this was mischief-making on an epic scale.

With their clamorings having thus been endorsed by the President of France, Quebec's separatists found new heart for the struggle to wrench the province away from the rest of the nation. The Parti Québecois was formed under the militant leadership of René Lévesque, and won 23 percent of the vote in the 1970 provinical elections. That same year the separatist movement turned nasty around its fringes, as the so-called *Front de Liberation du Québec* (FLQ) resorted

became a brushfire and Lévesque's Parti Québecois were swept into power in the provincial elections. Immediately Lévesque embarked on a campaign to emphasize Quebec's separation. In particular, strict language laws were passed to ensure that French, and only French, would be the official language of Quebec. Not only that, but a Commission de la Langue Française was created to operate as a kind of language police in stamping out every last trace of English in the province — even down to the humble apostrophe, if caught being used in

to outright terrorism, kidnapping the British Trade Commissioner and murdering the Canadian Labour Minister, Pierre Laporte. Prime Minister Pierre Trudeau responded by invoking the War Measures Act and sending 10,000 troops into the province. The crackdown succeeded; the FLQ was crushed and Laporte's killers were caught. Three years later the Parti Québecois won only six seats in the 110-seat provincial parliament.

Despite this electoral setback, and the Trudeau government's concessions to the Quebecois, including the Official Languages Act by which French became Canada's second official language, the flames of separatism refused to die out. Then in 1976, to widespread astonishment, the flames

a non-French way (e.g., to create a possessive noun).

Alarmed by the Anglophobia underlying this outbreak of cultural chauvinism, English-speaking people and businesses fled the province in droves — much to the delight of the Quebecois extremists but much to the detriment of Quebec's economy. Then, in 1980, the pendulum swung back the other way again; in a referendum on separation, Quebecois rejected the proposal by a large majority. And at the next election Lévesque's separatists were voted out of office. In 1987 the Conservative government of Brian Mulroney made a significant gesture towards the Quebecois when the prime minister signed a document recognizing them as a "distinct society". The following year, in what seemed like a reciprocal gesture of appreciation, Quebec gave Mulroney's Conservatives a large part of their majority in the national elections. It seemed, at last, that the flames of separatism had finally been extinguished.

Not so. As before, the desire for separation among the Quebecois simply smoldered unnoticed, waiting to be re-ignited into the burning issue it had so often been in the past. And, sure enough, it blazed back into prominence at the start of the nineties.

ment recommended that a new referendum on sovereignty for the province be held in 1992 and, if approved by the voters, that Quebec should become an independent sovereign state one year from the date of the referendum. Although the voters rejected the idea in 1992, the betting is that next time the proposition is put to them they *will* vote to let Quebec go its own way.

The reason is that *next* time — for the first time — the other Canadians are not going to beg them to stay. All across Canada I heard the same message: every time the people in

This time, however, nobody was able to say precisely what set it alight. The best explanation I heard came from Don Johnson, a columnist for the Toronto *Globe and Mail.* "We are merely advised that Quebeckers feel humiliated, the status quo is unacceptable and unhappiness prevails", he said with a helpless shrug. He then went on to compare it to the breakdown of a marriage — "where neither party can point to a specific cause, but there is a general feeling that a divorce would be preferable."

At any rate, whatever the cause of the latest "unhappiness", it looks increasingly likely that this 125-year-old marriage is headed for eventual divorce. In March 1991 a commission set up by the Quebec parlia-

Quebec throw a tantrum we give them what they want, and they're always demanding special treatment; if they want to go, let them go. That is obviously a crude paraphrase of a more complicated sentiment, but it is nonetheless a sentiment that I encountered everywhere I went in Canada. And my experience is borne out by a recent opinion poll showing that over 75 percent of English-speaking Canadians would be happy to bid *adieu* to Quebec. This means, among other things, that any federal government would be severely limited in the inducements it could offer the Quebecois to reconsider, which

The maple leaf or the fleur-de-lis? Will it be the national or the provincial flag that flies over Quebec in future?

in turn would hurt feelings that are already bruised. No, Canada's prospects of surviving in its present shape do not look good.

I suppose it is impertinent for a non-Canadian to offer an opinion in the matter, but I will anyway. I find it terribly, terribly sad to contemplate the idea of a great nation dismembering itself, especially when it had seemed so close to finding the right formula for becoming — multiculturally, bilingually — a near-perfect example to the rest of the world of how to build a terrific country. One can only hope that good sense and good will ultimately will prevail.

GEOGRAPHY AND CLIMATE

William Lyon Mackenzie King, Canada's longest-serving prime minister, observed at the beginning of his third term of office in 1936: "If some countries have too much history, we have too much geography."

It's hard to argue with that. Spread over almost 10 million sq km, Canada stretches more than 5,500 km (3,400 miles) from Cape Spear, Newfoundland, in the east to the Alaskan border in the west, and 4,600 km (2,900 miles) from Lake Erie's Pelee Island in the south to Cape Columbia on Ellesmere Island in the north (which is only 800 km or 500 miles from the North Pole). Yes, *much* geography.

Within this vastness, predictably, one finds stunning topographical extremes. Almost half the country, for example, is forested — one single forest zone of conifers extends for 6,000 km (3,730 miles) in a wide sweep from Newfoundland to the far north — while similarly enormous tracts of land are empty, treeless prairies. There are millions of acres of flood plains and marshy lowlands, and there are the majestic Rocky Mountains. (Canada's highest mountain, at 5,951 m or 19,525 ft, Mt. Logan, is not in the Rockies but in the St. Elias Mountains of the southwestern Yukon.)

And then there is the water. Canada is awash in lakes and rivers; they account for over seven percent of the country's total

The spectacular Mackenzie Mountains divide the Yukon from the Northwest Territories.

area. There are 400,000 of them in Ontario alone. Three of the 20 longest rivers in the world are to be found in Canada. In all, the country has a staggering 25 percent of the world's fresh water resources.

Geologically, Canada can be divided into five distinct regions, not counting the archipelago of islands inside the Arctic Circle. The **Appalachian** region is that hilly, wooded part of the country bounded on the west by the St. Lawrence River and on the east by the Atlantic, and includes the Maritime Provinces, Newfoundland, and the Gaspé Peninsula. It belongs to an ancient mountain system, now eroded to modest elevations, that reaches as far south as Alabama.

The **St. Lawrence Lowlands** comprise that swath of land from the mouth of the St. Lawrence River to the Great Lakes. This fertile flood plain is home to most of Canada's people, industry, and commerce.

The **Prairies** spread across the provinces of Manitoba, Saskatchewan, and Alberta, and on up into the Northwest Territories. The rich soil in the southern reaches, where the prairies join the Great Plains of the U.S., yields great golden seas of wheat which gradually dry up in Alberta, giving way to huge cattle ranches.

The **Western Cordillera** is bounded on the east by the Rocky Mountains and on the west by the Coast Mountains. In between is the spectacular diversity of British Columbia, a province of soaring mountain peaks, alpine lakes and meadows, large boreal forests, intricate networks of rivers, deep blue lakes and long green valleys.

The fifth region, the **Canadian Shield**, encompasses everything else: the immense, horseshoe-shaped land mass that surrounds Hudson Bay, and stretches from the coast of Labrador down to the St. Lawrence Lowlands, over to the Prairies, and up to the Arctic. Covering some 4.7 million sq km (1.8 million sq miles), about half the entire area of Canada, this rough-hewn, rock-strewn, lake-pitted wilderness is one of the oldest sections of the earth's crust.

Dotted throughout all of these regions are enclaves of particular note: Canada's 34 national parks. With a total area of over 140,000 sq km (54,000 sq miles), the national parks system is designed to protect

wildlife of all kinds — wild flowers as well as wild animals — from the predations of man.

The flora and fauna that decorate and populate the Canadian landscape naturally vary from region to region. There are, however, some animals that can be found just about everywhere: squirrels and chipmunks, rabbits and hares, porcupines and skunks. Equally widespread throughout the country's forests and woodlands are deer, moose, black bears, beavers, wild geese, and ducks. The richest fishing grounds in Canada — possibly in the world — are to be found in the Gulf of St. Lawrence and the waters of the continental shelf off Newfoundland: cod, herring, mackerel, tuna, oysters, clams, lobsters, and scallops are only the best-known of the 800 species of edible marine life with which the area teems.

In the St. Lawrence Lowlands the coniferous forests of spruce, firs, and pines that sweep from Labrador to the Rockies begin to be infiltrated by aspen, birch, oak, elm, beech, hemlock, and ash. In southern Quebec the sugar maples appear, and in southwestern Ontario the walnut and tulip trees, the hickories and dogwoods. As for its animal life, the region is better known for its bipeds than its quadrupeds.

In the prairies, one animal in particular is conspicuous by its absence: the plains buffalo. The few who have survived are now in the national parks, while their place has been taken by great herds of cattle. Denizens of the semi-arid grasslands of the southern prairies include kangaroo rats, hares, pronghorn antelopes, and the ranchers' nemesis, coyotes.

In the mountain ranges of the Western Cordillera one can find, if one tries hard enough, brown bears, elk, mountain goats, bighorn sheep, and the bosses of the upper slopes, grizzly bears. In the lakes and rivers there is some of the best trout and salmon fishing to be found anywhere in the world.

In the great expanse of forests across northern Canada are the largest concentrations of fur-bearing animals: mink, ermine, marten, muskrat, beaver, river otter, weasel, lynx, bobcat, wolves, and wolverines. Further north, in the tundra, are the arctic foxes, lemmings, musk ox, and caribou, as well as snow geese and trumpeter swans. Still further north, where the frigid waters are full of whales, seals, and walrus, the mighty polar bear patrols the ice packs of the Arctic.

Because words like "frigid" and "polar" and "ice" and "Arctic" — and even the subtly prejudicial "north" — are all words that we readily associate with Canada, most foreigners think that Canada's climate can probably be summed up in one word: cold. This is a mistake. True, Canada occupies the northern — and therefore colder — part of the continent, but this ignores the fact that Pelee Island, Ontario is on the same latitude

tion in Canada falls as snow, compared to a worldwide average of five percent. And the only national capital colder than Ottawa is Ulaan Bataar, the capital of Mongolia; Winnipeg is the coldest city in the world with a poulation of more than half a million; and residents of Montreal shovel more snow every year than residents of any other city.

But there is a bright side to all this. It's just that: brightness. Canada may be refrigerated half the time, but it is sunlit most of the time. Which means that it is beautiful all the time, brilliantly white in winter, infinitely

as Rome. True, the dominant images of western Canada are the snow-capped peaks of the Rockies, but this obscures the fact that those same Rockies form a protective wall that guarantees Vancouver milder winters than, say, Dallas. True, the eastern coast takes a beating from the Atlantic, but parts of it are also caressed by the Gulf Stream, creating swimming beaches equal to any in the Mediterranean.

Having said that, one has to admit that for much of the year Canada is a theme park called Winter. Harold Town, one of Canada's leading artists, once said: "We are a nation of thermometers monitoring cold fronts.... We jig to the crunch of snow." Indeed, over a third of the annual precipita-

and variously green the rest of year. What's more, its meteorological diversity mirrors its geographical diversity, so that the visitor has the luxury of choosing not only the scenery and activities that most appeal, but also the precise climate in which to enjoy both.

In the following chapters, and in the WHEN TO GO section of TRAVELERS' TIPS, I will give information about the sort of weather you can expect to find in different places at different times. For now, though, let me just assure you that in Canada there is truly a time and place for everything.

The Canadian prairies in bloom.

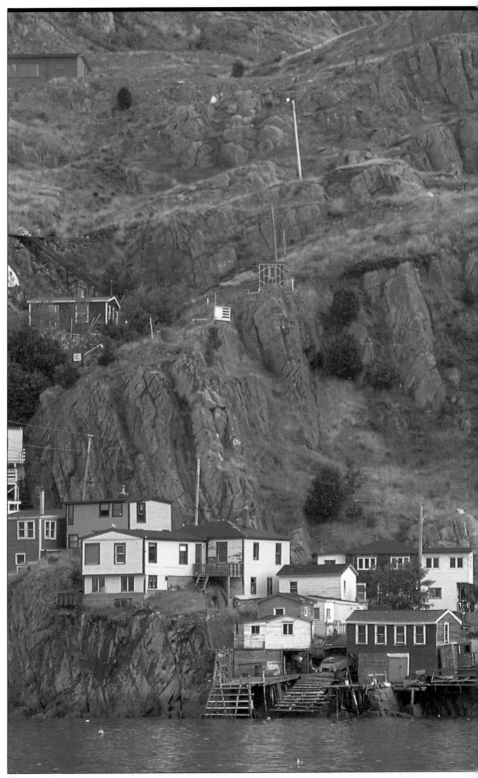

New-
foundland

IT IS ALMOST IMPOSSIBLE to read or hear anything about Newfoundland without coming across the word "rugged" to describe both the place and the people who live there. It is an apt word. The island is indeed rugged — although Labrador, on the mainland, is officially a part of the province, whenever people speak of Newfoundland they mean the island — very rugged, as you would expect of a land that only 10,000 years ago was still covered by glaciers, and today is regularly lashed by Atlantic winds and rain. And the people, or "Newfies" as they are known throughout Canada, are every bit as rugged as the landscape they inhabit.

They are also ruggedly independent. Although a confederated Canada was formed in 1867, and spanned the continent by 1905, the Newfies stubbornly refused to join the

Confederation until 1949. And they still refer to their compatriots from the mainland as "Canadians", while enquiring of visitors if they come "from Canada". They have their own distinctive accents and dialects, with their own colorful (if not always comprehensible) vocabulary. They even have their own time zone — "Newfoundland Time" — which is a half-hour ahead of Atlantic Time. And they are happy to point out that the provincial capital, St. John's, is closer to Europe than it is to Winnipeg in the middle of Canada.

Given this fiercely independent streak, it is not surprising that they have become the butt of countless "Newfie jokes" among other Canadians, rather like the Irish jokes that the English enjoy telling. The Newfies themselves take all this in their good-humored stride, and in turn seem to have made the island itself the butt of their own little jokes: just look at the map. There you will find places with names like Stinking Cove, Useless Bay, Sitdown Pond, Come By Chance, Blow Me Down, Tickle Cove, Witless Bay, Joe Batt's Arm, Jerry's Nose, Nick's Nose Cove, Cuckold Cove, Dildo Pond, Happy Adventure, Heart's Desire, Heart's Content, and Little Heart's Ease.

The island of Newfoundland, known to Newfies as "The Rock", is the 18th largest in the world, and was already inhabited by Inuit and American Indians when the Vikings first arrived a thousand years ago and established a settlement near L'Anse aux Meadows at the northern tip of the island. The next Europeans to arrive came with John Cabot, who arrived in the harbor of what is now St. John's in June, 1497. He reported back to Henry VII that he had discovered a "new founde lande" surrounded by rich fishing grounds. Thirty years later a Captain John Rut arrived and wrote back to the new king, Henry VIII, urging that a permanent settlement be established here. This was done the following year, but it was not until 1583 that Queen Elizabeth I sent Sir Humphrey Gilbert to officially claim the island for England. Thus did Newfoundland become the first British colony in the New World.

Anchored as it was in the rich Grand Banks fishing grounds, the island became the scene of repeated military confrontations between the British claimants and others, usually the French. Under the Treaty of Utrecht in 1713 Newfoundland was formally recognized as belonging to Britain, but there was another half-century of hostilities before the British finally secured undisputed control of the island when they decisively defeated the French at St. John's in 1762.

There followed a period of increased immigration from Britain, swelling the colony's population to 40,000 by 1800. In 1832 it was granted self-government in domestic affairs, and in 1855 achieved full dominion status in the British Commonwealth. Especially hard hit by the Depression, Newfoundland in 1934 suffered the dual humiliation of bankruptcy and reversion to being a mere colony. Finally, in 1949, but only by

the narrowest of margins, Newfies voted to end their long holdout and join the rest of Canada as the nation's tenth province.

With its population of 600,000 concentrated almost exclusively along its 9,660 km (6,000 miles) of deeply-indented coastline, Newfoundland's economy is still based on fishing, as it has been for 500 years. With its many glacial lakes and rivers as well as its offshore waters teeming with fish, the island's fishermen bring in an annual haul of over 500,000 tons of fish, mostly cod. (In fact, when Newfies say "fish" they always

mean cod; other types of fish are given their individual names.)

Despite these rich pickings, the province's economy is chronically depressed, with high unemployment. This could well change, however, in the foreseeable future, thanks to the recent discovery of oil beneath the continental shelf southeast of Newfoundland. If the find turns out to be as big as many think it is, then the sea could once again provide the people of Newfoundland with a good living. Until that time comes, they can still depend on the land — with its abundant game, enormous forests, beautiful lakes

Fishing boats now come to rest in Newfoundland where Viking ships landed a thousand years ago.

and ponds, rivers and streams — to provide them with an enviable quality of life.

ST. JOHN'S

First settled in 1528, St. John's can legitimately claim to be the oldest city in North America. And its past has not only been long but colorful, sometimes violently so. Given its strategic location as the nearest point to Europe in the New World, as well as being located near some of the richest fishing

board houses lining the narrow winding streets that climb away from the harbor where the fishing boats of many nations lie at anchor.

BACKGROUND

Although it has been settled only since 1528 (and then sparsely), the 175,000 citizens of St John's date their city from June 24, 1497, the saint's day of St. John the Baptist, when John Cabot sailed into the lovely little harbor and named the place after the saint.

grounds in the world, and blessed with a wonderfully sheltered natural harbor, it was a prize to be coveted, and repeatedly fought over, for two and a half centuries — until British supremacy was finally and lastingly established in 1762 at the end of the Seven Years' War. But just because there was peace afterwards doesn't mean that St. John's was suddenly peaceful. Far from it. It became a favorite haven for pirates who preyed on ships on their way to and from Europe. As a result, by the end of the eighteenth century there were 80 taverns in the town and over 200,000 gallons of rum were being imported annually.

It is markedly quieter today, but still colorful, with its brightly painted clap-

If the next three centuries were tumultuous, with the British and French (and occasionally the Dutch) fighting for control of the city, the nineteenth century was one of rapid growth interrupted by devastating fires: St. John's burned down no fewer than five times during the last century. And each time the townspeople, undaunted, rebuilt it — in wood. As it has escaped the flames so far this century, the oldest buildings in St. John's date back to the Victorian period.

One of these buildings, Cabot Tower on Signal Hill, is of particular historical interest. Built in 1897 to mark the fourth centenary of Cabot's landing as well as Queen Victoria's diamond jubilee, it was here on December 12, 1901 that Guglielmo Marconi received the first transatlantic radio message from his transmitter in Cornwall.

Now the colorful wooden houses that crowd the waterfront are beginning to be overshadowed by modern buildings and high-rises, but it can truthfully be said that after five centuries the oldest city in North America has lost little of its character. Perhaps the sailors who went to war over it, and the pirates who took refuge in it, would have trouble recognizing it today, but they would still find something awfully familiar about it.

WHAT TO SEE AND DO

Sights

The one thing you mustn't miss seeing in St. John's is the one thing you can't miss seeing: the **Cabot Tower** on **Signal Hill**. Signal Hill, which rises steeply at the mouth of the harbor, got its name because it was originally used by the various sailing companies to hoist their flags in order to signal to the dockworkers and merchants that one of their ships was approaching. At

GENERAL INFORMATION

The Newfoundland Department of Development and Tourism can be contacted at P.O. Box 2016, St. John's, Newfoundland A1C 5R8. ((709) 576-2830, toll-free (800) 563-6353. You can write to the St. John's Economic Development and Tourism Division at P.O. Box 908, St. John's, Newfoundland A1C 5M2, ((709) 576-8204, or you can visit their offices in City Hall on New Gower Street. There is also a Visitor Information Centre 16 km (10 miles) west of the city on the Trans-Canada Highway, which begins — or ends, if you're traveling east — at the St. John's City Hall.

the Cabot Tower, which is open daily ((709/772-5367), you can see the birthplace of modern telecommunications. Outside you can see cannon of the Queen's Battery dating from 1796 as well as ruined fortifications from the War of 1812. Halfway up the hill on the road from town is a Visitor Information Centre with a small museum.

Just over the hill on the north side is the picturesque fishing village of **Quidi Vidi** (pronounced Kiddy Viddy), an absolutely charming port community set on a small inlet. Among the little wharves and boats are some wonderful seafood restaurants.

Although St. John's is the oldest city in North America, almost all of its oldest buildings were built in this century.

Back in town, take a stroll along **Water Street**, one of the oldest streets in North America, which runs parallel to the harbor through the middle of town. At the corner of Duckworth and Prescott Streets is the **Newfoundland Museum** ((709/576-2460), which houses exhibits on the early native peoples of Newfoundland and on the history of St. John's, with particular emphasis on daily life in the nineteenth century. The museum also has a branch downtown off Harbour Drive which traces the history of the seafaring trades from the sixteenth century to the present, with an excellent section on the military and naval history of the province. Both museums are free, and are open every day as well as Thursday evenings.

The **Roman Catholic Basilica Cathedral of St. John the Baptist** (1855) on Military Road, ((709) 754-2170, is well worth a visit. It's the one with the Gothic facade and twin granite-and-bluestone towers that dominate the city's skyline. Further along Military Road is the distinctly more modest **St. Thomas' Church**, which dates from 1836 and is one of the few buildings to be spared in the terrible fires that swept the city in the nineteenth century. In fact it is the oldest church still standing anywhere in the province.

Next door to the church is **Commissariat House**, a clapboard structure with tall chimneys which dates from 1821. It, too, escaped the fires and was used by the military commissariat until 1871, when it became the rectory for the church. Beautifully restored and refurnished with period pieces, it is open daily during July and August. ((709) 753-9730.

At the corner of Allendale Road and Prince Philip Drive, near the university, is the **Arts and Culture Centre**, which includes two galleries featuring contemporary Canadian art, two theaters, three libraries, and a fine restaurant, Act III. In the summer there is a festival of the arts with free outdoor concerts. For general information call (709) 726-5978; for information about current and coming theatrical productions call (709) 576-3900, for reservations (709) 576-3901.

Here at Cabot Tower on Signal Hill Guglielmo Marconi received the first transatlantic radio message in 1901.

Outside St. John's, I would recommend a short excursion to **Cape Spear National Historic Park**, only 11 km (seven miles) southeast of the city. Here at North America's most easterly point you will get a stunning view of the ocean (which often includes the sight of whales heaving their way up and down the coast). There is also a square, white clapboard **lighthouse** dating from 1835, which makes it the oldest lighthouse in Newfoundland. The park is open daily, ((709) 772-5367, and from mid-June to mid-September there are conducted tours of the lighthouse.

Sports

The oldest annual sporting event in North America, the **St. John's Regatta**, which began in 1818, is held on the first Wednesday in August on Quidi Vidi Lake, just inland from the fishing village. Regatta Day is a truly gala occasion, with all sorts of peripheral games and much food and drink. ((709) 726-7596.

But that just lasts one day. What lasts all year — allowing, of course, for seasonal restrictions — is some of the best **hunting** and **fishing** to be found anywhere in Canada. For details regarding seasons, limits, equipment required and available, get a copy of the *Newfoundland and Labrador Hunting and Fishing Guide*, published and distributed free by the Newfoundland Department of Development and Tourism (see GENERAL INFORMATION above).

Shopping

Duckworth Street and **The Murray Premises** shopping center down on Water Street are the places to go for boutiques and luxury goods. Duckworth Street is also good for antique shops. For arts and crafts the area around the War Memorial at the eastern end of **Water Street** is the best hunting ground.

Nightlife

In keeping with its rum-soaked past, St. John's probably has more drinking spots per capita than any other city in Canada. Most of them seem to be clustered on and around **George Street** downtown, where you can find pubs, clubs, and discos to suit almost any state. I also like the **Ship Inn** at 265 Duckworth Street, down the stairs, off the alley, which has live music and is popular with the sailors. Upstairs and upmarket, the disco in the luxurious **Hotel Newfoundland** on Cavendish Square is very popular.

WHERE TO STAY

Luxury

The new **Hotel Newfoundland** is easily the grandest hotel in Newfoundland, with 288 elegantly furnished rooms and 14 suites, a formal dining room, restaurant, lounge, indoor swimming pool, sauna, whirlpool, squash courts and, as I've already mentioned, a disco. Very reasonable for what it has to offer — and it has discount weekend packages. Cavendish Square, St. John's, A1C 5W8. ((709) 726-4980, toll-free (800) 268-9411 in Canada, (800) 828-7447 in the U.S. The 11-story **Radisson Plaza Hotel** is another newish hotel. Overlooking the harbor, with 276 rooms and nine suites, it has non-smoking floors as well as the swimming and health facilities you would expect, and an excellent restaurant, Newman's. It's at 120 New Gower Street, St. John's A1C 1J3. ((709) 739-6404, toll-free (800) 333-3333.

So delightful that it ought to be in the Luxury category and so reasonably-priced that it ought to be in the Mid-range category, the **STEL Battery Hotel** on Signal Hill has 150 lovely rooms affording glorious views over the harbor and city, plus indoor swimming pool, saunas, etc. It's at 100 Signal Hill Road, St. John's A1A 1B3. ((709) 576-0040, toll-free (800) 267-STEL.

Mid-range

To begin with, there is Old Reliable: the **Holiday Inn** is at the intersection of Portugal Cove Road and MacDonald Drive, about two and a half kilometers (one and a half miles) from downtown, quite near the Arts and Culture Centre. It has all the amenities one associates with Holiday Inns, including here an above-average restaurant and 24-hour room service. ((709) 722-0506. About six kilometers (under four miles) from downtown on the Trans-Canada Highway is the **First City Motel**, which happens to be just about the first city motel you encounter when driving into St. John's. Very comfortable and quiet, its postal address is 479 Kenmount Road, St. John's A1B 3P9.

((709) 722-5400. Closer to town, and more lavishly appointed, is the **Travellers Inn** at 199 Kenmount Road, ((709) 722-5540, toll-free (800) 528-1234. The **Airport Inn**, P.O. Box 9432, St. John's A1A 2Y3, ((709) 753-3500, is right next to the airport, within walking distance of the terminal, about five kilometers (three miles) from downtown. Its 104 rooms are nicely furnished and its restaurant and lounge are both superior to what one expects to find nestling up against an airport, even a small one. But probably the best all-round value in this

Road. Smaller and cheaper, but further away from the city center at 34 Bonaventure Avenue is **Bonaventure House**, ((709) 753-3359. The **Sea Flow Tourist Home** at 53-55 William Street, St. John's A1C 2S3, ((709) 753-2425, is one of the best-situated and best-run tourist homes in the area. There are scores of other "tourist homes" and guest houses sprinkled throughout the city, indeed throughout the province. Get a copy of the *Newfoundland and Labrador Accommodations Guide*, available free from the Newfoundland Department of Development and Tourism.

category is the new **Journey's End Hotel** downtown on Water Street, ((709) 754-7788, toll-free (800) 668-4200.

Inexpensive

If you want a real bargain in civilized surroundings, head for the **Prescott Inn** at 17-19 Military Road, St. John's A1C 2C3, ((709) 753-6036, which has six large, balconied rooms overlooking the harbor, each splendidly and differently decorated and each with color TV and private bath. Complimentary continental breakfast. Also a good bet, and also in a good location, is the **Parkview Inn** at 118 Military Road, ((709) 753-2671. It has 15 comfortable rooms in a large green house at the corner of King's

WHERE TO EAT

Expensive

With one exception, the best restaurants in St. John's are in the luxury hotels. That exception is the **Stone House Restaurant** at 8 Kenna's Hill, near Quidi Vidi Lake, ((709) 753-2380. Set in a restored early nineteenth-century stone cottage, it can fairly claim to be one of the best restaurants anywhere in Canada. Innovative dishes featuring local game and seafood are complemented by an extensive wine list. Of the restaurants in the

Play ball! A St. John's softball team gets ready to take the field.

best hotels, I personally prefer the one in the **STEL Battery** on Signal Hill, ☎(709) 576-0040. Quite apart from the excellent food and service, it offers a stunning view to go with your meal. That said, I must also recommend highly the lovely restaurant in the **Hotel Newfoundland**, ☎ (709) 726-4980, and **Newman's** in the Radisson Plaza, ☎ (709) 739-6404.

Moderate

Act III in the Arts and Culture Centre, ☎ (709) 754-0790, offers an intimate ambience and warm service; in addition to its regular lunch and evening menus it has pre-theater and late supper specials. If you go to **The Fishing Admiral** on Water Street, and you should, be sure to go upstairs. Downstairs is the pub-like **Water Street 203** which is quite popular, but it's not quite the same thing as the elegant dining room upstairs (☎ 709/753-6203). Another upstairs/downstairs establishment is the **King Cod** seafood restaurant at 122 Duckworth Street, ☎ (709) 753-7006, where both the portions and the conversations are hearty downstairs, while the **Upper Flat** specializes in more interesting dishes in a quieter atmosphere. Nearby, at 108 Duckworth Street, the **Casa Grande** serves good Mexican food in cozy surroundings If you are willing to stray a bit further afield, I would suggest you stray out along Route 60 about 11 km (seven miles) to the **Woodstock Colonial Inn**, ☎ (709) 722-6933, where you will find some delicious food served (generously) in a delightful colonial setting.

Inexpensive

The **Duckworth Lunch** at 183 Duckworth Street is cheap and cheerful and popular with students. For fish and chips, **Ches's** is something of an institution in St. John's. Its two restaurants are at 655 Topsail Road, ☎ (709) 368-9473, and 9 Freshwater Road, ☎ (709) 726-2373. The **Curry House** at 106 Water Street serves very decent Indian food at very reasonable prices. And, of course, like every city of any size these days, St. John's has its full complement of fast-food places of which **Ports of Food** in the Atlantic Place Mall on Water Street is perhaps the most original.

How to Get There

Air Atlantic, a subsidiary of Canadian Airlines International, flies in to St. John's. For information or reservations call (709) 722-0222, toll-free in Newfoundland (800) 565-1800, in the U.S. (800) 426-7000.

THE REST OF THE ISLAND

The Avalon Peninsula may be home to Newfoundland's capital, St. John's, and most of its population, but the rest of the island has most of the land — land which includes two great national parks, a mountain range, mighty forests, and countless lakes and rivers.

Background

It is known that bands of Indians roamed the island up to 4,000 years before the Vikings landed about 1000 AD, including some who left behind stone tools that are among the most delicate ever discovered. Whether it was due to the arrival of the Vikings or to some other phenomenon, the island's original inhabitants disappeared about 1000 AD and were replaced by the Beothuck Indians. These were the Indians that Cabot and the later settlers encountered. As they tended to cover their bodies in a red powdered ochre, they became known as the "Red Paint People" — possibly the origin of the term "Red Indian". In any case, the arrival of the white man spelt doom for the red man. Over the next centuries the Beothucks were systematically exterminated by the settlers. The last known surviving Beothuck died in 1829.

Except at its edges, the island that the Beothucks and their predecessors occupied for millenia is still pretty much the way it was throughout its prehistory. Perhaps the only real difference, apart from the obvious inroads made by the modern world, is that the forests are being nibbled away — not devoured, just nibbled — by the timber, paper and pulp manufacturing industries

The clouds gather over Conception Bay, just north of St. John's.

which have now surpassed fishing in the economy of the western part of Newfoundland. Otherwise the land, or most of it anyway, retains the same wild beauty and the same abundance of fish and game that the Indians enjoyed long before Europeans ever set foot on it.

GENERAL INFORMATION

The primary source of information is, of course, the Newfoundland Department of Development and Tourism, listed above. In addition, the Department has Visitor Information Centres at Port aux Basques, Deer Lake, Notre Dame Junction, Clarenville, and Whitbourne. There are also regional centers to help tourists at Marystown, Gander, Grand Falls, Springdale, and Corner Brook. There are Visitor Reception Centres at Terra Nova National Park (℃ 709/533-2802), Gros Morne National Park (℃ 709/458-2066), and L'Anse aux Meadows National Historic Park (℃ 709/623-2608).

WHAT TO SEE AND DO

Bonavista Peninsula
Cape Bonavista at the northern tip of the peninsula is said to have been Cabot's first North American landfall. Anyway, he gave it its name in 1497 — accurately, one should add, because there is a beautiful view from the cape. The fishing village of **Bonavista**, five kilometers (three miles) away, has an outer harbor as well as a sheltered inner harbor for the smaller fishing boats. It was a favorite port of European fishing fleets in the sixteenth century before the British settled it, and now it is a favorite spot for whale-watchers in the early summer.

The picturesque little village of **Trinity** on Trinity Bay was discovered by the Portuguese navigator Jozo Vas Corte Real in 1500. Its settlement was so rapid that the first Admiralty Court in North America was convened here in 1615. Thanks to a program of renovation and restoration, the character of the village has been beautifully preserved.

Terra Nova National Park
The older and smaller of Newfoundland's two national parks, the 396 sq km (153 sq miles) of Terra Nova National Park are divided from north to south by the Trans-Canada Highway. To the east are the beaches, tidal flats, and rocky coast along Bonavista Bay, as well as the park's two developed campgrounds at **Newman Sound** and **Malady Head.** The one at Newman Sound has 400 campsites, a general store, laundry, cabins, showers, fireplaces, the works; the one at Malady Head is smaller (165 campsites) and a little more spartan. There are also more primitive campsites dotted around the park.

To the west of the highway are the woods, lakes, ponds, streams, and bogs so typical of the island's interior. And on both sides of the highway — indeed sometimes on the highway itself — the area teems with wildlife: black bear, moose, beaver, otter. There are 80 km (50 miles) of nature trails in the park, and both canoes and bicycles can be rented at the park's Visitor Reception Centre. There is even a nine-hole seaside golf course, from which in early summer you can see any number of icebergs floating in the coastal waters.

Gander
About the only thing Gander has going for it is its **airport**, which in the pre-jet era was the western take-off and landing point for transatlantic flights. It was chosen for this role not only because of its proximity to Europe, but also because it is far enough inland not to be affected by the fog that often shrouds the coast. It played a critical part in World War II as a refuelling stop for the thousands of military aircraft headed for Europe, but its importance has declined since the advent of the jet engine.

Gander's only other point of interest, unless you are excited by shopping centers, lies west of the town where the **Gander River** flows under the Trans-Canada Highway. Apart from being beautiful to look at, either from the bank or a canoe, it is one of the island's best salmon rivers. Bring your angling gear.

Gros Morne National Park
Gros Morne ("Big Knoll") is probably the most spectacular national park in all of eastern Canada. Within its 1,815 sq km

(700 sq miles) are mountains, gorges, lakes, and fjords of stunning beauty. The flat-topped **Long Range Mountains,** which rise to a barren plateau some 600 m (2,000 ft) high, are cut by deep lakes and fjords bordered by towering rock cliffs. The entire park is glorious, and crisscrossed by hiking trails, but there are two areas of especial beauty. One is **Western Brook Pond,** 29 km (19 miles) north of Rocky Harbour, which is reached by a walk of about four kilometers (two and a half miles) through the forest from the highway. When you get there, the "pond" turns out to be a lake 16 km (10 miles) long that resembles a fjord because of the soaring, near vertical cliffs that rise alongside it. It is truly breathtaking. There are three boat tours of the lake daily during the summer.

The other must-see scenic spot is **Bonne Bay,** which you can appreciate without getting out of the car. Bonne Bay is a deep fjord on the Gulf of St. Lawrence with two arms thrusting deep into the park. The drive along the South Arm must be one of the most gorgeous drives in the world, and only slightly less so is the drive up along the East Arm to Rocky Harbour.

L'Anse aux Meadows National Historic Park

Here, at the northern tip of Newfoundland's Northern Peninsula, is the site of the only authenticated Viking settlement in North America. It had long been known that Norsemen sailing from Iceland had landed somewhere along North America's Atlantic coast, and had named the spot Vinland after the wild grapes they found there, but it was not until 1960 that the Norwegian explorer Helge Instad came upon a cluster of overgrown mounds near L'Anse aux Meadows. For the next seven years he excavated the site and established beyond doubt that here were the remains of a 1,000-year-old Norse settlement.

In 1978 L'Anse aux Meadows was named the first UNESCO World Heritage Site. Today three of the original six sod houses have been reconstructed, and artifacts from the site, together with an exhibit on the Norse way of life, are on display in the Visitor Reception Centre.

Corner Brook

A population of a little over 30,000 makes Corner Brook Newfoundland's second largest town. With an economy based almost exclusively on the town's giant pulp and paper mill and the herring fishing industry, it cannot be said to have overpowering appeal for the visitor, unless one needs to buy the sort of goods and services generally unavailable in smaller places.

However, Corner Brook does have the advantage of being near some very appealing places indeed. To begin with, it is an ideal starting point for a drive along either the northern or southern shore of the scenic Humber Arm of the **Bay of Islands**. A drive out along the southern shore will take you to **Bottle Cove**, where there is a lovely public beach as well as campsites and hiking trails up into the mountains. Also, there is fabulous salmon fishing in the **Humber River** near Corner Brook: catches of salmon weighing over 30 pounds have been recorded here. Finally, there is excellent hunting nearby, and only eight kilometers (five miles) away is the **Marble Mountain Ski Resort**, the only proper ski resort in Newfoundland.

Port aux Basques

Named for the Basque fishermen who were fishing the waters of the Cabot Strait as early as 1500, and probably earlier, Port aux Basques is still an important fishing port as well as being the island's main ferry port. And if you arrive in Newfoundland by ferry, and you are intending to do some hunting and fishing, you will be happy to discover that you needn't go further than 200 km (125 miles) beyond Port aux Basques to find the best hunting and fishing on the island.

As you take the Trans-Canada Highway north towards Corner Brook, you go through the wooded valley of the **Grand Codroy River**, perhaps the best salmon river in Newfoundland. Moreover, this whole region, all the way to Corner Brook, is noted for its abundance of game, especially moose and caribou. In this corner of the island, the hills are alive with the sound of game.

OVERLEAF: The tranquil fishing village of Brugis in Conception Bay west of St. John's.

WHERE TO STAY

Bonavista Peninsula

On the Trans-Canada Highway (Route 1) at Clarenville, just before you turn off to head out on to the Bonavista Peninsula, there is a **Holiday Inn**, P.O. Box 967, Clarenville A0E 1J0. ((709) 466-7911, toll-free (800) HOLIDAY. With 64 rooms at mid-range prices, and the usual Holiday Inn amenities, plus the availability of whale-watching tours, this is probably your best bet for accommodation here. If you are keen on whale-watching, or other types of ocean-going expeditions, the **Village Inn** in Trinity (P.O. Box 10, Trinity A0C 2S0, (709/464-3269) organizes all sorts of trips and charters. It is small (12 rooms) and inexpensive, but very comfortable, with a licensed dining room and private bar.

Terra Nova National Park

Apart from the two big campgrounds already mentioned, at Newman Sound and Malady Head, there are two mid-range accommodations on the Trans-Canada Highway in the park. One is **Weston's Terra Nova National Park Chalets**, ((709) 533-2296, off-season ((709) 651-3434, which has 24 self-contained cabins. The other is the **Clode Sound Motel**, P.O. Box 10, Charlottetown A0C 1L0, ((709) 664-3146, off-season ((709) 664-4271, which has 19 housekeeping units, a heated pool, a tennis court, and is only 10 minutes from the nine-hole golf course at Twin Rivers.

Gander

The four best hotels in Gander are all mid-range in price, and all four belong to hotel chains. Easily the most expensive is the **Holiday Inn**, 1 Caldwell Street, Gander A1V 1T6, ((709) 256-3981, toll-free: (800) HOLIDAY. The **Hotel Gander**, a member of the Claytons Inn chain, is right on the Trans-Canada Highway in Gander, ((709) 256-3931, toll-free (800) 563-2988 from the Atlantic provinces. It is the largest and marginally the cheapest of the four. The other two, the **Albatross Motel** and **Sinbad's Motel**, are owned by Atlantic Inns. The Albatross is on the Trans-Canada High-

way — P.O. Box 450, Gander A1V 1W8, ((709) 256-3956, toll-free (800) 563-4894 from the Atlantic provinces — and has 111 very nicely furnished rooms. Sinbad's is on Bennett Drive across from the Gander Mall, ((709) 651-2678, but has the same postal address and shares the same toll-free number for reservations. Of its 120 rooms, only 49 are standard motel units; the rest are efficiency units.

Gros Morne National Park

Near Rocky Harbour there is a Visitor Reception Centre, where you can get details of all the campgrounds in the park. The handiest one is the **Juniper Campground** on Pond Road off Route 230 close to Rocky Harbour (P.O. Box 114, Rocky Harbour A0K 4N0, (709/458-2917). It has 40 campsites, 25 of them fully-serviced. In Rocky Harbour there are two comfortable and inexpensive places that I would recommend. One is the **Ocean View Motel**, P.O. Box 129, Rocky Harbour A0K 4N0, ((709) 458-2730, which has 35 rooms and two housekeeping units, plus an excellent dining room and organized boat tours of Bonne Bay and Western Brook Pond. The **Gros Morne Cabins**, P.O. Box 151, Rocky Harbour A0K 4N0, ((709) 458-2020, consists of 22 log cabins, fully-equipped housekeeping units, with a convenience store and recreation area.

L'Anse aux Meadows

The nearest good motel to the historic site is the inexpensive and appropriately named **Viking Motel** on Pistolet Bay at the junction of Routes 430 and 437. It has 11 rooms, a restaurant and bar, and even helicopter landing space; it is also only 30 minutes' drive from the local airport. The Viking's address is P.O. Box 552, Pistolet Bay, St. Anthony A0K 4S0, ((709) 454-3541. St. Anthony, only 27 km (17 miles) away from L'Anse aux Meadows, has two good motels. The **St. Anthony Motel**, 14 Goose Cove Road, P.O. Box 187, St. Anthony A0K 4S0, ((709) 454-3200, has a restaurant and night club to go with its 22 rooms, as well as a car rental office. The **Vinland Motel**, P.O. Box 400, St. Anthony A0K 4S0, ((709) 454-8843, is larger, fancier, and more expensive

— though still in the lower reaches of the mid-range category. In addition to its 27 motel rooms, it has 10 housekeeping units.

Corner Brook

As in Gander, the four best hotels in Corner Brook are chain-owned. And, again, the most expensive of these — though still moderately priced — is the **Holiday Inn** at 48 West Street, Corner Brook A2H 2Z2, ((709) 634-5381, toll-free (800) HOLIDAY. Then there is the **Mamateek Inn**, a Best Western hotel, on the Trans-Canada Highway at Maple Valley Road in Corner Brook, ((709) 639-8901, toll-free (800) 528-1234. Nearby at 41 Maple Valley Road is the least expensive of the four, the **Journey's End Motel**, ((709) 639-1980, toll-free (800) 668-4200. The best of the four, in my opinion, is the Tudor-style **Glynmill Inn**, a member of the Atlantic Inns group, at 1 Cobb Lane, P.O. Box 550, Corner Brook A2H 6E6, ((709) 634-5181, toll-free (800) 563-4894. Overlooking Glynmill Pond, it has 90 very handsome rooms and a splendid steak house, The Carriage Room, as well as a more intimate restaurant downstairs.

Port aux Basques

The best hotel is the **Hotel Port aux Basques**, which is still priced near the bottom of the mid-range hotels. It is on the Trans-Canada Highway just two kilometers from the ferry terminal (P.O. Box 400, Port aux Basques A0M 1C0, (709/695-2171) and has 50 rooms and a good restaurant. Equally near the ferry terminal, at the end of Grand Bay Road, is the **Grand Bay Motel**, P.O. Box 538, Port aux Basques A0M 1C0, ((709) 695-2105. It has 29 rooms, all inexpensive, and all with lovely views of the bay. Another bargain hostelry is **St. Christopher's Hotel** on Caribou Road (P.O. Box 2049, Port aux Basques A0M 1C0, (709/695-7034), which has a nice restaurant and a lounge with a large-screen TV showing sports and movies via satellite.

WHERE TO EAT

See above. Seriously. All of the best places to eat in the rest of the island are located in the best places to stay. But you can eat well

almost anywhere because of the super-abundance of delicious seafood.

HOW TO GET THERE

There are airports at Gander, Stephenville, Deer Lake, and St. Anthony. To find out about services contact Air Atlantic at ((709) 722-0222, toll-free (800) 565-1800 in Newfoundland, (800) 426-7000 in the U.S. For information about the ferry from North Sydney, Nova Scotia to Port aux Basques contact Marine Atlantic at P.O. Box 250,

North Sydney, Nova Scotia B2A 3M3, ((902) 562-9470, toll-free from the U.S. (800) 341-7981.

LABRADOR

At the top of the Gulf of St. Lawrence there is a strip of water 16 km (10 miles) wide that separates Newfoundland island from Labrador, the mainland part of the province. Covering 293,347 sq km (113,261 sq miles), Labrador is almost three times the size of the island, yet has only 35,000 inhabitants. Until fairly recently it was virtually uninhabited except for the Air Force base at Goose Bay and the dozens of tiny villages huddled in coves and inlets along the eastern seaboard.

 Though Labrador remains one of the world's last great wilderness areas, it is beginning to be opened up thanks to its

Boats tied securely and colorfully to a pier in Conception Bay.

fabulous natural resources. At Labrador City and Wabush near the Quebec border large mining complexes produce almost half of Canada's iron ore, while a giant hydroelectric plant at Churchill Falls supplies power to the eastern United States. At the same time, Labrador's other great natural resources, its fish and wildlife, are beginning to attract anglers and hunters in ever increasing numbers.

BACKGROUND

You could say that Labrador looks its age: it forms the eastern edge of the Canadian Shield, one of the oldest unchanged geological formations on the planet. As a result, it apparently looks very much the same as it did before animal life appeared on earth.

The first humans are thought to have arrived in Labrador almost 9,000 years ago. In any case, it is known that the native Indians and Inuit were here for thousands of years before the arrival of the first Europeans, Basque whalers who established a settlement at Red Bay, just across the strait from the northern tip of Newfoundland, in the sixteenth century. New arrivals since then have been few and far between, but this will undoubtedly change as more people begin to realize the extent of the unspoilt beauty that awaits them here.

GENERAL INFORMATION

Information about holidays in Labrador can be obtained from the Department of

Development and Tourism, P.O. Box 490, Wabush, Labrador. ((709) 282-5600, toll-free (800) 563-6353.

WHAT TO SEE AND DO

There is not much in the way of specific sights you ought to see or specific things you ought to do at a particular time or place. Labrador is just *there*, in all its vastness and prehistoric splendor, to be enjoyed by anyone who likes to hunt or fish or hike or ski or camp or simply breathe fresh, unpolluted air.

Having said that, I would definitely recommend a visit to the **Labrador Straits Museum** if you are in the area (and "the area" includes northernmost Newfoundland, a short ferry-ride away). It is located on Route 510 between Forteau and L'Anse-au-Loup, ((709) 927-5659. It is open every day during the summer, and has a fascinating collection of artifacts showing how life was lived here centuries ago. Likewise, if you are in the vicinity of **Goose Bay**, you should drop in at the **Labrador Heritage Museum** on the Air Force base, ((709) 896-2762. It has a good collection of photographs depicting the history of Labrador as well as tools used by the early trappers.

For details of organized hunting and fishing excursions by airplane into the interior, contact Labrador's Department of Development and Tourism.

WHERE TO STAY

As you might expect, Labrador is not exactly chock-a-block with hotels. As you might not expect, what accommodations there are tend to be, in my opinion, over-priced — although none of those I know about is yet in the Luxury category where prices (or amenities) are concerned.

Goose Bay has three first-rate hotels. The largest and plushest is the **Labrador Inn**, P.O. Box 58, Station C, Goose Bay A0P 1C0, ((709) 896-3351, toll-free in Newfoundland (800) 563-2763. It also has a superb restaurant. The **Aurora Hotel** is similarly comfortable, and cleverly offers a fax and photocopying service to guests. It is at 382

Hamilton River Road in Hamilton Heights (mailing address: P.O. Box 201, Station C, Goose Bay A0P 1C0), ((709) 896-3398, toll-free (800) 563-3066. The smallest and in many ways the most charming of the three is the **Royal Inn** at 5 Royal Avenue in Happy Valley (mailing address: P.O. Box 69, Station B, Happy Valley A0P 1E0), ((709) 896-2456.

One place that is *not* over-priced is the **Northern Light Inn** on Route 510 in L'Anse-au-Clair (mailing address: General Delivery, L'Anse-au-Clair A0K 3K0), ((709) 931-2332. Although inexpensive, it offers most of the same facilities as the pricier hostelries, plus housekeeping units and all kinds of recreational opportunities and facilities nearby.

WHERE TO EAT

What goes for eating in Newfoundland outside St. John's goes double for eating in Labrador: hotels will be your best bet, but almost any eatery will be a good bet.

HOW TO GET THERE

If you are coming from the island of Newfoundland, Air Atlantic flies to Goose Bay from St. John's, and Labrador Airways has flights from St. Anthony to several coastal communities as well as Goose Bay. Air Atlantic's telephone numbers are given in the previous section; you can get in touch with Labrador Airways by writing P.O. Box 310, Station A, Goose Bay A0P 1S0, or by calling (709) 896-3387.

Marine Atlantic operates a ferry service from Lewisporte, near Gander, to Goose Bay via Cartwright, Labrador, during the summer months; details from Marine Atlantic, P.O. Box 520, Port aux Basques, A0M 1C0, toll-free (800) 563-7336 in Newfoundland. There is also a daily ferry from May to November between St. Barbe, on Newfoundland's Northern Peninsula, and Blanc Sablon, Quebec, just across the border from L'Anse-au-Clair.

If you are coming from Quebec, there is a train link from Sept Isles to Labrador City, and Quebecair flies to Blanc Sablon from Montreal, Quebec City, and Sept Isles.

Nova
Scotia

APPROPRIATELY FORMED as if to honor its most celebrated culinary delight, the lobster-shaped province of Nova Scotia is Canada's anchor in the Atlantic. Its 55,490 sq km (21,425 sq miles) is divided into two parts: a long peninsula connected to the adjoining province of New Brunswick by the narrow Isthmus of Chignecto, and Cape Breton Island, which is linked to the peninsula by a mile-long causeway. With Prince Edward Island and New Brunswick, it is one of the three Maritime Provinces.

Like Newfoundland, Nova Scotia is thought to have been visited by the Vikings around 1000 AD, but dates its "discovery" to 1497 when John Cabot arrived at the northern tip of Cape Breton Island and claimed the territory for England. The first settlement, however, was French: Samuel de Champlain founded Port Royal, now Annapolis Royal, on the peninsula's southwest coast in 1605. Sixteen years later, King James I, a Scot, granted the region to another Scot, Sir William Alexander, so that he might establish a "New Scotland" there. Which he did, though using the Latin form of the name in the original charter.

For the next century Nova Scotia was caught up in the Anglo-French struggle for possession of eastern North America. Finally, in 1737 it was agreed that the British would have sovereignty over the peninsula while the French would control Cape Breton Island. Then in the early 1740s the French completed building a great fortress in a commanding position at Louisbourg on the east coast of the island, prompting Britain to send a large group of settlers to establish a fortified settlement at Halifax, as a counterweight to France's military stronghold to the north.

In 1755, as Britain and France squared up to fight another war, the British governor of Nova Scotia ordered the deportation of all French settlers, or Acadians, who refused to take an oath of allegiance to the British Crown. Over the next few years 15,000 Acadians were forcibly removed from their homes and shipped off to the American colonies, where they found themselves equally unwelcome. Most of them eventually settled in the bayou country of Louisiana, where they survive to this day as Cajuns.

After the end of the Seven Years' War in 1763 all of Nova Scotia, including Cape Breton Island, came under British rule. The anglicization of the region received a further boost after the American Revolution, when 30,000 Loyalists fled the new republic and resettled in Nova Scotia, mostly along the Atlantic coast. In 1867 it became one of Canada's four founding provinces.

Fishing, naturally, has always been at the heart of the province's economy, and today still accounts for a third of its revenues. There is also a thriving timber industry to go alongside the agricultural output of the orchards and dairy farms of the Annapolis Valley. But probably its fastest growing industry is tourism. Thanks to its great natural beauty, which includes the spectacular Cape Breton Highlands National Park, and its excellent recreational facilities, Nova Scotia is the most popular of the Maritime Provinces with both American and European tourists.

HALIFAX

Originally founded for purely strategic reasons, Halifax still remains militarily important as the home of Canada's largest naval base. But as a bustling provincial capital with a metropolitan population of around 300,000, which makes it the largest city in the Maritime Provinces, Halifax is more important today as the commercial center of the Maritimes.

Situated on a small peninsula on the western shore of a deep inlet of the Atlantic, Halifax has a superb natural harbor — and indeed the busiest port on Canada's east coast. The historical as well as the contemporary center of the city is that part which lies between the harbor installations and the hilltop Citadel that dominates the peninsula. As the oldest British town on the Canadian mainland, and home of Canada's first Protestant church, Halifax wears its age very gracefully. At the same time, as a modern financial center and seat of government, the city has a liveliness and sophistication seldom found in cites of comparable size. In

Lunenberg, once a haven for pirates, is now home to a less swashbuckling breed of seafarers.

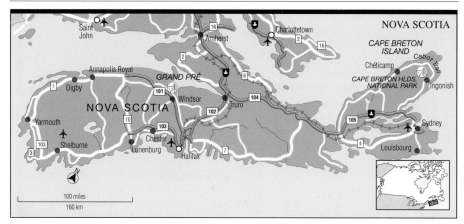

short, Halifax is in the enviable position of being able to boast both big-city amenities and small-town virtues.

BACKGROUND

Although the area had long been inhabited by the Micmac Indians, the town of Halifax came into being almost overnight when in 1749 Colonel Edward Cornwallis led a flotilla of 20 ships, carrying 3,000 settlers, into the harbor and immediately began work on constructing a town. Built in response to the perceived threat posed by the new French fortress at Louisbourg, it was named after the Earl of Halifax, who was then the president of England's Board of Trade and Plantations.

Ironically, having been established in the first place solely because of its strategic location in case of war, Halifax went on to prosper greatly from wars fought in other lands. First, the British victory in the Seven Years' War removed any potential threat from Louisbourg. Then during the American War of Independence the harbor became an important naval base for British warships, which pumped a lot of money into the local economy; and after the British were defeated the resulting influx of fleeing loyalists, many of whom were well-educated and well-to-do, further invigorated the local economy as well as having a profound and beneficial impact on the local culture. Then came the War of 1812, which brought the warships back from Britain, and with them more money to swell the municipal coffers. Even the American Civil War led to in-

creased military activity in Halifax, and thus increased military spending, and thus increased employment.

This century's wars, too, have been profitable for the town. During World War I, thanks to its 16 sq km (10 sq miles) of deepwater anchorage in the harbor's Bedford Basin, it was used as a distribution center for the supply ships heading for Europe. And during World War II it was the port from which the great convoys — some 17,000 ships in all — sailed across the North Atlantic.

Only once, in 1917, has Halifax suffered a war wound of its own — but it was a horrible wound, and left a permanent scar on the collective memory of its citizens. In December 1917 a French munitions ship, the *Mont Blanc*, loaded with explosives headed for Europe, collided with a Belgian relief ship in the harbor and blew up. The explosion leveled the entire north end of town, killing over 2,000 people and injuring 9,000, of whom 200 were blinded by the blast. It is not the sort of thing a community recovers from quickly or easily.

But recover it did, and during the past half-century has shown that it can flourish in peacetime just as well as in wartime.

GENERAL INFORMATION

For a copy of the *Nova Scotia Travel Guide*, which is packed with almost 300 pages of information for visitors, write to the Nova Scotia Department of Tourism and Culture, P.O. Box 456, Halifax, Nova Scotia B3J 2R5. Nova Scotia also has a free reservation and travel information service called Check In, which you can call toll-free for the answers to any questions you may have as well as guaranteed reservations for every kind of accommodation. The number to call in the U.S. is (800) 341-6096 and in Canada (800) 565-0000; in Halifax itself you dial 425-5781.

The Halifax office of the Department of Tourism is in the Red Store building, Historic Properties, on the downtown harbor boardwalk. ((902) 424-4247. There is also a tourist information counter in the Halifax airport, ((902) 426-1223. The City of Halifax Tourism office is in the Old City Hall at Barrington and Duke Streets, ((902) 421-8736.

WHAT TO SEE AND DO

Sights

Thanks to a city ordinance banning the construction of buildings that interfere with various "view planes" across the city, Halifax has been uniquely successful in preserving the "human scale" as it has grown. The center of Halifax since its founding has been the **Grand Parade**, a square running along the west side of Barrington Street, Halifax's main shopping thoroughfare. At the north end of the square is **City Hall**, with its enormous wooden flagpole, and at the south end is the timber-framed **St. Paul's** (1750), the oldest Protestant church in Canada. Going up George Street from the Grand Parade towards The Citadel, you come upon the **Old Town Clock**, erected in 1803, the symbol of Halifax. Further up is **The Citadel** itself, a many-angled, star-shaped fortress that towers over the city. Originally built by Cornwallis on his arrival in 1749, it was rebuilt and expanded after the American Revolution and then again after the War of 1812. Finally, in 1828, the Duke of Wellington ordered that a permanent fortress of masonry be built. Every day at noon a cannon is fired from the grounds of The Citadel.

On the other side of the hill from the downtown area, at 1747 Summer Street, ((902) 429-4610, is the **Nova Scotia Museum**. Open daily, free of charge, it has exhibits covering every aspect of the province's history — geographical, natural, social, and industrial. The **Public Gardens** just south of the museum were first opened in 1867 and

remain to this day seven hectares (17 acres) of classic Victoriana: a bandstand, duck pond, fountains, statues, and formally planted Oriental trees. Even more attractive for would-be strollers and picnickers is **Point Pleasant Park** at the southern tip of the Halifax peninsula. This heavily-wooded, 79-hectare (186-acre) park has a restaurant and a beach in addition to its many walking trails and picnic spots.

Down on the harborfront north of Duke Street you will find the **Historic Properties**, a group of old wharves and buildings dating

from as early as 1800, now restored and refurbished, in an all-pedestrian area which includes shops, galleries, restaurants, and street entertainers. The buildings include the **Privateers' Warehouse**, the oldest structure in the area, where nineteenth-century pirates stashed their loot, and the **Old Red Store** building, which now houses the tourist office. A few blocks south of the Historic Properties is the **Maritime Museum of the Atlantic** at 1675 Lower Water Street, ((902) 429-8210. Its displays include ship models, naval instruments, weapons, and many other items illustrating Halifax's maritime history.

The Victorian bandstand is the focal point of Halifax's Public Gardens.

Fittingly, the best tours of Halifax are waterborne. A replica of Canada's most famous boat, the unbeaten racing schooner *Bluenose II*, is moored at the wharf beside Privateers' Warehouse and goes on two-hour cruises of the harbor three times a day during July and August, ((902) 422-2678. Also leaving from Privateers' Wharf is the *Haligonian III*, a 200-passenger sightseeing boat with a cafeteria and bar which offers harbor cruises from mid-May to mid-October, together with an excellent commentary on the sights seen. ((902) 423-1271.

SHOPPING

Apart from the colorful selection of shops dotted in and around the **Historic Properties**, there are two shopping centers at opposite ends of Barrington Street where you will be able to find just about anything you could possibly want. The larger of the two, the **Scotia Square** complex near the Historic Properties, has over 100 shops and restaurants on two levels, with an information booth on the lower level. The **Maritime**

SPORTS

There are public **tennis** courts on Halifax Common, and five 18-hole golf courses within 16 km (10 miles) of downtown. The **Ashburn course** in Halifax ((902/443-8260) and the **Brightwood Golf and Country Club** ((902/466-7688) in Dartmouth, just across the harbor, are both particularly popular and both welcome non-members. For either **swimming** or **jogging** Point Pleasant Park is the place to go. The nearest good **fishing** is to be found in the lakes and rivers along the coast northeast of Halifax; for Atlantic salmon the best place is the St. Mary's River near Sherbrooke.

Mall, at 1505 Barrington Street near the corner of Spring Garden Road, has about 30 shops.

If you would like to see the work of local artists, potters, jewelers, ceramicists, and weavers, ask the Department of Tourism for a copy of its free *Buyer's Guide to Arts and Crafts in Nova Scotia.*

NIGHTLIFE

Halifax is surprisingly lively at night, especially along **Argyle Street**, which on Friday and Saturday nights appears to be the scene of one long party. Meanwhile, there is a tall party going on at **Privateers' Warehouse** in the Historic Properties: below the excellent

Upper Deck restaurant (see WHERE TO EAT) is the **Middle Deck**, a lounge where rock, blues, and jazz bands play, and below that the **Lower Deck**, where robust maritime folk music fills the air. The **Misty Moon** at 1595 Barrington Street, ((902) 454-6666, has live rock bands nightly and stays open until 3 am. The **Palace** at 1721 Brunswick Street across from The Citadel, ((902) 429-5929, is also open nightly and offers more varied musical fare. On Granville Street, not far from the Historic Properties, try the **Split Crow Pub** and **Scoundrel's**, while

at 1919 Upper Water Street, Halifax B3J 3J5, ((902) 421-1700, toll-free (800) 325-3535. Although large (356 rooms) and modern and equipped with all the luxuries, it has been so well designed and decorated that it manages to blend in beautifully with the historic buildings around it. Not far away, in the new Scotia Square complex, is the **Chateau Halifax** at 1990 Barrington Street, Halifax B3J 1P2, ((902) 425-6700, toll-free in Canada (800) 268-9411, in the U.S. (800) 828-7477. As it is attached to the largest shopping mall in Nova Scotia, this 300-room Canadian Pacific

Ginger's on Hollis Street offers mostly folk and blues to go along with its own beer. In addition, all of the larger hotels have lounges with live entertainment.

Concerts of all kinds are performed regularly at the **Metro Centre** on Brunswick Street near The Citadel ((902/451-1202 for recorded information), while the intimate **Neptune Theatre** at 5216 Sackville Street, ((902) 429-7070, stages both dramas and comedies.

Hotel offers not only the amenities you would expect of a luxury hotel, but also the convenience of having every conceivable type of shop within easy walking distance. Connected by underground walkway to the new Metro Centre is the **Prince George Hotel** at 1725 Market Street, Halifax B3J 3N9, ((902) 425-1986, toll-free (800) 565-1567. Opened in 1986, this elegantly-appointed hotel has not only a handy location next to the convention center but also boasts an award-winning restaurant.

WHERE TO STAY

Luxury

The most luxurious address in Halifax is the **Halifax Sheraton** in the Historic Properties

OPPOSITE: Lobster pots piled up on Cape Breton Island. ABOVE: The restored Historic Properties on the harborfront in Halifax.

Mid-range

Halifax is blessed with a large number of superb mid-range hotels. The **Citadel Inn Halifax**, a sister hotel of the Prince George, is perhaps marginally the best of these. Located at 1960 Brunswick Street, Halifax B3J 2G7, ((902) 422-1391, toll-free in Canada (800) 565-7162, the Citadel Inn has 270 luxurious rooms, some of which are on no-smoking floors and some of which overlook the harbor. Another top-class hotel in this category is the **Delta Barrington** at 1875 Barrington Street, Halifax B3J 3L6, ((902) 429-7410, toll-free in Canada (800) 268-1133, in the U.S. (800) 887-1133. Near the Historic Properties, here is another classic example of how to build a very modern hotel without upsetting the neighbors — in this case by dismantling the century-old facade and then replacing it once the building was completed. For elegance and charm it would be hard to beat the **Halliburton House Inn** at 5184 Morris Street, Halifax B3J 1B3, ((902) 420-0658. This registered Heritage Property with 44 rooms was built in 1820, and it has been completely renovated and modernized without sacrificing any of its original charm. It also has one of the best restaurants in Halifax.

The **Holiday Inn Halifax Centre** is at 1980 Robie Street, Halifax B3H 3G5, ((902) 423-1161, toll-free (800) HOLIDAY. This high-rise has an indoor pool, a good restaurant and piano bar, and free underground parking. The **Halifax Hilton**, 1881 Hollis Street, Halifax B3H 2P6, ((902) 423-7231, toll-free in Canada (800) 268-9275, in the U.S. (800) 445-8667, is a rather elderly hotel next to the railway station, but it has been tastefully refurbished and now enjoys the addition of a number of luxury rooms as well as a swimming pool and tennis court. It also runs a free shuttle service to downtown. The **Lord Nelson** is another venerable hotel, located opposite the Public Gardens at 1515 South Park Street (corner Spring Garden Road), Halifax B3J 2T3, ((902) 423-6331, toll-free (800) 565-2020. Finally, there is the **Waverley Inn** at 1266 Barrington Street, Halifax B3J 1Y5, ((902) 423-0167. This friendly 32-room inn has been here since 1876, and numbers Oscar Wilde among its former guests. Now fully modernized, it is an attractive bargain.

Inexpensive

Although it is some way from downtown, the **Chebucto Inn** is probably the best of the inexpensive hotels. It has 32 air-conditioned rooms, with all the standard facilities, in an attractive two-story building at 6151 Lady Hammond Road, Halifax B3K 2R9, ((902) 453-4330. Another good value is the **Travelers Motel** right on the Halifax city limits at 773 Bedford Highway, Bedford B4A 1A4, ((902) 835-3394. It has 25 motel units and 10 cottages, a pool, a restaurant, and free movies. Next door at 771 Bedford Highway, Bedford B4A 1A1, ((902) 835-3367, is the **Motel Esquire**, which has 30 units, pool, and restaurant, for the same prices. Across the harbor from Halifax in Dartmouth are two places that represent excellent value. The first is the **Dartmouth Inn** at 9 Braemar Drive, Dartmouth B2Y 3H6, ((902) 469-0331, which has 116 air-conditioned rooms, a licensed lounge and dining room, a gift shop, and a steak house. Also in Dartmouth at 7 Yorkshire Avenue Extension, ((902) 465-4000, toll-free (800) 465-4000, is the **Country Inn & Suites**, which has an innovative array of complimentary services in addition to its creature comforts.

For really cheap accommodation, contact **Halifax Metro Bed and Breakfast**, P.O. Box 1613, Station M, Halifax B3J 2Y3, ((902) 434-7283. They have a register of member B&Bs with details of rates.

WHERE TO EAT

Expensive

As with any smallish city, the best restaurants generally are in the best hotels. In Halifax, I would recommend two in particular: **The Grand Banker** in the Sheraton Halifax, ((902) 421-1700, and the superb restaurant in the **Halliburton House Inn**, ((902) 420-0658. Also, as I have already mentioned, the **Upper Deck** restaurant on the third floor of Privateers' Warehouse in the Historic Properties ((902/422-1289) has excellent food as well as courteous service to go with its maritime decor. Also on the waterfront at Privateers' Wharf is **Clipper Cay**, ((902) 423-6818, where the seafood is unsurpassed anywhere. Of course, it's difficult not to find wonderful seafood in Halifax, but if you want to find it in an unusual and lovely setting, go to **Five Fishermen** at 1740 Argyle Street across from the Grand Parade, ((902) 422-4421. The restaurant is upstairs in a converted schoolhouse and is lit by genuine Tiffany lamps. But wherever you go, be sure to include a visit to **Old Man Morias**, a marvelous Greek restaurant run by two Greek emigrés, Vasilios and Panagiota Migas. It is in an old townhouse at 1150 Barrington Street, ((902) 422-7960.

Moderate

Ryan Duffy's Steak and Seafood in the Spring Garden Place shopping center at 5640 Spring Garden Road, ((902) 421-1116, is as moderate (or as expensive) as you want it to be. If you order a steak, for example, the meat is cut and trimmed to your specifications at your table before it is cooked, and the price is strictly according to the weight of the cut you have chosen. A very good deal. **Scanway**, 1569 Dresden Row, ((902) 422-3733, is a delightful Scandinavian restaurant in a little cluster of shops called The Courtyard, near Spring Garden Road. **Thackeray's** at 5407 Spring Garden Road, ((902) 423-5995, is in a renovated eighteenth-century townhouse, where the service is exceptionally jolly and the food exceptionally good. The **Silver Spoon** at 1865 Hollis Street, ((902) 422-1519, would be a splendid place to eat even if it didn't back on to a dessert shop of the same name — but it does. Oh my, yes it does. Opposite the Maritime Museum of the Atlantic at 1680 Lower Water Street, ((902) 421-6161, is **McKelvie's**, which serves delicious seafood in a converted firehall.

Inexpensive

Argyle Street alongside the Grand Parade has a large number of budget eateries, of which I would single out three. The **Guru** at 1580 Argyle Street, ((902) 422-6347, is a very comfortable and reasonable Indian restaurant. **Lawrence of Oregano** at 1727 Argyle Street, ((902) 422-6907, is a very cheerful and popular Italian restaurant serving excellent pizzas and spaghetti dishes. **The Graduate** at 1567 Argyle Street, ((902) 423-4703, has middle-of-the road fare (steaks, chicken, etc.) at off-the-wall prices. **Mariano's** at the corner of Grafton Street and Blowers Street serves good, inexpensive Mexican food, while the **Midtown Tavern** at the corner of Grafton Street and Prince Street is extremely popular with students for its draught beer and hearty meals in a friendly, noisy atmosphere.

HOW TO GET THERE

Air Canada has daily flights to Halifax from New York, Boston, Toronto, and Montreal, while Canadian Airlines International flies

in daily from many Canadian cities. Canadian Airlines' affiliate, Air Atlantic, connects Halifax with the rest of the Maritimes and with Newfoundland. For flight information call toll-free (800) 565-1800 in Canada or (800) 426-7000 in the U.S.

If you are driving, highways from all over the U.S. and Canada join the Trans-Canada Highway which crosses from New Brunswick into Nova Scotia at Amherst. Similarly, Greyhound buses from the U.S. and Voyageur buses from Montreal link up with the SMT bus lines in New Brunswick

A fisherman with his catch in picturesque Peggy's Cove, west of Halifax.

which in turn connects with the Acadian Lines in Nova Scotia at Amherst.

There are no ferries into Halifax, but there are ferries from Newfoundland to North Sydney, discussed in the preceding chapter, and there is a ferry from Wood Islands, Prince Edward Island, to Caribou, Nova Scotia, daily May to December, operated by **Northumberland Ferries**, P.O. Box 634, Charlottetown, Prince Edward Island C1A 7L3, toll-free in the Maritimes (800) 565-0201. There are also ferries to Yarmouth from Bar Harbor, Maine and Port-

GENERAL INFORMATION

The Department of Tourism and Culture in Halifax is, of course, your best source of information about the province as a whole, while the free Check In service is your best bet for getting up-to-date travel information or for making reservations. In addition there are Tourist Information Centres in the following locations around the province.

The South Shore: Lunenburg (℃ 902/ 634-8100) and Shelburne (℃ 902/ 875-4547)

land, Maine. These will be discussed at the end of the next section.

OUTSIDE HALIFAX

Nova Scotia may divide into two parts geographically — the peninsula and Cape Breton Island — but ethnically it is a jigsaw puzzle. While Halifax is very English both in its history and its character, the rest of the province shows the cultural influences of the English, the Irish, the French, the Germans, and the Scots — whose descendants today make up over a third of the population. As you travel around Nova Scotia these influences will become very apparent.

both have tourist offices, while there is a Tourist Information Centre in Yarmouth up the hill from the ferry terminal, on the right. ℃ (902) 742-5033.

Annapolis Valley: There is a Tourist Information Centre, ℃ (902) 245-2201, in Digby on Shore Road en route from the ferry terminal. The one in Annapolis Royal is at the Annapolis Tidal Power Project on Route 1, ℃ (902) 532-5454.

Cape Breton Island: There is a Tourist Information Centre in Port Hastings on the right after crossing the causeway. ℃ (902) 625-1717. There is also a Cape Breton Highlands National Park information office (℃ 902/285-2270) and a Louisbourg Visitor Centre (℃ 902/733-2280).

PEGGY'S COVE

I have a suspicion that Peggy's Cove, 43 km (27 miles) west of Halifax on Route 333, is secretly sponsored by Kodak, for it must be the most photographed fishing village in all of Canada. Dating from 1811, the village is built around a narrow ocean inlet and is dominated by a lighthouse perched on massive granite boulders. Here brightly-colored clapboard houses cling to the granite cliffs surrounding the lovely little harbor where

name Shoreham), it is still the summer home of quite a few American families — as well as a favored retirement home of wealthy Canadians. Although visitors are welcome to use its tennis courts and its 18-hole golf course on a promontory overlooking the bay, most people come for the sailing and yachting. Indeed, the high point of the summer season is Chester Race Week in the middle of August, the largest sailing regatta in the Maritimes.

The little town of **Mahone Bay**, 21 km (13 miles) southwest of Chester on Route 3,

the fishing boats are moored and where the fishermen's shacks stand on stilts in the water.

Unfortunately, such is the fame of Peggy's Cove, it is packed with tourists during the summer, so if you want to see it then the best time to go is early morning, and if you're driving the best place to park is in the public lot at the top of the village.

THE SOUTH SHORE

On Route 3 southwest of Halifax, the charming seaside village of **Chester** is situated on a peninsula at the head of scenic, island-strewn Mahone Bay. Settled by New Englanders in 1760 (who originally gave it the

is today best known as a crafts and antiques center, with its trademark three churches standing side by side at the head of the harbor. But there was a time, in the century after its founding by Captain Ephraim Cook in 1754, when it was known primarily as a haunt of pirates and smugglers. In fact, the name mahone is thought to be derived from the old French *mahonne*, a type of raiding boat used by pirates. One of the most delightful aspects of the town is that many of its shops, studios, galleries, and restaurants

Two approaches to harvesting the sea: ABOVE, lobster pots in Cape Breton Highlands National Park and, OPPOSITE, fishing boats moored in Peggy's Cove.

are housed in historic early nineteenth-century buildings.

Just down the coast from Mahone Bay is **Lunenburg**, long considered Nova Scotia's premier fishing port. Like its neighbor, it was a favorite haven for pirates until well into the nineteenth century. Settled in 1753 by Protestants from the German town of Lunenburg, it has a long and colorful seafaring heritage, but is probably best known as the town that in 1921 built the *Bluenose*, the famous racing schooner that never lost an international race and which is depicted on

stantly created a prosperous town where there had been nothing but wilderness. That is to say, nothing but wilderness and one of the best natural harbors in the world. Within a few years the population had quintupled, making it the largest community in British North America. However, the population shrank again almost as quickly as it had expanded, whereupon the settlers who stayed on began turning Shelburne into a fishing and shipbuilding center — in fact, it went on to become the birthplace of many of the world's great yachts. There are still

the back of the Canadian dime. (In 1963 Lunenburg also built its replica, *Bluenose II*, which can usually be seen in the harbor at Halifax.) Situated on a picturesque peninsula with a front and back harbor, Lunenburg has lately become an important tourist stop-over, with shops, galleries, and all sorts of recreational facilities, including the nine-hole **Bluenose Golf Course** overlooking Front Harbour. It is also home to the interesting **Fisheries Museum of the Atlantic**, ((902) 634-4794, with three floors of exhibits and an aquarium.

Further down Route 103 is **Shelburne**, "The Loyalist Town", settled in 1783 when 3,000 Loyalists fleeing New York City, many of them rich, arrived in 30 ships and in-

quite a few houses in Shelburne that date from the Loyalist period, but two in particular deserve mention: the **Ross-Thomson House**, built in 1784, which was originally a general store and is today a Loyalist museum that includes shelves still stocked with goods that were in demand in the 1780s, and the **David Nairn House**, built in 1787, which now is the home of the Shelburne County Museum.

Although **Yarmouth**, with a population of 7,700, is Nova Scotia's largest seaport west of Halifax and has a great shipping tradition going back to its settlement in 1761, it is principally of interest today as the "Gateway to Nova Scotia", the terminus for ferries from Portland and Bar Harbor in

Maine. It is also notable for its well-preserved Victorian architecture and for its famous **Runic Stone** on Main Street, which bears inscriptions suggesting that the Vikings reached here, too, 1,000 years ago.

ANNAPOLIS VALLEY

To go up Route 1 from Yarmouth to Windsor, through the beautiful Annapolis Valley region, is to go up the **Evangeline Trail**, named after the eponymous heroine of Longfellow's famous poem about the trag-

the area. Finally, in 1710, the English triumphed and renamed the town Annapolis Royal in honor of Queen Anne. Although it then became the capital of Nova Scotia until the founding of Halifax, it remained an English island in a sea of French-speaking Acadians until 1755 when the Acadians were expelled from the province. The centerpiece of the town is the **Fort Anne National Historic Site** (℃ 902/532-2397) with its well-preserved earthwork fortifications, a museum, and a gunpowder magazine dating from 1708. Also well worth a visit are

edy of the Acadians who were expelled from here in 1755. This is the heartland of Acadia.

The first town of any size that you come across is **Digby,** home of the (justly) celebrated Digby scallops. In fact, the town itself celebrates its best known product with the Digby Scallop Days in August. Almost as well known are the locally cured smoked herring, called Digby Chicks. Digby's situation, on an inlet of the Bay of Fundy, is not only beautiful but handy: it is the terminus for the ferry from Saint John, New Brunswick.

Founded in 1605 by Samuel de Champlain, Annapolis Royal was originally called Port-Royal and for over a century was at the center of the battles that raged between the French and English for control of

the **Annapolis Royal Historic Gardens** (℃ 902/532-7018) near the fort on Upper George Street, where you can see the history of the area in its gardens. At Port Royal National Historic Site, 10 km (six miles) west of Annapolis Royal, you will find **Champlain's Habitation** (℃ 902/532-2898), a restoration of the original French fur-trading post that stood here from 1605 to 1613.

Grand Pré, the "great meadow" of dyked lands along the shore a few kilometers east of Wolfville, was the most important Acadian settlement before the Deportation

ABOVE: Annapolis Royal's Historic Gardens.
OPPOSITE: The church in Grand Pré National Historic Site that memorializes the deported Acadians.

and was the setting for Longfellow's *Evangeline*. Grand Pré National Historic Site (℡ 902/542-3631) features a bronze statue of Evangeline, as well as an Acadian well, a blacksmith's shop, and a stone church that stands as a memorial to the Acadians and houses an exhibit on the Deportation.

The Evangeline Trail ends at **Windsor**, at the eastern end of the Annapolis Valley, which also happens to be located exactly midway between the Equator and the North Pole. Settled by the Acadians at the end of the seventeenth century, not long after the founding of Grand Pré, it disappeared as an Acadian town in 1755 and became a Loyalist stronghold shortly thereafter. Today it is best known as the home of Judge Thomas Chandler Haliburton, the "Canadian Mark Twain" who created the memorable character of Sam Slick, many of whose coinages are now everyday expressions. Haliburton's house, which he built in 1833, is now a museum.

CAPE BRETON ISLAND

Connected to the mainland by the mile-long Canso Causeway, Cape Breton Island consists of 10,300 sq km (3,980 sq miles) of some of the most beautiful scenery in North America. Once across the causeway, most visitors continue on up the Trans-Canada Highway as far as Baddeck, where they join the **Cabot Trail**, a 294-km (184-mile) loop that rivals California's famous Highway 1 for unbelievably spectacular views.

After leaving the Trans-Canada Highway, heading clockwise, you follow the Cabot Trail over Hunter's Mountain into the Middle River Valley before joining the Margaree River in a lush valley renowned for its salmon pools. The highway then cuts across gentle farmland until it reaches Margaree Harbour on the coast, where it crosses the estuary of the Margaree River and heads up the coast, affording excellent views of the Northumberland Strait and the Gulf of St. Lawrence. About half an hour's drive up the coast from Margaree Harbour is **Chéticamp**, an Acadian, French-speaking fishing

Mother Nature with infant settlements: Cape Breton Island.

village known for the hooked rugs and mats hand-made by the local women. In addition to the large number of crafts shops, the **Musée Acadien** has a splendid collection of hooked rugs as well as a cafe and a shop where all kinds of locally made items are for sale.

About five kilometers (three miles) east of Chéticamp is the entrance to **Cape Breton Highlands National Park**, 958 sq km (370 sq miles) of steep mountains, stony shores, deep forests, green valleys, sandy beaches, and stunning ocean views — not to mention all kinds of wildlife — in a wilderness area furnished with many campgrounds and picnic sites. The most important resort area along the Cabot Trail is in the **Ingonish** region at the eastern entrance to the park, 105 km (65 miles) from Chéticamp. Here you will find the park's administrative headquarters and a great variety of recreational facilities: a golf course, tennis courts, supervised swimming, campsites, picnic areas, hiking trails, boating, sailing, and, in winter, skiing. Ingonish Beach, south of Ingonish, is also the home of the Keltic Lodge, one of the finest resort hotels in eastern Canada. From there you climb the 366 m (1,200 ft) of Cape Smokey, a mist-capped promontory whence the Trail plunges back to the coast and continues along the "North Shore", an area originally settled by Highland Scottish pioneers, down to South Gut St. Ann's, below St. Ann's Harbour, where it rejoins the Trans-Canada Highway for the final 18 km back to Baddeck, completing the loop.

If you take the Trans-Canada Highway (Route 105) in the other direction — east — it will take you to North Sydney, where it is met by the ferry to Newfoundland. Before entering North Sydney, if you turn right on to Route 125 it will take you across the Sydney River to the outskirts of Sydney, the "Steel City", Nova Scotia's third largest (and certainly drabbest) urban area. From there you take Route 22 south for 37 km (23 miles) to reach the **Fortress of Louisbourg National Historic Site**, the largest in Canada. The fortress itself, guarding the entrance to the St. Lawrence and therefore the approach to Quebec, took the French a quarter of a century to build

(1719–1744) and really wasn't completely finished when it was attacked in 1745 by an army of 4,000 New Englanders who captured it after a 49-day siege. It was handed back to France in 1748 under the Treaty of Aix-la-Chapelle, but was retaken by the British in 1758. Two years later Prime Minister William Pitt ordered the fortifications blown up. Since 1961 the fortress and the town have been the site of the largest historical reconstruction project ever undertaken in Canada. Over 40 buildings have been meticulously reconstructed, while the streets and shops are full of people in period dress and the inns and taverns serve authentic eighteenth-century food and drink. It is remarkable in the way that it captures the feel of a French colonial outpost of the time.

I would add just one word of caution. As the weather at Louisbourg is often foggy and cold, bring along a sweater and a raincoat just in case.

WHERE TO STAY

Peggy's Cove

The two nicest places to stay in Peggy's Cove are next to each other in Indian Harbour, two and a half kilometers (one and a half miles) to the northwest on Route 333. The **Clifty Cove Motel**, Box 10, Site 30, RR 1, Tantallon, Nova Scotia B0J 3J0, ((902) 823-3178, has 10 units with full bath/shower and TV. Next to it, owned by the same family, are the **Lover's Lane Cottages by the Ocean**, Box 4, Site 31, RR 1, Tantallon B0J 3J0. The six cottages are, like the motel units, fully equipped and inexpensive. Nearby on Route 333 is the **King Neptune Campground**, ((902) 823-2582, which has a boat dock and launching area in addition to the usual facilites.

The South Shore

In **Chester** your best bet is the **Windjammer Motel** on Route 3 at the southern turn-off to the town (Box 240, Chester B0J 1J0, (902/275-3567). It has 18 units set in landscaped grounds, with small fridges and mini-bars as well as picnic tables, barbecues, miniature golf, and a pool. And it's not expensive. Even less expensive is the **Casa Blanca Guest House and Cabins** at 463

Duke Street, Chester B0J 1J0, ((902) 275-3385. Four of its eight rooms have private baths, the other four share two baths. There is also a two-unit cabin next door, with all facilities. Full breakfast.

Nearby in **Hubbards** there are two delightful places on Shore Club Road. One is the **Anchorage House & Cabins**, RR 2, Hubbards B0J 1T0, ((902) 857-9402, which has seven housekeeping cottages, two cabins, and five rooms in the main lodge. It has fishing charters and small-boat rentals from its own private wharf. Very reasonably priced.

half private baths, a walking trail, beach bikes, a pond. The price, which is in the mid-range category, includes full breakfast.

The two most elegant hostelries in **Lunenburg** are the **Boscawen Inn** and the **Bluenose Lodge**, both of which are restored Victorian mansions full of antiques and period pieces. The Boscawen Inn, 150 Cumberland Street, Lunenburg B0J 2C0, ((902) 634-3325, is slightly more expensive than the Bluenose Lodge, and somewhat larger, with 17 rooms. The Bluenose Lodge is at 10 Falkland Avenue, Lunenburg B0J 2C0,

At 167 Shore Club Road, Hubbards B0J 1T0, ((902) 857-1790, is the rather more expensive **Dauphinee Inn**, which has only six rooms but has a licensed dining room and lounge, a gift shop, and boat docking facilities.

In **Mahone Bay** there are two charming B&Bs. The **Sou'Wester Inn** at 788 Main Street, Mahone Bay B0J 2E0, ((902) 624-9296, has four rooms with one private bath, one shared bath, and one shared powder room. Furnished with antique furniture and with a veranda overlooking the bay, the inn's inexpensive price includes full breakfast and evening tea. **Longacres Bed & Breakfast** is in a house that dates from 1800 at 122 Clearland Road, Mahone Bay B0J 2E0, ((902) 624-6336. It has three rooms with two and a

((902) 634-8851, and like the Boscawen Inn has a licensed dining room serving three meals daily. An excellent bargain is the **Homeport Motel** at 167 Victoria Road, Lunenburg B0J 2C0, ((902) 634-8234, which has nine air-conditioned units as well as six new housekeeping units, cable TV, whirlpool tub, queen-size beds, etc., at very competitive rates. There is also a campground right next to the tourist information center on Blockhouse Hill Road.

In **Shelburne** you should try to get into **The Cooper's Inn**, 36 Dock Street, Shelburne

ABOVE: Stop Press! Long after the flames died, the story of a terrible forest fire still lives in Cape Breton Highlands National Park. OVERLEAF: The rugged beauty of Cape Breton Island's coastline.

B0T 1W0, ((902) 875-4656, a splendidly refurbished 1785 house on the waterfront with an excellent licensed restaurant. It has three rooms with private baths; breakfast is included in the inexpensive price. More inexpensive still is the **Loyalist Inn** downtown at 160 Water Street, Shelburne B0T 1W0, ((902) 875-2343, which has 18 air-conditioned rooms with bath and cable TV. Another bargain is the **Ox Bow Motel** on the shores of Lake George about five kilometers (three miles) east of Shelburne (Box 459, RR2, Shelburne B0T 1W0, (902/875-3000). It has 47 units, including 13 housekeeping, a heated pool, licensed dining room and lounge, and a coffee shop.

The poshest hotel in **Yarmouth** is easily the **Rodd Grand Hotel** at 417 Main Street, Yarmouth B5A 4B2, ((902) 742-2446, toll-free in the Maritimes (800) 565-0207, in Quebec and Ontario (800) 565-0241, and in the U.S. (800) 565-9077. Its 138 luxurious rooms occupy seven floors overlooking Yarmouth harbor, with all the usual trimmings at mid-range prices. Its lower-priced sister hotel, the **Rodd Colony Harbour Inn**, is across from the ferry terminal at 6 Forest Street, Yarmouth B5A 3K7, ((902) 742-9194, toll-free numbers the same as the Rodd Grand. The hotel's Colony Restaurant is deservedly celebrated, while its Hawthorne's Lounge is a most convivial watering hole. It has 65 rooms, 20 more than the **Best Western Mermaid Motel** at 545 Main Street, Yarmouth B5A 1J6, ((902) 742-7821, toll-free (800) 528-1234, which has a lounge and English-style sports pub as well as a heated swimming pool and gift shop, only minutes away from the ferry terminal. Four kilometers (two and a half miles) from Yarmouth on Route 1 at Dayton is the **Voyageur Motel**, Box 1020, RR1, Yarmouth B5A 4A5, ((902) 742-7157, toll-free in the Maritimes (800) 565-5026. Overlooking Doctors Lake, it has 29 motel units and four housekeeping units. All of its rooms, even the de luxe ones, are priced in the middle range. Nearby, two and a half kilometers (one and a half miles) from Yarmouth on Route 1, is **Doctors Lake Camping Park**, one of the best-equipped

campgrounds anywhere in Nova Scotia, ((902) 742-8442.

Annapolis Valley

If you know anything about **Digby**, you know it is the home of the **Pines Resort Hotel** on Shore Road, Digby B0V 1A0, ((902) 245-2511, toll-free (800) 341-6096 in the U.S., where the 83 rooms in the main lodge and the 61 rooms in the 30 cottages are, yes, expensive — and well worth it. The Pines, which is one of three grand resort hotels operated by the provincial government, has its own 18-hole golf course, floodlit tennis courts, heated and glass-enclosed swimming pool, croquet lawns, hiking trails, you name it. The best of the rest is the **Admiral Digby Inn** on Shore Road, Digby B0V 1A0,

The forested mountains and steep, verdant valleys of Cape Breton Highlands National Park provide a paradise for hikers and campers.

((902) 245-2531, only half a mile from where the New Brunswick ferry docks. It has 44 motel units and two deluxe cottages, a heated indoor swimming pool and the full range of amenities at moderate prices. For inexpensive but extremely comfortable accommodation try the **Kingfisher Motel** on Warwick Street, Digby B0V 1S0, ((902) 245-4747. Its 37 rooms are well appointed and its restaurant is good.

In **Annapolis Royal** there is no shortage of delightful places to stay. For creature comforts, you can't do better than the **Auberge Wandlyn Royal Anne Motel** with its modern rooms, sauna, whirlpool baths, cable TV, and restaurant. It is just west of town on Route 1 (Box 628, Annapolis Royal B0S 1A0, (902/532-2323, toll-free in the Maritimes

800/561-0000). For charm and taste (and convenient location) I would recommend three places. **The Bread and Roses Country Inn** at 82 Victoria Street, Annapolis Royal B0S 1A0, ((902) 532-5727, is a brick mansion built in 1882 where the nine rooms all have baths en suite and antique furnishings. **The Garrison House Inn** at 350 St. George Street, Annapolis Royal B0S 1A0, ((902) 532-5750, is directly across from Fort Anne and was built in 1854. **The Queen Anne Inn** at 494 Upper St. George Street, Annapolis Royal B0S 1A0, ((902) 532-7850, is a registered Heritage Property with 10 rooms, all with private bath, and cable TV in the sitting room.

In the **Grand Pré** area my favorite place is the **Old Orchard Inn**, P.O. Box 1090, Wolfville B0P 1X0, ((902) 542-5751, which is only five kilometers (three miles) from Grand Pré National Historic Park, off Exit 11 from Route 101. Set in an attractive apple orchard overlooking Wolfville, it has 110 well-appointed rooms, 30 rustic chalets, an indoor heated pool, tennis courts, saunas, playground and ski trails — all for mid-range prices. The **Blomidon Inn** at 127 Main Street, Wolfville B0P 1X0, ((902) 542-2291, has 27 rooms, elegantly furnished, as well as recreational facilities and a first-class dining room. Also moderately priced. If you're looking for a bargain, you need look no fur-

Cape Breton Island

On the **Canso Causeway** at the junction of Routes 19, 104, and 105, are two very comfortable and moderately priced motels. **Keddy's Inn**, Box 50, Port Hastings B0E 2T0, ((902) 625-0460, toll-free (800) 561-7666, is the larger and slightly more expensive of the two. **Skye Motel**, Box 190, Port Hastings B0E 2T0, ((902) 625-1300, has the better restaurant.

On the way up the **Cabot Trail** the **Normaway Inn** in the Margaree Valley is a rewarding place to stop (Box 100, Margaree Valley B0E 2C0, (902/248-2987, toll-free 800/565-

ther than the **Evangeline Motel**, Grand Pré B0P 1M0, ((902) 542-2703, at the intersection of Route 101 and the road into the park. Its 21 rooms are comfortable, there is a pool and restaurant, and it costs what you would pay in tax alone at some other places.

In **Windsor** the pick of the accommodations is easily the **Hampshire Court Motel and Cottages**, 1081 King Street, Windsor B0N 2T0, ((902) 798-3133. In beautiful surroundings, with air conditioning, tennis courts, cable TV, and a lovely picnic area, it is surprisingly inexpensive.

9463). There are nine rooms in the main lodge and 17 cabins, tennis courts and arrangements for canoeing, horseback riding, salmon fishing and many other activities. Fairly expensive. In **Chéticamp** the cream of the crop is **Laurie's Motel** on Main Street, Chéticamp B0E 1H0, ((902) 224-2400. It has 55 rooms, some with private balcony, and a superb restaurant. Mid-range. Slightly cheaper is the **Park View Motel**, Box 117, Chéticamp B0E 1H0, ((902) 224-3232. It has a view of the entrance to the park as well as a view of the Gulf of St. Lawrence, with a licensed dining room and friendly late-night lounge. The **Ocean View Motel**, Box 419, Chéticamp B0E 1H0, ((902) 224-2313, is about the same price, and offers ocean swimming and barbecue pits.

On Cape Breton Island, Ethel obviously aims to attract motorists already blinded by hunger.

In **Ingonish**, the **Glenhorm Resort** (Box 39, Ongonish B0C 1K0, (902/285-2049), offers astonishingly good value for its mid-range prices. It has 74 motel units and 11 housekeeping cottages on 22 acres with ocean frontage and a swimming pool. Near the eastern entrance to the park at Ingonish Beach is the spectacular, and spectacularly expensive, **Keltic Lodge**, another resort complex operated by the provincial government. Set on a peninsula jutting out into the Atlantic, it features a baronial main lodge with 32 rooms, the White Birch Inn with 40 rooms, and nine cottages with 26 bedrooms. It has its own 18-hole golf course and absolutely everything else that the dedicated vacationer might want. Box 70, Ingonish Beach B0C 1L0. ((902) 285-2880. Much more basic, and much cheaper, but still very comfortable are the **Skyline Cabins** run by Joyce Marra a few hundred yards from the park entrance (Box 26, Ingonish Beach B0C 1L0, (902/285-2055). Of the 11 cabins, six are housekeeping and all have full bath/shower. There are also three excellent **campgrounds** nearby in the park.

In **Baddeck**, the moderate-to-expensive **Inverary Inn** offers a wide variety of motel rooms and cottages — 160 in all — in addition to a private beach on Bras d'Or Lake, spacious grounds, indoor and outdoor swimming pools, tennis courts, and a wonderful restaurant. Box 190, Baddeck B0E 1B0. ((902) 295-2674. Just across the road is the **Silver Dart Lodge**, Box 399, Baddeck B0E 1B0, ((902) 295-2340, which is smaller and less expensive, but nonetheless has its own private waterfront, playground, swimming pool, luxury suites, chalets, jacuzzis, and so on.

There are a number of perfectly adequate B&Bs in **Louisbourg**, but the place I would stay is the **Louisbourg Motel** at 1225 Main Street, Louisbourg B0A 1M0, ((902) 733-2844, which is quite inexpensive and yet has all the conveniences of a modern motel plus an excellent licensed dining room.

WHERE TO EAT

Peggy's Cove

Peggy's Cove is mostly distinguished, if that's the word, for its snack bars and fast-food places: pit stops for the hungry tourist. There is, however, **The Sou'Wester,**((902) 823-2561, on Route 333 at the top of the hill near the lighthouse, which specializes in lobster live from the tank.

The South Shore

In **Chester**, if you are staying in the Windjammer Motel, as I've recommended, eat there. Otherwise go down Route 3 to **The Galley Restaurant & Lounge**, between Exits 98 and 9, ((902) 275-4700, which has a lovely view over the marina at Marriott Cove as well as lovely food. In **Mahone Bay**, **Zwicker's Inn** at 662 Main Street, ((902) 624-8045, serves especially delicious chowders, pasta, breads, and ice creams — all homemade — in a refurbished 1805 post house. Also worth trying is **The Innlet Cafe**, ((902) 624-6363, at Kedy's Landing in Mahone Bay. Smartly decorated, in the wing of a 200-year-old house, it specializes in various coffees and desserts, but what comes before is quite edible.

In **Lunenburg**, the best dining is to be found in the **Boscawen Inn** and the **Bluenose Lodge**, both mentioned above. Also good is the **Capt'n Angus Seafood Restaurant** on the second floor of the Fisheries Museum of the Atlantic, ((902) 634-3030, which offers several traditional Lunenburg dishes.

In **Shelburne**, apart from **The Cooper's Inn** and the **Loyalist Inn**, in one of which you should be staying anyway, there is **McGowan's**, a licensed dining room and lounge at 1 Dock Street on the upper level, ((902) 875-3602, above Bruce's Wharf.

In **Yarmouth**, once again, the best places to eat are in the best places to stay: **Rodd Colony Harbour Inn** and the **Rodd Grand Hotel**. After those you ought to check out **Captain Kelley's Kitchen** at 577 Main Street, ((902) 742-9191, which serves very good food at popular prices. Also, out on Route 1 across from the Voyageur Motel, there is the unpromisingly named **Harris' Quick 'n' Tasty,**((902) 742-3467, which is much better than it sounds, and also boasts of "cholestrol-free frying".

Annapolis Valley

In **Digby** the place to eat is **The Pines Resort Hotel**. The other place is the **Admiral Digby**

Inn. To introduce a little variety into your diet, the **House of Wong** at 110 Water Street in Digby, ((902) 245-4125, has been serving delicious Chinese food for half a century. Just outside Digby, in Smith's Cove, there is the **Harbourview Inn**, ((902) 245-5686, where one can dine very well indeed.

In **Annapolis Royal**, the **Historic Gardens Restaurant** at 469 St. George Street, ((902) 532-7062, serves delicious seafood in a Victorian house overlooking beautiful gardens. At 218 St. George Street is **Newman's**, ((902) 532-5502, which is more for gourmands than gourmets, but its basic and well-prepared dishes are very reasonably priced.

In **Wolfville**, the best place to eat is **Chez La Vigne** at 17 Front Street, ((902) 542-5077, where you will find classic French cuisine in a romantic setting. The chef and owner, Alex Clavel, was voted the "1989 Canadian Chef of the Year". More homespun is the **Colonial Inn Restaurant**, ((902) 542-7525, on Main Street across from the post office in the center of town. Everything here is homemade, including the pastries, and served in a colonial setting. For elegant food in an elegant atmosphere, you can't beat the Acadian Room in the **Old Orchard Inn**, followed closely by the dining room at the **Blomidon Inn**.

Cape Breton Island

One of the best places to eat in Cape Breton Island is also one of the first you come across: the restaurant in the **Skye Motel** on **Canso Causeway**. On the **Cabot Trail**, the **Normaway Inn** in Margaree Valley has a wonderful dining room in the main lodge. In **Chéticamp**, **Laurie's Motel** has a very fine restaurant, although it closes a bit early. The **Harbour Restaurant**, on Main Street, ((902) 224-2042, has a patio overlooking the sea as well as a dining room, and serves fresh lobster after season. You probably don't have to be told that the place to eat in Ingonish is the **Keltic Lodge**, which probably has the best food on the island — and the dearest. In **Baddeck**, the restaurant in the **Inverary Inn** is worth a visit even if you're not staying there, as indeed is **McCurdy's Restaurant** in the **Silver Dart Lodge** just over the road. I also like the **Bell Buoy Restaurant** on Chebucto Street downtown, ((902) 295-2581. In **Louisbourg**, the dining room of the **Louis-**

bourg Motel is more than adequate, but do plan to have at least one meal in one of the period restaurants in the fortress itself. Probably the two best are **The Grubstake Restaurant** at 1274 Main Street, ((902) 733-2309, and **Anchors Aweigh Restaurant** at 1095 Main Street, ((902) 733-3131, both of which have their own bakeries attached.

How to Get There

If you want to fly directly to Cape Breton Island without going through Halifax, Air

Atlantic ((902/564-4545) connects Sydney with the rest of Atlantic Canada.

If you are planning to come to Nova Scotia by ferry from Maine, there are daily ferries from Bar Harbor and Portland.

The ferry from Bar Harbor which takes about six hours, is operated by Marine Atlantic. For information or reservations write to them at P.O. Box 250, North Sydney, Nova Scotia B2A 3M3, or call them in Bar Harbor at (207) 288-3395, toll-free (800) 432-7344 in Maine, (800) 341-7981 in the rest of the U.S.

The ferry from Portland, which sails overnight and takes about 11 hours, is run by Prince of Fundy Cruises. For information and reservations you can write to them at International Terminal, Portland ME 04101 or call them at (207) 775-5616, toll-free (800) 565-7900 in the Maritimes, (800) 428-0955 in Maine, and (800) 341-7450 in the rest of the U.S.

Nova Scotia from the inside and outside. OPPOSITE TOP: A barn and farmhouse in their wooded context and BOTTOM: The shingled exterior of a barn. ABOVE: Preparing salmon for smoking.

Prince
Edward
Island

A GLANCE at some of the sobriquets given to Prince Edward Island tells you a great deal about the province. Variously and affectionately known as Canada's "million-acre farm", "Spud Island", and "the Garden of the Gulf", it is indeed small (over half a million hectares or 1.4 million acres actually, spread over an island 224 km or 140 miles long and six to 64 km or four to 40 miles wide), it is mostly rolling farmland, it is famous for its potatoes, and it is lovely and unspoiled.

Separated from the mainland by the Northumberland Strait, the island was inhabited by Micmac Indians when Jacques Cartier in 1534 came upon "the fairest land 'tis possible to see", named it Ile St-Jean, and claimed it for France. French settlers didn't begin to arrive in any numbers, however,

until the early eighteenth century, to be reinforced in 1755 by Acadians expelled from Nova Scotia by the British and again in 1758 by French colonists fleeing Nova Scotia after the fall of the fortress at Louisbourg. But it didn't remain a safe haven for very long. Later that same year, 1758, a British expeditionary force under Lord Rollo captured the island and deported most of the French-speaking population. Five years later Ile St-Jean was renamed the "Island of St. John" and annexed to Nova Scotia. In 1764, Charlottetown, named in honor of Queen Charlotte, the wife of George III, was designated as the capital, and in 1769 the island became a colony in its own right.

In the years following the American Revolution both the colony's population and its

ture, tourism is now the island's most important industry.

CHARLOTTETOWN

This lovely little city of tree-shaded streets and squares, stately Victorian clapboard houses and monumental churches is not only the provincial capital but also the center of the island's commerce and tourism. It is situated on an arm of Hillsborough Bay, off the Northumberland Strait, 55 km (34 miles) from the ferry landing at Wood Islands. Known as the "cradle of Confederation", it was here that the discussions were held in 1864 that led to the birth of the Dominion of Canada.

BACKGROUND

Charlottetown lies just across the harbor from the spot where the first European settlement on Prince Edward Island was founded in 1720 by 300 French colonists, who named it Port-La-Joye. After the British captured it in 1758 they built Fort Amherst on the site, and six years later founded Charlottetown. Over the next century, despite the influx of Loyalists following the American Revolution, and successive waves of immigrants from Ireland and the Scottish Highlands, the town's population grew at a slow but steady pace — much like the pace of life in Charlottetown today. Then in 1864 it became the

Anglophile orientation received a boost from the arrival of Loyalists fleeing the new republic to the south, and in 1799 it was renamed one final time, in honor of Prince Edward, later Duke of Kent and father of the future Queen Victoria. In 1851 the colony was granted self-governing status, and in 1864 it hosted the historic conference that led to the confederation of Canada in 1867. Prince Edward Island joined the Confederation in 1873.

Although the island's population is only 130,000, it is nonetheless Canada's most densely populated province — because it's easily the smallest province. And it is even more densely populated in the summer, when it attracts over half a million visitors who come to enjoy its idyllic scenery and long sandy beaches. Indeed, after agricul-

birthplace of Canada when delegates from Britain's North American colonies convened in Province House and signed the articles that led to the Canadian Confederation.

With much of its colonial architecture still handsomely preserved, Charlottetown is a delightful and attractive place to start any visit to the island.

GENERAL INFORMATION

Like Nova Scotia's excellent Check In system, Prince Edward Island has a toll-free "Dial The Island" information and reservation service. In the Maritimes the toll free number to call is (800) 565-7421, in the rest

A typical corner of Canada's "million-acre farm".

of North America it is (800) 565-0267. For a copy of the province's free 200-page Visitor's Guide, write to Visitor Services, P.O. Box 940, Charlottetown, Prince Edward Island C1A 7M5. The Charlottetown Visitor Information Centre is in the Oak Tree Place shopping mall on University Avenue (which is also the Trans-Canada Highway) at Summer Street, ℂ (902) 368-4444. There are also Visitor Information Centres in Borden, Portage, Summerside, Brackley Beach, Cavendish, Stanhope, Wood Islands, Montague, and Souris. If you are thinking of holding a

large get-together on the island, contact the P.E.I. Convention Bureau at 11 Queen Street, Charlottetown C1A 4A2, ℂ (902) 368-3688.

WHAT TO SEE AND DO

Charlottetown

The heart and soul of Charlottetown is to be found in the **Confederation Centre of the Arts** on Queen Street between Richmond and Grafton Streets, ℂ (902) 566-2464. Built in 1964 to commemorate the 100th anniversary of the historic conference where the first steps were taken towards a united, confederated Canada, it covers two city blocks and contains a memorial hall, a theater, an art gallery, a museum, a library, and a restaurant. It is the principal venue of the annual, summer-long Charlottetown Festival, which always includes a popular musical based on the classic children's book, Anne of Green Gables. Opposite the Centre on Richmond

The House that Anne Built: Green Gables House, near Cavendish, is a perennial tourist attraction.

Street is **Province House**, a three-story, neo-Georgian sandstone edifice built in 1843–47, which is where the delegates met in 1864 to begin the process that created Canada. The room on the second floor where their meetings were held is now called the Confederation Chamber and is set out exactly as it was in 1864. The building also houses the provincial Legislative Assembly.

South of Province House on Richmond Street is **St. Dunstan's Basilica**, one of Canada's largest churches, easily recognizable by its twin Gothic spires. Inside you will find some exceptionally fine Italian carvings. On Church Street is **St. Paul's Anglican Cathedral**, which dates from 1747, making it the oldest Protestant church in the province. Its interior is distinguished by several murals by the portraitist Robert Harris.

Golf enthusiasts will want to pay a visit to the lovely, semi-private Belvedere Golf and Winter Club, a few minutes' drive northeast of downtown on Riverside Drive, ℂ (902) 892-7838. The best spectator sport in town is the **harness racing** held three evenings a week at the Charlottetown Driving Park on Kensington Road, ℂ (902) 892-6823.

Shoppers will find Prince Edward Island a treasure trove of traditional **crafts** such as stitchery, quilting, pottery, glasswork, leather, woodwork, and weaving. For information contact The Manager, Craft Development, Dept. of Community and Cultural Affairs, P.O. Box 2000, Charlottetown C1A 7N8, ℂ (902) 368-5280, or the P.E.I. Crafts Council, 156 Richmond Street, Charlottetown C1A 1H9, ℂ (902) 892-5152.

The North Shore

If you take Route 2 north of Charlottetown you will come to Route 6 just beyond Dunstaffnage; Route 6 will then take you to **Dalvay** at the eastern entrance to **Prince Edward Island National Park**, the province's premier tourist attraction. The park stretches for 40 km (25 miles) along the north shore and is hugely popular thanks to having some of the finest white sand beaches in North America and beautiful clear water warmed by the Gulf Stream. **Dalvay Beach** is usually the least crowded of the park's beaches, while **Cavendish Beach** at the other end of the park is one of the busiest in all of Canada. All of these beaches are accessible from Route 6, which after **Brackley Beach** becomes part of the scenic Blue Heron Drive that loops around the central part of the island. The drive is named for the beautiful blue herons who make their home in **New London Bay**, just beyond Cavendish at the western end of the park.

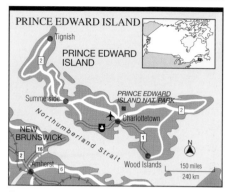

Off Route 6 in Cavendish is **Green Gables House**, the old green and white farmhouse that belonged to the cousins of Lucy Maud Montgomery, who used it as Anne's home in her novel, *Anne of Green Gables*. Now carefully restored, it is visited by thousands of people every year. Nearby is the **Rainbow Valley** amusement park, ((902) 836-3610, which has 30 acres of rides and entertainments.

WHERE TO STAY

Charlottetown

The biggest and best hotel is the new 10-story **Prince Edward Hotel and Convention Centre** overlooking the waterfront at 18 Queen Street, Charlottetown C1A 8B9, ((902) 566-2222, toll-free (800) 268-9411 in Canada, (800) 828-7447 in the U.S. A Canadian Pacific hotel, its 211 rooms enjoy the use of saunas, jacuzzis, spas, swimming pool, mini-bars in every room, two restaurants and a lounge. The other really top-flight hotel is **The Charlottetown**, a Rodd Classic hotel at the corner of Kent and Pownal Street, Charlottetown C1A 7K4, ((902) 894-7371, toll-free (800) 565-0207 in the Maritimes, (800) 565-0241 in Quebec and Ontario, (800) 565-9077 in the U.S. It is marginally less expensive than the Prince Edward, and about half the size, but offers the same basic range of amenities in the heart of downtown.

Of the mid-range hotels my pick would be **The Inn on the Hill** at the corner of University Avenue and Euston Street, P.O. Box 1720, Charlottetown C1A 7N4, ((902) 894-8572. It is quite modern, well situated and has a very good restaurant, Samuel's. The **Kirkwood Motor Hotel** at 455 University Avenue, Charlottetown C1A 4N8, ((902) 892-4206, is larger and has two restaurants and a swimming pool with sun deck. The **Dundee Arms Inn and Motel** at 200 Pownal Street, Charlottetown C1A 3W8, ((902) 892-2496, is a restored turn-of-

the-century mansion furnished with antiques and situated in a tree-lined residential area. Its restaurant, the Griffon Room, is probably the best on the island. Rooms in the motel wing are less expensive than those in the inn. Three kilometers west of Charlottetown on the Trans-Canada Highway is the **Auberge Wandlyn Inn**, P.O. Box 9500, Charlottetown C1A 8L4, ((902) 892-1201, toll-free (800) 561-0000 in Canada, (800) 561-0006 in the U.S. With a swimming pool and licensed dining room it offers very good value. So, too, in a different way, does the **Elmwood Heritage Inn** on elm-lined North River Road, P.O. Box 3128, Charlottetown C1A 7N8, ((902) 368-3310. In a lovely setting, this large Victorian house is furnished with antiques and distinguished by its friendly, personal service.

Of the less expensive accommodation, the three best equipped places are conveniently clustered together on the Trans-Canada Highway just a couple of kilometers west of the city. The fanciest of these is the **Queen's Arms Motel**, West Royalty RR 7, Charlottetown C1A 7J9, ((902) 368-1110. Its 66 rooms are all air-conditioned and have color cable TV, and there is a restaurant and swimming pool. The **Journey's End Motel** at 112 Trans-Canada Highway, Charlottetown C1E 1E7, ((902) 566-4424, toll-free (800) 668-4200, is a typical representative of this chain: 81 nicely furnished rooms with color cable TV at very reasonable prices. The smallest and cheapest of the three places is the **Royalty Maples Court**, West Royalty RR7, Charlottetown C1A 7J0, ((902) 368-1030. It has 16 housekeeping units, 10 of them cottages, set in spacious grounds near a shopping mall and golf course. Happily for the bargain-hunter, there is an abundance of tourist homes and **B&Bs** in Charlottetown, as well as in the rest of the island. A full list of these is available from the Visitor Services office in Charlottetown.

The North Shore

At the eastern end of the national park near **Dalvay Beach** is the magnificent old **Dalvay-by-the-Sea Hotel**, P.O. Box 8, York C0A 1P0, ℂ (902) 672-2048, winter (902) 672-2546. Built in 1895 as the summer residence of Alexander Macdonald, a Standard Oil tycoon, it is set in lovely grounds only 180 m

and sailboats. At **Brackley Beach** the class act is **Shaw's Hotel** on Route 15, Brackley Beach C0A 2H0, ℂ (902) 672-2022. Run by the Shaw family since 1860, it has 22 rooms in the hotel proper and 12 cottages (including six luxury chalets) on the well-manicured grounds, which are only about 500 m (1,640 ft) from the beach.

Around **Rustico Bay** there are three delightful places to stay, all very reasonably priced. In South Rustico there is the **Barachois Inn**, P.O. Box 1022, Charlottetown C1A 7M4, ℂ (902) 963-2194. It is a Victorian house

(590 ft) from the beach, with an excellent resturant, a two-hole fairway, a bowling green, a lake with canoes, tennis courts, playgrounds, and nature trails. Its 26 rooms are expensive, but what do you expect for a little bit of paradise? Further west, on Route 25 overlooking Covehead Bay, is the moderately priced **Stanhope by the Sea**, P.O. Box 9, York C0A 1P0, ℂ (902) 628-7899, winter (902) 672-2047, which has been a country inn since 1817. There are 35 rooms in the original inn, 24 in the new inn, 17 motel units, and one expensive apartment; all have been recently renovated. The inn is near the beach and has its own tennis courts

on Route 243, built in 1870, recently refurbished, with five tastefully decorated rooms and one suite. In **Rusticoville, The Breakers by the Sea** on Route 6, Box 38, Hunter River C0A 1N0, ℂ (902) 963-2555, has deluxe two-bedroom cottages with cable color TV and propane barbecues overlooking the harbor and the ocean. In **North Rustico**, the **Gulf View Cottages**, P.O. Box 119, North Rustico C0A 1X0, ℂ (902) 963-2052, also offer well-equipped two-bedroom cottages in spacious grounds overlooking the sea.

As you would expect, given the presence of Green Gables House as a mecca for tourists, not to mention the enormous popularity of Cavendish Beach, the entire area around **Cavendish** is crammed with places to stay. A

The oyster beds in Malpeque Bay.

few hundred meters to the east of Cavendish on Route 6 is the **Island Wild Resort**, Hunter River RR2, Cavendish C0A 1N0, ((902) 963-2193, which offers 11 deluxe cottages with satellite TV, gas barbecues, and heated pool at moderate rates. Within walking distance are the **Sundance Cottages**, Hunter River RR1, Cavendish C0A 1N0, ((902) 963-2149, which also offers 11 deluxe cottages with the same amenities. In the heart of Cavendish, the **Kindred Spirits Country Inn and Cottages**, Cavendish C0A 1N0, ((902) 963-2434, is a charming, antique-filled inn on a beautiful estate right next to Green Gables House and Golf Course. There are 10 large rooms in the inn and 13 cottages, plus a large swimming pool. Also next to Green Gables Golf Course is the **Lakeview Lodge and Cottages**, Cavendish C0A 1M0, ((902) 963-2436, which has 10 rooms in the lodge and 22 cottages. On Route 13 in the center of Cavendish is the **Shining Waters Country Inn and Cottages**, Cavendish C0A 1M0, ((902) 963-2251, another moderately-priced and delightful inn. It has 10 rooms in the main lodge and 20 cottages, with a splendid array of recreational facilities.

Nor should one forget that all along this coast there are excellent **campgrounds** everywhere, including three run by the national park itself, in addition to budget accommodations in farmhouses and tourist homes.

WHERE TO EAT

Charlottetown

The best place to eat in Charlottetown, perhaps in the whole province, is the colonial-style **Griffon Room** in the Dundee Arms Inn, ((902) 892-2496. It is expensive, of course, but not quite as expensive as the **Lord Selkirk Room** in the Prince Edward Hotel, ((902) 892-9052. In any case, both are excellent, as is the **Confederation Room** in The Charlottetown, ((902) 894-7371, which is somewhat easier on the wallet. **Samuel's** restaurant at the Inn on the Hill, ((902) 894-8572, has delicious seafood at reasonable prices.

Charlottetown has a good selection of moderately-priced eateries serving above-average food. One such is the **Lobsterman's Landing** on the Prince Street Wharf overlooking the harbor, ((902) 368-2888, where

the clams and mussels are exceptionally delicious. The **Queen Street Cafe** at 52 Queen Street, ((902) 566-5520, offers some very tasty bargains on its menu in addition to its very attractive decor. Another popular place is the **Town & Country Restaurant** at 219 Queen Street, ((902) 892-2282, which has good steaks and salads.

Surprisingly, perhaps, Charlottetown also has quite a few worthwhile ethnic restaurants. My favorite is **The Dispensary** in the basement of Apothecaries' Hall at 99 Grafton Street, ((902) 894-5990, which serves up Mexican food with live entertainment on weekend nights. For Chinese food the place to go is the **King Palace Restaurant** at 161 Queen Street, ((902) 894-9644. **Cedar's Eatery** at 81 University Avenue, ((902) 892-7377, is a welcoming sort of place that specializes in Lebanese dishes and mountainous servings. For Italian food, **Casa Mia** at 186 Prince Street, ((902) 892-8888, is a good bet, but everybody's favorite is **Pat's Rose and Grey Room** at 132 Richmond Street across from the Confederation Centre, ((902) 892-2222. This high-ceilinged, mahogany-stained, leaded-windowed restaurant has a very pleasant ambience to go with its appetizing food.

The North Shore

If you have taken my advice on where to stay along the north shore, then you will be well-placed to eat well. The dining room at **Dalvay-by-he-Sea** is excellent, with an Anglo-French accent to its seafood. ((902) 672-2048. The seafood dishes are similarly scrumptious, if not as elaborate, at **Stanhope by the Sea**, ((902) 672-2047. And when you get to **Brackley Beach**, you are in for a treat at the dining room of **Shaw's Hotel**, ((902) 672-2022, especially if you arrive in time for their Sunday buffet. A bit further down the road, on Route 6 in Oyster Bed Bridge, you can enjoy a delightful meal in delightful surroundings at **Cafe St. Jean**, ((902) 963-3133, at delightfully reasonable prices.

In **North Rustico** the whole world, or so it seems, heads for **Fisherman's Wharf** on the harbor, ((902) 963-2669, where it is claimed that 10 tons of live lobsters are kept for the hundreds (yes, hundreds) of customers who can be accommodated at one sitting. For somewhat quieter dining in North Rustico,

I would recommend the **Idle Oars Restaurant** on Route 6, ((902) 963-2534, which has first-rate steaks in addition to its seafood, and has views which look out over rolling farmland.

In **Cavendish** there are many — too many — diners, snack bars, and fast-food places, but not many really decent places to eat. One is **The Galley** on Route 13, ((902) 963-3383, which also has steaks as well as seafood. But for fun with your food I would go to **Fiddles & Vittles** next to the Bay Vista Motor Inn on Route 6, ((902) 963-3003. The fiddles in the background are mostly western and unobtrusive, the vittles in the foreground are mostly seafood and delicious, while the service in the middle is unfailingly friendly.

HOW TO GET THERE

If you are coming by air, Air Canada ((902/892-1007 in Charlottetown; toll-free 800/426-7000 from the U.S.) has daily flights to Charlottetown from several cities across Canada, while Air Atlantic ((902/892-3581 in Charlottetown) flies to Charlottetown from Halifax and Montreal, where there are connecting flights from many other cities. Details from your travel agent or from Visitor Services in Charlottetown as well as from "Dial the Island", the toll-free service.

There are also two regular ferry services from the mainland. Marine Atlantic operates a year-round service from Cape Tormentine, New Brunswick, to Borden, Prince Edward Island. The ferry leaves every half-hour during the summer, and the crossing only takes about 45 minutes. However, reservations are not accepted so it is advisable to get there early in the day, whether coming or going. The same is true of the ferry that crosses from Caribou, Nova Scotia, to Wood Islands, P.E.I. which leaves about every hour or so during the summer and takes 75 minutes to make the crossing. Information and schedules are available from Visitor Services or from Marine Atlantic, 180 Kent Street, Charlottetown C1A 1N9, ((902) 855-2030, toll-free (800) 565-9470 in the Maritimes, (800) 341-7981 in the U.S.; and from Northumberland Ferries, P.O. Box 634, Charlottetown C1A 7L3, ((902) 894-3473, toll-free (800) 565-0201 in the Maritimes.

A small Prince Edwardian takes it easy.

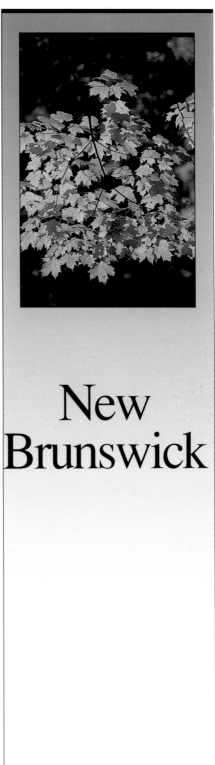

New Brunswick

NEW BRUNSWICK, the "gateway to Atlantic Canada", can lay claim to two of the wonders of the natural world: the tides in the Bay of Fundy and the leaves on its trees. Twice a day 100 billion tons of water swirl up the funnel-shaped Bay of Fundy, creating tides of up to 15 m (50 ft), the highest in the world. And once a year the trees of New Brunswick put on such a spectacular show of color — as their leaves in the autumn turn to gold, red, orange, and purple — that the Department of Tourism operates a toll-free hotline which people from all over North America can call to get daily updates on the colors the leaves are turning.

And there are a lot of leaves to turn, because over 80 percent of New Brunswick's 74,437 sq km (28,354 sq miles) is covered in forest. Bordered in the west by Maine, in the north by Quebec, and joined to Nova Scotia in the southeast by the Isthmus of Chignecto, New Brunswick still has approximately 2,250 km (1,400 miles) of coastline. Along these shores are to be found dozens of first-rate beaches in addition to hundreds of charming little fishing villages.

Like the other Maritimes, New Brunswick was inhabited by the Micmac Indians for at least 2,000 years before it was "discovered" by Jacques Cartier in 1534. Seventy years later Samuel de Champlain established a settlement on St. Croix Island, but the French settlement of the province didn't begin in earnest until the early eighteenth century. In 1751, with British pressure mounting, the French built Fort Beausejour to protect the settlers. It failed. Four years later, in 1755, it fell to the British under Colonel Moncton, and shortly thereafter the order for the deportation of the French-speaking Acadians was proclaimed.

In 1783 the first ships bearing Loyalists from the former American colonies arrived at Parrtown (now Saint John). By the following year the Loyalist population had grown to 14,000, and in response to their demands the new province of New Brunswick was formally established and named after the German duchy then still ruled by the British Crown. In 1785 Saint John became Canada's first incorporated city, while Fredericton was named the provincial capital. Around this time, some of the Acadians who had been deported 30 years before began to return, and today one-third of the province's 725,000 people are French-speaking. In fact, New Brunswick in 1969 was the first province to become officially bilingual.

FREDERICTON

As the home of the provincial legislature and the University of New Brunswick, Fredericton is the political and intellectual center of the province. Thus, with a popula-

tion of only about 50,000, it is not surprising that a majority of its inhabitants work either for the government or the university, nor that Frederictonians seem to spend most of their free time planning or attending gala dinners, charity balls, and garden parties. This "City of the Stately Elms", with its tree-lined avenues and elegant houses, is definitely and observably the heartland of New Brunswick high society.

It is also, thanks to lavish benefactions from the city's most famous native son, Lord Beaverbrook, an important cultural center, with an excellent art gallery, theater, and library. In addition, the city in recent years has become a center for all kinds of crafts, making it an ideal place to look for hooked rugs, batik, pottery, enamelware, jewelry, stained glass, and pewterware. Fredericton, in other words, has managed the difficult feat of providing the perfect setting for both gentility and creativity.

OPPOSITE: St. Andrew's Church in Fredericton.
ABOVE: The Saint John River at Fredericton.

BACKGROUND

Although the French built a fort here where the Nashwaak River joins the Saint John River as early as 1692, it was several decades before there was a French settlement of any size. Called Pointe Ste-Anne, it lasted only until 1759, when British troops drove the settlers out and renamed it Fredericton after the second son of George II. With the arrival of the Loyalists in 1783 it came into its own as a British town, the first major inland

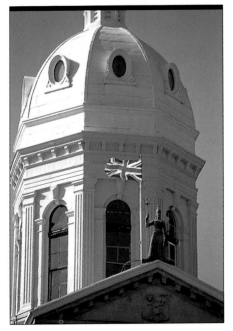

settlement. The following year New Brunswick was declared a province with Thomas Carleton as its first governor, and in 1785 Carleton decided that the provincial capital should be Fredericton rather than the larger Saint John because it was less vulnerable to attack from the sea. It quickly grew into an attractive and prosperous city — and remains one to this day.

GENERAL INFORMATION

For the most comprehensive and up-to-date information about holidaying in New

The dome of the Legistlative Building in Fredericton, under which lies one of the rare copies of the original Domesday Book.

Brunswick, get a copy of the complimentary *New Brunswick Travel Guide* from Tourism New Brunswick, P.O. Box 12345, Fredericton, New Brunswick E3B 5C3, toll-free (800) 442-4442 in New Brunswick, (800) 561-0123 in the rest of North America. These are also the numbers to call to get the latest reports on the turning leaves in the autumn.

There are two Tourist Information Centres in Fredericton. One is in the City Hall downtown, ((506) 452-9500, and the other is just off Route 2, the Trans-Canada Highway, at Exit 290.

WHAT TO SEE AND DO

Most of the places you will want to visit in Fredericton are centrally located on Queen Street. **Christ Church Cathedral**, a fine Gothic edifice modeled on the parish church of St. Mary in Snettisham, Norfolk, was consecrated in 1853 and has the distinction of being the first new cathedral foundation on British soil since the Norman Conquest of 1066. The silver-domed **Legislative Building**, ((506) 453-2527, built in the 1880s, has one of the rare copies of the original Domesday Book. Opposite the Legislative Building is the **Beaverbrook Art Gallery**, ((506) 458-8545, which houses one of the most impressive art collections in North America. Lord Beaverbrook designed the original building himself and gave it, along with his personal art collection, to the people of New Brunswick. First opened in 1959, it has expanded considerably in recent years and is particularly renowned for its wide range of masterpieces by British artists, although its most striking work is the huge *Santiago El Grande* by Dali that hangs by the entrance.

Another of Lord Beaverbrook's gifts to the city where he grew up is **The Playhouse**, ((506) 458-8345, built in 1964 and now the home of Theatre New Brunswick. Also on Queen Street is **Officers' Square**, ((506) 453-3747, an old parade ground that is now the site of lunchtime theater on weekdays during July and August as well as free weekly band concerts. Between Queen Street and the river is **The Green**, a large and beautiful landscaped park.

If you are a sports enthusiast, you should know about the **Mactaquac Provincial Park**,

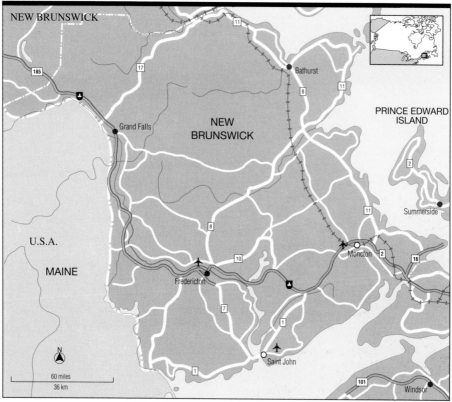

((506) 363-3011, just 24 km (15 miles) west of Fredericton on Route 105, off the Trans-Canada Highway. This 570-hectare or 1,400-acre "superpark", the largest park in New Brunswick, stretches along the north shore of the headpond of the Mactaquac Dam and offers sailing, boating, waterskiing, fishing, and lovely beaches for swimming. It also has an 18-hole golf course, supervised playgrounds, guided nature trails, and 300 campsites. Futher along the Saint John River, 37 km (23 miles) west of Fredericton, is **King's Landing**, ((506) 363-3081, toll-free (800) 561-0123, a reconstruction of a typical nineteenth-century Loyalist village. Beautifully situated on the banks of the river, the village has over 50 buildings, including a working sawmill and grist mill, and 100 "villagers" who go about their daily routines exactly as they would have done in the last century, all the while explaining to visitors what they are doing. Typical food and drink of the period is served in the King's Head Inn, and there is a special tour for children.

WHERE TO STAY

The good news is that even the best hotels in Fredericton — and there are some very good ones — are moderately priced. In fact, at this writing, it is difficult to find a double room in Fredericton costing over $105 a night. The venerable **Lord Beaverbrook Hotel** is the best in town. Conveniently located across from The Playhouse at 659 Queen Street, Fredericton E3B 5A6, ((506) 455-3371, toll-free (800) 561-7666, it has all the luxuries one would expect, including an indoor heated pool, and many of its 165 rooms overlook the river. It also has one of the city's best restaurants. Similarly priced and equipped is the **Auberge Wandlyn Inn** at 58 Prospect Street West, Fredericton E3B 2T8, ((506) 452-8937, toll-free (800) 561-0000 in eastern Canada, (800) 561-0006 in the U.S. Also in this category are the **Fredericton Motor Inn** at 1315 Regent Street, Fredericton E3B 1A1, ((506) 455-1430, and the **Howard Johnson Motor**

New Brunswick

Lodge, P.O. Box 1414, Fredericton E3B 5E3, ((506) 472-0480, toll-free (800) 654-2000, with the edge going to Howard Johnson.

Dropping down in price, there are four particularly good hotel bargains in Fredericton: the **Diplomat Motor Hotel** overlooking the river at 225 Woodstock Road, Fredericton E3B 5A6, ((506) 454-5584; **Keddy's Inn** at 368 Forest Hill Road, Fredericton E3B 5G2, ((506) 454-4461, toll-free (800) 561-7666, which is also in a delightful location and has a heated indoor swimming pool; the **Town and Country Motel**, RR3, Fredericton E3B 4X4, ((506) 454-4223, overlooking the river just west of the city; and the **Carriage House Inn** at 230 University Avenue, Fredericton E3B 4H7, ((506) 452-9924, a Victorian mansion built in 1875 for the city's mayor, adjacent to The

Green, with excellent facilities for its seven guest rooms, but no restaurant. In Mactaquac Park, near King's Landing, there is the **Chickadee Lodge**, ((506) 363-2759, a superb Bed & Breakfast overlooking the headpond. And of course there are all those campsites.

WHERE TO EAT

If you are staying at the Lord Beaverbrook Hotel, you could stay there for weeks without exhausting its dining possibilities. To begin with, there is the hotel's elegant **Terrace Room**, one of the finest restaurants in the city; in the basement there is the popular **Maverick Room**, which has excellent steaks and a lively bar that stays open till midnight; the **River Room** stays open even later, and

New Brunswick

For Greek food, **Dimitri's** at 596 Queen Street, ((506) 452-8882, is the place to go. Finally, there are two restaurants next to each other on Queen Street that both deserve a visit; **The Barn** at N° 540 ((506/455-2742) and **Benoit's** at N° 536 ((506/459-3666). The Barn is more of a family restaurant, while Benoit's has higher culinary ambitions.

HOW TO GET THERE

Fredericton is served by both Air Atlantic (from the other Atlantic provinces and elsewhere in New Brunswick) and by Air Canada (from more distant cities). Full details from Tourism New Brunswick or the airlines themselves. For information on Air Atlantic call toll-free (800) 565-1800 in New Brunswick, (800) 426-7000 in the U.S.; for Air Canada dial (506) 652-5440 in New Brunswick, or toll-free (800) 4-CANADA in the U.S.

If you are coming by car, the Trans-Canada Highway passes through Fredericton, entering New Brunswick from Nova Scotia across the Isthmus of Chignecto and from Quebec near Edmundston, whence it follows the Saint John River Valley into Fredericton. Coming from Maine, the I-95 enters New Brunswick near Woodstock, where it links up with the Trans-Canada Highway on its way down the Saint John River Valley.

has live entertainment every evening; while on the roof the **Top Deck** serves meals under large umbrellas throughout the summer. Probably the best restaurant in the city, however, is **Eighty Eight Ferry** at 88 Ferry Street, ((506) 472-1988. During the summer cocktails are served on the lawn beside a little brook and meals are served on the porch of a charming old farmhouse. It isn't cheap, but the food and the service are both exquisite.

For excellent steaks and seafood at reasonable prices in a genuine Victorian setting, head for the **Victoria & Albert** at 642 Queen Street, ((506) 458-8310. For Chinese food, oddly enough, you can hardly better the Cantonese dishes at the dining room of the **Diplomat Motor Hotel**. For Szechuan cooking, **Mei's** at 74 Regent Street, is very good.

SAINT JOHN

Known as "Loyalist City" to its inhabitants and as "Fog City" in the rest of New Brunswick, Saint John is never known as St. John. It is Canada's oldest incorporated city, having been incorporated by its Loyalist settlers in 1785, and New Brunswick's largest, with a population of 77,000. Situated in the estuary of the Saint John River, it has long been an important port and shipbuilding center, although today most of its income comes from its oil refineries and its big pulp and paper mill.

More often than not the city is shrouded in fog, hence its nickname, but the sea mists can have a welcome cooling effect on summer

The happy, proud countenances of Legionnaires in Fredericton.

days when the rest of the province is sweltering. And while Saint John has never been best known for its beauty, the city has been transformed in recent years by an ambitious development and restoration project that has done wonders for the waterfront and has skillfully blended the past with the present elsewhere in the city. Now, when the fog lifts, it can be quite a pleasant city to look at.

BACKGROUND

On St. John the Baptist's Day in 1604 Samuel

The growth and prosperity that the city had enjoyed almost uninterrupted since the arrival of the Loyalists came to an abrupt end in the latter part of the century. As wooden sailing ships became obsolete, Saint John's shipyards sank into bankruptcy. Then, as if to demonstrate the cruelty of the fates, a devastating fire in 1877 swept through the city's wooden buildings, wiping out over half of the city. It was a long time before Saint John recovered. But recover it did, so that the Saint John of today once again resembles the proud, bustling Saint John of yesterday.

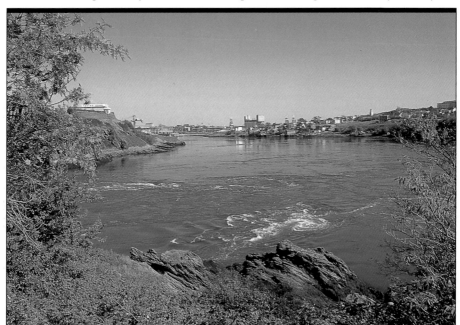

de Champlain landed at the mouth of the river, and in 1631 Charles de la Tour founded a fort and a trading post there. For the next century and a half the history of Saint John mirrored the history of the region, with the Acadian population being dispossessed by the British in 1755 and the city itself being formally ceded to England in 1763. But its real birthday was May 18, 1783 — the day that ships carrying more than 3,000 Loyalists arrived. What had been an obscure trading post instantly became a thriving Loyalist town, growing into a flourishing Loyalist city that so prospered from its trade and shipbuilding that it became known in the nineteenth century as the "Liverpool of America".

GENERAL INFORMATION

In addition to the more comprehensive information available from Tourism New Brunswick in Fredericton, specific enquiries regarding Saint John may be addressed to the Saint John Visitor and Convention Bureau, P.O. Box 1971, Saint John E2L 4L1, ((506) 658-2990. The bureau is on the eleventh floor of City Hall on King Street. There is also a Tourist Information Centre at Market Slip near the Market Square complex, ((506) 658-2855, and one on Route 100 at Reversing Falls Bridge, ((506) 635-1238. For up-to-the-minute information on Saint John's amazing tides, call Dial-A-Tide, ((506) 648-4429.

WHAT TO SEE AND DO

There are sights and sights to see in Saint John, and then there is The Sight: the famous phenomenon of the **Reversing Falls** that occurs twice daily when the mighty tides in the Bay of Fundy confront the Saint John River and drive it back upstream. At the point where the river empties into the bay the level of the river is over four meters (14 ft) above that of the bay at low tide, but at high tide the river is over four meters

652-3590, a Georgian mansion built in 1816 and one of the very few existing buildings to have survived the terrible fire of 1877. East of King Square, the old **Loyalist Burial Grounds** has tombstones dating all the way back to 1784, the year after the Loyalists arrived. Across the street, on the harborfront, is **Barbour's General Store**, ((506) 658-2939, a red clapboard building dating from 1867, stocked with merchandise of the time and staffed by people in period costume. It also includes a vintage barbershop. Another historical attraction is the **Carleton**

below the oncoming sea water — which has now risen by 8.5 m (28 ft)! — so the river is forced to reverse its course. And because the river narrows dramatically and curls around a sharp bend just before it reaches the bay, whirlpools and plunging rapids are created: reversing falls. There is an observation point at Reversing Falls Bridge which is ideal for witnessing this trick of nature.

Most of the sights in the city itself are within easy walking distance of King Square, and most have a distinctly Loyalist flavor. **King Square** itself advertises the city's past and present orientation: flowerbeds are laid out in the form of a Union Jack. Nearby, at the corner of Union Street and Germain Street, is **Loyalist House**, ((506)

Martello Tower, ((506) 648-4957, a stone fortification built during the War of 1812 and which today provides a commanding view of the city and the estuary. The **New Brunswick Museum**, at 277 Douglas Avenue, near Reversing Falls Bridge, ((506) 658-1842, is Canada's oldest museum, having been founded in 1842. It features national and international art treasures, historic artifacts, and a natural science gallery.

Saint John is also the home of Canada's oldest market, the **Old City Market**, which has been held in the same building since 1876 and where many of the same families

OPPOSITE: The famous Reversing Falls at Saint John. ABOVE: Saint John's Old City Market, the oldest market in Canada.

have operated stalls for generations. In addition to the fish, fruit, and vegetables on sale there is a wide variety of crafts and antiques. But if you're interested in either crafts or antiques, the place to go is **Prince William Street**, which is packed with shops and galleries. For more contemporary shopping, the **Market Square** complex, opened in 1983, offers several levels of shops to go along with its hotel and convention center.

Rockwood Park with its five lakes in the heart of the city has camping facilities, swimming, a waterslide, bumper boats, a

and more expensive than the Hilton is **The Delta Brunswick** at 39 King Street, Saint John E2L 4W3, ☎ (506) 648-1981, toll-free (800) 268-1133. Luxurious and comfortable, it is also centrally located.

Below these two are several moderately priced hotels of exceptional quality, each one a member of a chain known for its high standards. There is the **Howard Johnson Hotel** at 400 Main Street, Saint John E2K 4N5, ☎ (506) 642-2622, toll-free (800) 654-2000, with 100 nicely appointed rooms, indoor heated pool, sauna, etc. **The Holiday**

recreation area, an aquatic golf driving range, miniature golf — and the 18-hole course of the Rockwood Park Golf Club, ☎ (506) 658-2933.

WHERE TO STAY

The best hotel in Saint John is the **Saint John Hilton** at One Market Square, Saint John E2L 4Z1, ☎ (506) 693-8484, toll-free (800) 268-9275 in Canada, (800) HILTONS in the U.S. Along with all the luxury comes the splendid location in Market Square, with direct access to over 60 shops, boutiques, and restaurants in the complex as well as to the convention center, and beautiful views out over the harbor. Even larger (255 rooms)

Inn at 350 Haymarket Square, Saint John E2L 3P1, ☎ (506) 657-3610, is somewhat cheaper but is not air-conditioned, although in every other respect its amenities are first-rate. For my money, the best bargain in Saint John is **Keddy's Fort Howe Hotel** at Main and Portland Street, Saint John E2K 4H8, ☎ (506) 657-7320, toll-free (800) 561-7666. It has all the amenities of a luxury hotel — air conditioning, cable color TV, indoor heated pool, sauna, exercise room, on-site parking — and yet is very moderately priced. And its top-floor restaurant overlooking the city and harbor is one of the best. Not quite so central, but again offering good value, is the **Colonial Inn** at 175 City Road, Saint John E2L 3V6, ☎ (506) 652-3000, toll-free (800) 561-

INNS. Apart from the usual amenities, it has a 24-hour restaurant. There is no restaurant at the **Country Inn & Suites**, 1011 Fairville Blvd., Saint John E2M 4Y2, ((506) 635-0400, toll-free (800) 456-4000, but there are compensations, such as free videocassette players in all the rooms and free video movies, complimentary Continental breakfasts, and microwave ovens in the two-room suites.

In the western part of Saint John, just north of and parallel to Route 100 (Fairville Boulevard) is Manawagonish Road. Along

Manawagonish Road, Saint John E2M 3X5, ((506) 672-1273, which is the least expensive of the lot and has 17 units, all with color cable TV, overlooking the bay.

WHERE TO EAT

Easily the three best places to eat in Saint John are the **Turn of the Tide** restaurant in the Hilton, ((506) 693-8484, the **Top of the Town** restaurant at Keddy's Fort Howe Hotel, ((506) 657-7320, and the restaurant in the **Delta Brunswick**, ((506) 648-1981. You

this road you will find motels and guest houses of every type and description, all inexpensive. Five of the best: The **Island View Motel** at 1726 Manawagonish Road, Saint John E2M 3Y5, ((506) 672-1381, which has a heated pool and kitchenettes; the **Fundy Ayre Motel** at 1711 Manawagonish Road, Saint John E2M 3Y2, ((506) 672-1125, which also has housekeeping units and apartments; the **Seacoast Motel** at 1441 Manawagonish Road, Saint John E2M 3X8, ((506) 635-8700, overlooking the bay; the **White House Lodge Motor Hotel** at 1400 Manawagonish Road, Saint John E2M 4X9, ((506) 672-1000, which is very comfortable and has a good restaurant, McGuire's Steak House; and the **Hillside Motel** at 1131

will pay handsomely to eat at these places, but you will eat handsomely as well.

For less sumptuous dining your best bet is to go to Market Square, where you will find an array of restaurants and cafes to appeal to every appetite and every budget. As difficult as it is to single out any one of them, I would mention **Grannan's**, ((506) 634-1555, a seafood restaurant and oyster bar which has delicious dishes at quite moderate prices. If you have trouble choosing between all the restaurants, or if you are just in a hurry, there is the **Food Hall at Market**

OPPOSITE: The golf course in Fundy National Park, halfway between Saint John and Moncton.
ABOVE: Pumpkins for sale outside Fredericton.

Square, which is full of fast-food places selling pizzas, burgers, sandwiches, fried chicken, ribs, and so on. A short walk from Market Square is the popular **Incredible Edibles** at 42 Princess Street, ((506) 633-7554, which specializes in pastas and local desserts. If you fancy New Orleans-style cooking, the **Cafe Creole** on King Square, ((506) 633-8901, is admirably authentic. For even more far-flung flavors, the **Mediterranean Restaurant** at 419 Rothesay Avenue, ((506) 634-3183, is reliable and reasonably priced. And if you appreciate fine dining with attentive service in nineteenth-century surroundings, you will want to head for **La Belle Vie** at 325 Lancaster Avenue, ((506) 635-1155.

HOW TO GET THERE

Like Fredericton, Saint John is served by both Air Atlantic and Air Canada. For details contact your travel agent or Tourism New Brunswick, or call the arlines at the numbers given above.

If you are traveling to Saint John by car, the principal north-south highway into the city is Route 1, which links with the Trans-Canada Highway about 70 km (43 miles) to the north at Sussex and in the south crosses the border into Maine at St. Stephen and becomes U.S. 1. From Fredericton the main road is Route 7, but the meandering Route 102, which follows the Saint John River, is much more picturesque.

If you are coming by train, you will take the VIA Rail network to Moncton and then change for one of the two daily trains to Saint John.

Marine Atlantic operates a year-round ferry service across the Bay of Fundy between Digby, Nova Scotia and Saint John. For information and reservations call Marine Atlantic at (506) 648-4048 in Saint John or (902) 245-2116 in Digby; toll-free (800) 565-9470 in the Maritimes, (800) 565-9411 in central Canada, (800) 432-7344 in Maine, and (800) 341-7981 in the rest of the U.S.

Farm boys cycling on the road north from Saint John.

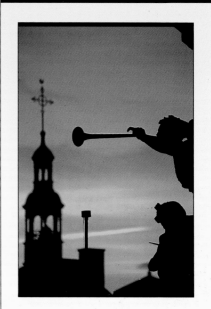

Quebec

QUEBEC, the largest of Canada's provinces, is very large indeed: it covers over 1.5 million sq km (almost 600,000 sq miles), one-sixth of Canada. Or to put it another way, it is twice the size of Texas and three times the size of France. But it is as "La Belle Province", a bastion of French culture in an Anglo-dominated continent, that Quebec is best known. And rightly so, because for almost four centuries the people of Quebec have stubbornly resisted every effort by others to interfere with their way of life — first by the Indians who wanted to drive

them out, then by the British who wanted to stamp them out, and latterly by their fellow Canadians who have tried to buy them out. All to no avail. The Quebecois are determined not to surrender any part of the heritage left them by their ancestors. This determination is succinctly captured in the province's defiant motto, which is displayed on all Quebec license plates: *Je me souviens* ("I remember").

And they have much to remember from their unique history. Although Jacques Cartier landed at Gaspé in 1534 and claimed the region for France, it was not until 1608 that the French-speaking history of the province began when Samuel de Champlain arrived at a place on the St. Lawrence River that the Indians called *Kébec*, which means "narrowing of the waters". Here he established a small fur trading post. Three years later he established another trading post on the river at a spot now occupied by Montreal. Permanent settlements followed

A sylvan scene in the Laurentians, north of Quebec City.

at Trois Rivières in 1634 and Ville Marie (now Montreal) in 1642. Although constantly raided by the hostile Iroquois Indians, the settlements grew steadily and more were founded along the shores of the St. Lawrence. By 1700 there were 25,000 French colonists living along the St. Lawrence, while the French colony of New France stretched from Hudson Bay to the Gulf of Mexico, and from the St. Lawrence almost to the Rockies.

French dominion over Quebec continued more or less undisturbed for the next half-century, but the outbreak of the Seven Years' War in 1756 changed all that. Or, to be precise, it was the 15-minute battle on the Plains of Abraham, where the British forces under Wolfe routed the French under Montcalm, that broke forever France's political hold on Quebec. Under the Treaty of Paris in 1763 France ceded all its Canadian possessions to England. In 1774 Parliament passed the Quebec Act, recognizing the right of French Canadians to keep their language, religion, property, and legal system. Incensed by these and other concessions to the French Canadians, especially regarding special advantages in the fur trade, the American colonists sent an army under General Richard Montgomery to attack Montreal and Quebec City. Montreal fell, but Quebec City held out, and the following year Montreal was recaptured by the British.

In 1791 Parliament passed the Consititutional Act dividing Quebec into mainly English-speaking Upper Canada (present-day Ontario) and mainly French-speaking Lower Canada (present-day Quebec). The arrangement worked reasonably well for the next four decades, despite growing resentment among the people of Lower Canada against being swamped by English-speaking immigrants and being governed by a British lieutenant-governor with his hand-picked legislative council. This led to a violent but unsuccessful rebellion by French Canadians in 1837. While the insurrection itself may have been put down, the desire for more control over their own affairs would linger on. And on.

In 1867 the newly-created provinces of Quebec and Ontario joined Nova Scotia and New Brunswick in the confederated

Dominion of Canada. Quebec City was made the provincial capital. During the rest of the century, Quebec's economy remained largely dependent on trade and agriculture, as Quebec City consolidated its position as the center of government as well as chief custodian of French Canadian heritage and culture, while Montreal emerged as a great port and the province's financial and industrial center. By 1911 Montreal's population had reached half a million — and it doubled in the next two decades.

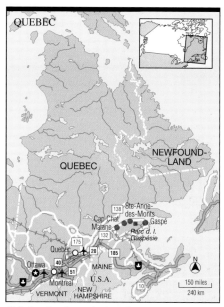

Unfortunately, the suspicions and enmities that had long bedeviled Quebec's relations with the other provinces surfaced again, with renewed virulence, in 1917 when Canada was forced to introduce conscription to replace the horrific numbers of servicemen lost in the fighting in Europe. To the French Canadians, conscription was a sinister ploy to use them as cannon fodder in Britain's war with Germany. To the rest of Canada, the revolt of the Quebecois against conscription was little short of treasonable.

The old wounds, thus reopened, never really healed. And when the Union Nationale party of Maurice Duplessis took control of the provincial government in the 1930s the estrangement looked set to become permanent — all the more so when the fight over conscription flared up again during World War II. Indeed, by 1960, when the Union Nationale finally lost power to the Liberals, Quebec was not only far apart from the rest of Canada. It was far behind as well. Industrial expansion had been sacrificed in an attempt to preserve Quebec's traditional agrarian economy, science and economics had been woefully neglected in the province's Church-run schools, and most progressive ideas for revitalizing the province had been successfully suppressed.

In 1960, however, the Liberals under Jean Lesage gained power and set in motion the "Quiet Revolution", an ambitious program of economic and social reform which nudged Quebec towards a modern society and a dynamic economy. At the same time, alas, it exposed the lack of French Canadians who had been properly trained for managerial responsibilities, which meant that most of the bosses were Anglos — a situation guaranteed to sow further discord. And it

did. In the late sixties the separatist Parti Québecois rose to prominence under René Lévesque, taking 23 percent of the vote in the 1970 provincial elections and then, astonishingly, taking power in the 1976 elections. But Lévesque's radicalism, tinged with Anglophobia, frightened Anglo-run businesses out of the province, which in turn frightened the people who somehow thought they could lose their bosses without losing their jobs. In a 1980 referendum the voters of Quebec overwhelmingly rejected the idea of declaring independence, and in 1985 the Parti Quebecois was turned out of office in favor of the Liberals. But now the pendulum seems to have swung back towards the separatists. Only time will tell — and it, I think, is running out.

Whichever path the people of Quebec decide to take — continued provincial status with perhaps enhanced autonomy, or independent nationhood — one thing is certain: in either version Quebec will be a formidable economic power. Its natural resources alone guarantee that. With 16 percent of the world's freshwater resources, it is able to generate (and sell) vast amounts of hydroelectric power. With its gigantic forests, it has a thriving lumber industry and is the top producer of paper in North America. With more than its share of the ancient rocks of the Canadian Shield, it is rich in such minerals as iron, copper, gold, silver, lead, zinc, and nickel; it is one of the world's foremost producers of aluminum. With the fertile flood plain of the St. Lawrence, its farmland supports a thriving agriculture industry. With all of these blessings, and with a population of only 6.7 million, it is no wonder that Quebec is able to export 40 percent of its total production.

And what to say of those 6.7 million Quebecois? Are they merely an Anglophobic sub-species of counterfeit Frenchmen? Far from it. To begin with, they are not as homogeneous as they may appear at first glance. At least 10 percent are of British ancestry, most of whom live in Montreal, and another 10 percent are immigrants from Europe, Asia, Latin America, and the Caribbean. And while French may be the official language of Quebec, with English as the widely-understood second languge, there are 35 other languages one can hear spoken in the province, such is the ethnic diversity of its immigrant population. Nor are the French-speakers the fanatical malcontents they are often portrayed to be. On the contrary, they are warm, garrulous, hospitable, informal, and affectionate, with a *joie de vivre* that underlines their Norman and Breton ancestry.

If it is their destiny to carry the torch of French civilization in the Americas, they do it not only proudly, but with a big smile.

QUEBEC CITY

It is somehow appropriate that the only city in North America to have been designated by UNESCO a "world heritage treasure" is also the only walled city in North America. It is as if the only way to preserve and protect an Old World gem in the hurly-burly of the New World is to build a wall around it.

Perched on a cliff 110 m (360 ft) above the St. Lawrence River, Quebec City is not only one of the most beautiful cities in North America, it is one of the most *French* cities anywhere — including France. As Charles Dickens wrote, "It is a place not to be forgotten, or mixed up in the mind with other places." Indeed, how could one forget a walled, clifftop city with cobbled streets,

many seventeenth- and eighteenth-century stone buildings, breathtaking views, lively bistros and outdoor cafes, magnificent churches, a city redolent of history, a city that not only speaks but breathes in French — here in North America? It would be like forgetting or confusing Gibraltar with some place else; in fact, Churchill once referred to Quebec City as "the Gibraltar of America".

Actually, one should probably refer to it as Quebec Cities, because there is the *Haute Ville* (Upper Town), which includes the romantic and historic Old City with its walled fortifications, lovely residential areas, and the Plains of Abraham, as well as some extramural concessions to the twentieth century in the form of modern office buildings and shopping malls, and there is the *Basse*

Ville (Lower Town) wrapped around the foot of the cliff and extending into the valley of the St. Charles River, where the industrial suburbs begin. And although the city has an official population of about 600,000, it never has that few people in it because its attractions make it one of the most visited cities on the entire continent.

BACKGROUND

The first European to visit the spot the Indians called *Kébec* was Jacques Cartier in 1535. Optimistically, he named the cliff Cap aux Diamants ("Diamond Cape") in honor of the great mineral wealth he hoped (and failed) to find there. When Samuel de Champlain arrived in 1608 he took a much more

realistic view of the site's potential importance. Recognizing its strategic location, he established a trading post at the foot of the cliff, and then in 1620 built a fort at the summit. It was captured by the British under Admiral David Kirke in 1629, but was regained by the French three years later. For the next 130 years it found itself repeatedly under siege by either the British or the Iroquois, finally falling on the morning of September 13, 1759 when Wolfe's troops surprised the French forces under the Marquis de Montcalm on the Plains of Abraham.

In 1763, with the signing of the Treaty of Paris, the city that had been the heart and

The Bassin Louise marina in Quebec City's Lower Town.

soul of New France became the capital of a new British colony. After the American attack on the city in 1775 was repulsed, the British strengthened the fortifications and built the Citadel, but, happily, they were never needed. Although the city continued to prosper into the nineteenth century, thanks to its fur trading, shipbuilding, and timber industries, it was gradually overtaken by Montreal and Toronto as an economic center. Today the city's principal business is government.

GENERAL INFORMATION

Information and a variety of free publications are available from Tourisme Quebec, Case postale 20,000, Quebec G1K 7X2. Alternatively, you can call toll-free (800) 363-7777 from anywhere in Canada or the U.S. Specific enquiries are also dealt with by the Quebec City Region Tourism and Convention Bureau, 339 rue St-Joseph Est, Quebec G1K 8E2, ((418) 522-3511. There is a tourist information office at 12 rue Ste-Anne in the Place d'Armes, across from the Château Frontenac, ((418) 643-2280.

WHAT TO SEE AND DO

Sights

Divided into Haute Ville and Basse Ville, the city has stairways and a funicular to bring you up (or down) the escarpment. With the attractive old stone buildings, narrow winding streets, pleasant squares and parks, there's a lot to see within a small area, which is comforting news for the visitor as the narrow and sometimes pedestrianized streets make walking by far the best means of getting about.

Situated in the heart of Haute Ville, the **Place d'Armes** is a good place to begin a tour and makes a useful orientation point. For a very relaxed sightseeing tour you can take a ride in one of the horse-drawn calèches that you'll find waiting here. The square, and indeed the city, is dominated by the imposing **Château Frontenac**, an enormous red brick structure with a profusion of towers, turrets, and parapets that gives it the air of a medieval castle. Built on the site of Château St. Louis, the residence of the gov-

ernors of New France, it takes its name from a former governor, the Comte de Frontenac. The Canadian Pacific Railway Company built it in 1893 as a luxury hotel and it became the city's most famous and unignorable landmark.

Next to Château Frontenac is the **Jardin des Gouverneurs**, once the garden of the Château St. Louis. At the center of this little park stands a monument which pays tribute to both General Wolfe and General Montcalm, and in the summer there's often some kind of entertainment to be found

here. Running along the south side of the park the **avenue Ste-Geneviève** is lined with European-style inns.

Just off the Place d'Armes is the lively and colorful **rue de Trésor**, so named because the royal treasury once stood here. During the summer months it's filled with artists of varying talent displaying their works and sketching visitors' portraits. At the end of the rue de Trésor turn left on to the rue Buade and at the corner of Côte de la Fabrique you'll find the **Basilique Notre-Dame-de-Québec**. This somber gray stone cathedral has an ornate interior and some interesting paintings. Champlain and Frontenac are among the many people interred in its vast crypt.

To the left of the basilica stands the **Semi-nary**, the entrance to which is at 9 rue de l'Université. It was founded in 1663 by Quebec's first bishop, François Xavier de Laval, and developed into the Université Laval. It has a beautiful and tranquil inner

The Place d'Armes in Quebec City.

courtyard and its main chapel is notable for its relics and the beautifully-crafted tomb of Laval. In order to visit other parts of the seminary you have to take a guided tour for which a small fee is charged. Tours run daily from mid-May to mid-August. Situated within the seminary is the **Musée de Séminaire de Québec**, ((418) 692-2843, which has sizable and wide-ranging art collections from Quebec and Europe, and there's also an interesting collection of old scientific instruments. The museum is closed on Mondays.

exquisite examples of their embroidery on show. The recently restored **Chapelle des Ursulines** contains some interesting relics and Montcalm is buried here (at least in part: his skull is in the museum). The convent, museum, and chapel are open Tuesday-Saturday and Sunday afternoons. Just along the rue des Jardins is the **Holy Trinity Anglican Cathedral**, a fine building in the English Baroque style. Built in 1804, it was the first Anglican cathedral built outside the U.K.

If by now you feel the need to blow away the cobwebs, behind Château Fronte-

Nearby in rue Charlevoix is the **Hôtel-Dieu**, a large hospital founded by the Augustine nuns in 1639. It houses the **Musée des Augustines** (32 rue Charlevoix, (418/692-2492), where some religious paintings and relics of the hospital's past can be seen. The museum is closed on Mondays and admission is free.

Moving back south and still on a religious note, at 12 rue Donnacona stands the **Convent des Ursulines** ((418) 694-0694. Founded in 1693, it is the oldest girls' school in North America. The **Musée des Ursulines**, ((418) 694-0694, lies within the convent walls. Here displays show you how the Ursulines lived under French rule, and there are paintings, furniture and some

nac you'll find the **Terrasse Dufferin**, a wide boardwalk stretching south overlooking the St. Lawrence and offering good views of the Basse Ville and the opposite shore. It leads to the **Promenade des Gouverneurs**, a stairway and boardwalk clinging to the edge of the cliff and taking you by the Citadel and on to the Plains of Abraham.

From Terrasse Dufferin either the funicular or the Côte de la Montagne leading to the Casse-cou (Breakneck) stairway will bring you down to rue Petit Champlain, the oldest and narrowest street in the city. It's a bustling, arty area where an abundance of craft shops and cafés tempt you to indulge yourself or just stroll and browse. North and slightly to the east is **Place**

Royale, a small eighteenth-century square. The square was once the hub of the city's thriving commercial center until business moved away in the nineteenth century. Now the whole area has been carefully restored and in the square some of the beautiful steep-roofed buildings now house museums, art galleries, restaurants, and shops, making it once again the lively center of Basse Ville.

On the south side of Place Royale stands **Notre Dame des Victoires**. This little church was built in 1688, and was extensively

man, society, and culture, and has a particularly good exhibition on Quebec's history and society. It's at 85 rue Dalhousie, ((418) 643-2158. Open daily but closed on Mondays off-season. At the south side of the Louise Basin is the newly restored **Old Port** which now holds theaters, shops, condominiums and marinas. The days when it functioned as one of the world's great ports are recalled in **Port of Québec in the 19th Century** on rue St-André where you can see films, displays, and demonstrations on shipbuilding and the lumber trade.

restored after the bombardment of 1759. It has some interesting features such as the fort-shaped altar, and a wooden model of a boat that hangs from the ceiling. Across the square at 1 Place Royale is the **Maison des Vins** ((418/643-1214) where the Québec Société des Alcools sells its very best rare and vintage wines. It's worth a visit to look around the cool and candlelit vaults of the old building. It's closed on Sundays and also on Mondays off-season. Admission is free.

Just north of Place Royal in the Old Port area stands the **Musée de la Civilisation**, an interesting modern building designed to integrate with the surrounding architecture. It has some lively multimedia exhibitions on

The Fortifications

Returning to Haute Ville, Quebec's fortifications warrant a tour to themselves. Built mainly by the British to protect the city from American attack, they were never needed but instead have added to the unique character of the city. The city wall encircles the old town and has four Portes or gates. Standing at the south end is the Citadelle, the large star-shaped fortress that looms high over the banks of the St. Lawrence. It was constructed (1820–1832) at great expense and is now occupied by the Royal 22e Régiment.

OPPOSITE: Quebec City, dominated by the mighty Château Frontenac, overlooks the St. Lawrence River. ABOVE: The horse-drawn calèche remains the most leisurely way to tour the city.

Guided tours of the fortress and its museum are given and you can watch the Changing of the Guard and Beating of the Retreat ceremonies during the summer. The entrance to the fortress is on the Côte de la Citadelle, ℂ (418) 648-3563.

Near the Porte St-Louis the **Poudrière de L'Esplanade** (Powder Magazine) at 100 rue St-Louis now holds an interpretation center explaining the development of the fortifications. Guided tours of the fortifications run from here, and it's the place to start a walk of the ramparts. Moving north along the

passes the Plains of Abraham, on which the bloody battle of 1759 was fought. Two early nineteenth-century Martello towers remind us of this with their displays on the battles fought here. At the south end of the park is the **Musée du Québec** at 1 ave Wolfe-Montcalm, ℂ (418) 643-2150, a neo-classical building which houses a fine collection of old and contemporary Quebecois art. The museum and park are closed on Mondays from mid-September to mid-June and open daily during the rest of the year. Admission is free.

wall, slightly north of Porte St-Jean is the **Parc de l'Artillerie**, 2 rue d'Auteuil, ℂ (418) 648-4205, a complex of buildings dating from the early eighteenth century, and which have served a variety of purposes over the years, mainly military. There's an interpretation center, and the exhibitions on offer are mostly on military themes. The park is open daily and is closed in December and January.

Outside the Walls

West of the fortress is the **Parc des Champs de Bataille** (National Battlefields Park), large and pleasant, sprinkled with gardens and monuments and offering impressive views of the St. Lawrence. The park encom-

From here head for the **Grande Allée**, the beautiful avenue that is alive with cafés, bars, and restaurants, and at the north side near the corner of avenue Dufferin you'll come to the Parliament buildings. The **Assemblée Nationale** (Legislative Building) is a stately Renaissance-style building built in 1886 and is the home of the provincial government. There are free guided tours of some of the most splendid rooms. Call (418) 643-7239 for details.

Further north, about two miles from the Porte St-Jean on the banks of Rivière St-Charles, lies the **Cartier-Brébeuf National Historic Park**. Here an interpretive center focuses on the exploration and development of the colony and also the harshness of the conditions in which Cartier and his crew lived. There's a replica of the *Grande Hermine* on which Cartier sailed to North America. The park is a true de l'Espinay, ((418) 648-4038.

Make time if you can for a trip to the Île d'Orléans in the St. Lawrence, which is a sanctuary of seventeenth- and eighteenth-century houses, churches, mills and farms, and a picture of rural life in early Quebec. Throughout the island local produce and woven goods are on sale. Route 368 makes a 64-km (40-mile) circular tour of the is-

land going through all six villages. Take Route 440 East, then Route 138 to the island.

You can see things from a different perspective by taking a **cruise** on the St. Lawrence aboard *M/V Louis Jolliet*. Excursions leave from Chouinard Pier, 10 rue Dalhousie, ((418) 692-1159. For an excursion that includes dinner on the Île d'Orléans contact Beau Temps, Mauvais Temps, ((418) 828-2275. There's a variety of cruises available and the tourist office in the Place d'Armes or the one in the Place Royale area, by the funicular, will give you information on what's available.

In early July, the town is busy with the annual **Québec Festival d'Eté**. It's a cultural celebration with concerts, theater, jazz, folk

music, and dancing. Book your accommodation in advance. For festival information write to the festival office, P.O. Box 24, Station B, Quebec City G1K 7A1 or telephone (418) 692-4540. The **Carnaval d'Hiver** is an altogether more rumbustious affair. This 10-day celebration is usually held towards the end of February, and it's when Quebec really lets its hair down. It starts when the two-meter (seven-foot) snowman is erected and activities center around the wonderful ice and snow sculptures in the Parc de l'Esplanade. There are snow-sculpting contests, concerts, dances, parades, ice-skating, skiing, and an awful lot of Caribou, the local mixture of alcohol and wine, is consumed. Book accommodation well in advance as this is a really big event and the city is flooded with revellers. For information contact Québec Carnaval, 290 Joly, Quebec City or telephone (418) 626-3716.

Sports
Hockey fans can watch the Québec Nordiques, the National Hockey League team, play between mid-September and April in the Colisée de Québec at 2205 ave du Colisée, Parc de l'Exposition, ((418) 523-3333. **Horse racing** takes place at the Hippodrome de Québec, C.P. 2053, Parc de l'Exposition, ((418) 524-5283.

For those who want to play rather than watch, there are 18 **golf** courses within 20 miles of the city. The best is widely considered to be the one in the **Parc du Mont Sainte-Anne** on Route 360 north of the city in Beaupré, ((418) 827-3778. If you're planning on playing during the summer months you need to make reservations. **Tennis** enthusiasts should go to the Montcalm Tennis Club at 901 blvd Champlain, ((418) 687-1250, where there are indoor and outdoor courts; there are six indoor courts at Tennisport, 4230 blvd Hammel, Ancienne Lorett, ((418) 872-0111. Battlefields Park, just outside the city walls, is a good place for **jogging** and **bicycling**.

The **skating** season is roughly from December until March. You can join the throng in the Parc d'Esplanade or skate

OPPOSITE: The entrance the Séminaire de Quebec, founded in 1663. ABOVE: The statue of Joan of Arc in Quebec City's Jardin Jeanne d'Arc.

along the stretch of the rivière St-Charles between Samson and Marie l'Incarnation bridges. North of the city in the Village des Sports at Valcartier you can skate through the woods or go tobogganing. If you're a **skiing** enthusiast, Battlefields Park has cross-country skiing trails as do many of the nearby parks. Call Quebec City Bureau of Parks and Recreation, ((418) 691-6071, for further information. For downhill skiing Mont Ste-Anne is the place. It's situated northeast of the city at C.P. 400 Beaupré, ((418) 827-4561, and has 40 downhill trails,

14 lifts and over 160 km (100 miles) of cross country trails. There are another three alpine ski resorts around the city accessible by car or by the Skibus service which runs from certain downtown hotels and from Ste-Foy.

If you want to go **fishing** the Quebec authorities insist you have a permit. Most sports shops can provide you with one or you can get one from the Ministry of Recreation, Hunting, and Fishing, 150 blvd St-Cyrille E, ((418) 643-3127. Armed with your permit you can then go north to the lakes of the Réserve Faunique des Laurentides, ((418) 848-2422.

Shopping

Shopping hours are generally 9:30 to 5:30 from Monday to Wednesday, with late-night shopping on Thursdays and Fridays till about 9 pm and until 5 pm on Saturdays. In the summer months many shops open on

ABOVE: A knees-up in the Lower Town.
OPPOSITE: Carnival time in the Upper Town.

Sundays and shopping hours are often extended.

Some of the most unusual and fun shopping is on and around the **rue Petit-Champlain** in the Basse Ville. Here Quebec arts and crafts of all kinds abound and the cafés and restaurants add to the enjoyment of a visit. Also in the Lower Town is the **antique shop district** along the rue St-Paul in the Old Port district. Once a run-down area, its cafés and galleries have made it one of the city's most fashionable spots.

In the Haute Ville, outside the city walls is the **Place Québec**, a multi-level shopping mall that has about 70 shops, some restaurants, and two cinemas. It is near the Assemblée Nationale at 5 Place Québec, ((418) 529-0551. The suburb of Ste-Foy has many more malls, the largest being **Place Laurier** with over 300 shops. It's at 2700 blvd Laurier, Ste-Foy, ((418)653-9318.

Nightlife

There's plenty to do in Quebec City at night, mostly in or just outside the Old City. Check the *Quebec Chronicle-Telegraph* for arts and entertainment listings.

A lot of the action is centered around the clubs and bars of the rue St-Jean, and with part of the street closed to traffic in the summer it's a great place to stroll or just sit and watch. The Grande Allée and Old Port areas are also lively nightspots where the bars and clubs tend to attract a slightly older crowd.

Bar Élite, 54 rue Couillard, ((418) 692-1204, is popular with younger people, whereas a more sophisticated crowd frequents the **Café St-Honoré** at 570 Grande Allée, ((418) 529-0211. There's a café terrace and a small disco at **Le d'Orsay**, 68 rue Buade, ((418) 694-1582, jazz and blues in **Bar 1123** at 1123 rue St-Jean, while blues music sometimes adds to the already congenial atmosphere on the café terrace at **Croque-Mitaine**, 33 rue d'Auteuil, ((418) 694-1473.

Some of the best jazz can be heard in **L'Emprise** in the Hôtel Clarendon at 57 rue Ste-Anne, ((418) 692-2480, while rock and folk music plays at **Le Foyer** at 1044 rue St-Jean, ((418) 692-0708. For those who want to dance, **Le Bistro** at 1036 rue St-Jean is one of the most popular places for the young and energetic to bop their socks off,

while those who like sights with their sounds might prefer the more rarefied air of **Eden**, perched at the top of the Quebec Hilton, where, as may be expected, prices are more expensive.

Theater productions are all in French. At the **Grand Théâtre de Québec**, 269 blvd St-Cyrille E, ((418) 643-8131, classic and new plays are performed by le Théâtre du Trident; the open-air **Agora** in the Old Port at 160 rue Dalhousie, ((418) 692-0100, stages shows and plays, but for obvious reasons only in the summer. If you like theater in a

WHERE TO STAY

During the Carnaval d'Hiver in February hotels get very booked up, so if you're planning your visit then it's essential to book far in advance.

Luxury

The **Château Frontenac**, 1 rue des Carrières, ((418) 692-3861, may no longer be the ultra-luxury hotel that it was in its heyday, but there's still an air of romance about staying

casual café atmosphere, go to **Théâtre Petit-Champlain** at 70 rue Petit Champlain.

L'Orchestre Symphonique de Québec plays at the Grande Théâtre de Québec at 269 blvd St-Cyrille E, ((418) 643-8131. Classical music can also be heard at the **Bibliotèque Gabrielle-Roy** at 350 rue St-Joseph, ((418) 529-0924, and at the Agora.

At most cinemas the films shown are French or dubbed into French, but at **La Boîte à Films** at 1044 3rd Ave, ((418) 524-3144, some English films are also shown, and **Cinéma Place Québec** at 5 Place Québec, ((418) 525-4524, shows English films.

ABOVE: Dining in the Château Frontenac. OPPOSITE: The rue St-Louis, where small hotels and guesthouses abound.

in the most famous — and obvious — landmark in Quebec City. Situated on Terrasse Dufferin and right by the Place d'Armes, its location could not be better. There's a huge ballroom, a piano bar and a cafe, shops and a very good restaurant called Le Champlain, and an air of decaying splendor. There are 525 rooms and they vary widely in size and location. Also, the Château is currently undergoing a massive and badly-needed renovation, so you really should check details of your room to make sure it's been refurbished.

The more contemporary **Hôtel des Gouverneurs** at 690 blvd St-Cyrille E, ((418) 647-1717, is part of a luxury hotel chain found throughout Quebec. This high-rise hotel faces the Parliament buildings and has 377 large, well-appointed rooms, indoor pool, an excellent health club, a piano bar, and restaurant. Nearby, at the **Hôtel Hilton** at 3 Place Québec, ((418) 647-2411, toll-free (800) 268-9275, in the U.S. (800) HILTONS, you'll find service that cannot be bettered. The 564 rooms are spacious, the decor is modern, and the facilities are typically Hiltonesque. It has a health club, two restaurants, and a rooftop nightclub. Close to the Parliament buildings, the location is good, and to make life even easier it's connected underground to a large shopping complex. For a superb view of the Old Town, make sure you get a room on one of the upper floors.

Overlooking the Parc des Champs de Bataille, the **Hôtel Loews Le Concorde** at 1225 Place Montcalm, ((418) 647-2222, is just a short and pleasant walk from the heart of the city, and ideally placed for the cafés and nightlife of Grande Allée. Among the luxury facilities there's a health club, a business center, VIP floors, café terrace, disco, and, perched on top of this soaring concrete tower, a revolving restaurant.

Mid-range

In the Upper Town, the **Clarendon**, at 57 rue Ste-Anne, ((418) 692-2480, is in itself a landmark. It's the city's oldest hotel with a wonderful Art Deco interior and loads of character. It has 89 pleasantly decorated rooms, each with private bathroom, and it boasts an excellent jazz bar, a cocktail lounge, and atmospheric French restaurant. Standing next to City Hall, its location is ideal for sightseeing. Further along at 115 rue Ste-Anne, the **Fleur de Lys**, ((418) 694-0106, is a bit of a surprise as it's a modern hotel in the heart of the Old Town. Service is very good here, and there are 32 well-equipped and smartly decorated rooms.

Le Château de Pierre at 17 ave Ste-Geneviève, ((418) 694-0429, is a charming Victorian mansion, elegantly decorated throughout. Its 15 rooms have a genteel look but with modern conveniences. The **Manoir Ste-Geneviève**, at 13 ave Ste-Geneviève, ((418) 694-1666, overlooks the Jardin des Gouverneurs. This early nineteenth-century building is filled with old English country house furniture, creating a cozy and comfortable atmosphere. It offers nine accommodations, air-conditioned and with TV.

Outside the city walls, **Château Laurier** at 695 Grande Allée, ((418) 522-8108, offers 55 simple, well-equipped rooms, and the restaurants and nightlife of the Grande Allée are literally (and noisily) on the doorstep.

Inexpensive

Many small family-run hotels and guesthouses can be found in the rue St-Louis,

including the **Auberge St-Louis** at 48 rue St-Louis, ((418) 692-2424, which offers 23 very pleasant rooms and very good value, and, at N° 71, **Le Clos St-Louis**, ((418) 694-1311, where the rooms are clean and neat. A good choice of similar accommodation can be found along the peaceful rue Ste-Ursule, where at N° 68 **La Maison Demers**, ((418) 692-2487, offers eight cozy rooms, and at N° 40 the **Hôtel Maison Ste-Ursule**, ((418) 694-9794, offers 15 rooms, the majority of which have private bathrooms. There's also a hostel at N° 19, **Centre International de Séjour**, ((418) 656-2921.

For details of **Bed and Breakfast** in and around the Old City, contact Bed & Breakfast — Bonjour Québec, 3765 blvd

Monaco, ((418) 527-1465, or Bed & Breakfast in Old Quebec, 35 rue des Ramparts, ((418) 655-7685, which lists more expensive accommodation in the old houses of the Old Town.

The University offers **campus accommodation** from May to August. For details contact Service des Résidences de l'Université Laval, Pavilion Parent Local 1634, Université Laval, Ste-Foy, ((418) 525-9826.

WHERE TO EAT

Expensive

À la Table de Serge Bruyère at 1200 rue St-Jean, ((418) 694-0618, is the city's most famous restaurant and arguably its best. Here you can enjoy classic French cuisine in the elegant interior of a nineteenth-century building. There's only one sitting per night, hardly surprising as the seven-course "menu découverte" (discovery menu) is a popular choice. French haute cuisine can also be found at **Le Saint-Amour**, 48 rue St-Ursule, ((418) 694-9259, an attractive restaurant with a warm and informal atmosphere. Rabbit is always a good choice here, and the chocolate desserts are famous. The **Restaurant au Parmesan** at 38 rue St-Louis, ((418) 692-0341, offers fine Italian food

Seafood Italian-style is the specialty at **Gambrinus**, 15 rue du Fort, ((418) 692-5144. This cozy restaurant also serves meat dishes, but the pastas with seafood sauce are splendid. Probably the best seafood dishes are to be found at **Le Marie Clarisse**, situated in the Lower Town at 12 rue du Petit Champlain, ((418) 692-0875. The fish is cooked to perfection and with great flair, but committed carnivores are also well catered for.

Moderate

Au Chalet Suisse is at 32 rue Ste-Anne, ((418) 694-1320, and no prizes for guessing the cuisine here. The extensive menu offers some particularly good fondues, and with its umbrellaed sidewalk terrace and exceptionally late opening hours, it's an ideal place to spend an evening. Further along, **Le Biarritz** at 136 Ste-Anne, ((418) 692-2433, is a small and snug restaurant where the sea-

food is particularly recommended. Moving east in culinary terms, the **Fleur de Lotus** at 50 rue de la Fabrique, ((418) 692-4286, offers delicious Vietnamese, Thai, and Cambodian food at reasonable prices.

For traditional Quebecois food it's difficult to better **Aux Anciens Canadiens**, 34 rue St-Louis, ((418) 692-1627. Situated in a seventeenth-century house, there's a wonderful warmth about both the setting and the service, and it's a good place to try the pea soup, a Canadian specialty.

Inexpensive

Chez Temporal at 25 rue Couillard, ((418) 694-1813, is a very French café in look and taste, and makes an ideal place for breakfast or a snack. At **Au Relais de la Place d'Armes**, 16 rue Ste-Anne, ((418) 694-9036, you can sit outside on the square and enjoy some good, hearty food; while in the Lower Town **Le Trompe L'Oeil**, at 89 Sault-au-Matelot, ((418) 694-0152, serves bistro-style food and has some very good set-price lunches. For reliably good Italian fare try **Pizzeria d'Youville** at 1014 rue St-Jean, ((418) 694-0299, and **Restaurant Le Petit Italie**, 49A rue St-Louis, ((418) 694-0044.

How to Get There

Although Quebec City is served by Air Canada and a few other major airlines, most airborne visitors to the city come via Montreal or Toronto, both of which offer a number of daily flights on regional and commuter airlines.

If you are driving from the Maritime Provinces you will want to take the Trans-Canada Highway. From Montreal either the TCH (Route 20) or Route 40 will take you to Quebec City. From the Atlantic coast of the U.S. (except Maine) the best route is up I-91, which goes through Vermont and becomes Route 55 when it crosses the border. This soon joins Route 10 which in turn becomes Route 51 before joining the TCH at Drummondville, 155 km (96 miles) southwest of Quebec City.

A guard at the Citadelle, the nineteenth-century fortress overlooking the St. Lawrence.

MONTREAL

I must admit that it didn't occur to me until I had left the city, but Montreal has a lot in common with Manhattan: it is an island, it was once occupied by native American Indians, it is a major port, it is the most cosmopolitan and "European" city in the nation, it has hosted a memorable World's Fair, it has the largest Jewish population in the country, it is noted for its excellent restaurants and exciting nightlife, it is home to more than 100 different ethnic groups, and it has a National League baseball team which is the annual source of much hope and much suffering among its devoted fans.

But this train of thought will take you only so far, after which point the landscape becomes notable — and illuminating — for the differences between the two places. *Unlike* Manhattan, Montreal is a large island (51 km or 32 miles long, and at its widest 16 km or 10 miles wide), a thousand miles from the ocean, with a large and safe Metro (or subway) system — and the overwhelming majority of its citizens speak French as a first language. Indeed, it is the second largest French-speaking city in the world. And there is also a certain *je ne sais quoi* — let's call it *joie de vivre* — that clearly distinguishes Montreal from Manhattan, or from almost any other urban center that one can think of.

Built around a long-extinct volcano (Mont Royal, known locally simply as "the mountain"), Montreal stands as a living monument to happy co-existence, for here one finds happily co-existing two principal languages, two cultures, two traditions, two school systems (one Catholic, one Protestant), and even two eras: that of New France, which celebrates the past by preserving its landmarks, and that of the new Quebec, which began celebrating the present and future with EXPO '67, the World's Fair that brought 50 million visitors to the city, and continued with the 1976 summer Olympics, and has now produced a city that is gleamingly, efficiently modern without having sacrificed any of its Gallic zest for life.

As a result, a global survey of the quality of life in all the major metropolitan areas in

45 countries published at the end of 1990 showed Montreal tied with Melbourne and Seattle as the best city in the world to live in. Nobody who has ever been to Montreal was in the least surprised.

BACKGROUND

Whereas Montreal's name apparently dates from 1535, when Jacques Cartier is said to have described the island's volcanic peak as "un mont réal" ("a royal mountain"), the city's foundation dates from 1611, when Samuel de Champlain established a fortified trading post on the island. Some 31 years later, in 1642, Paul de Chomedey, Sieur de Maisonneuve, arrived with 53 Frenchmen and founded a permanent settlement named Ville Marie on the site of what is now known as Vieux Montréal. For the remainder of the century the settlers were under constant attack by the Iroquois, but during the eighteenth century the threat faded and the bustling town of Montreal — it ceased to be called Ville Marie during this period — prospered thanks to its ever-expanding fur trade.

When the city fell to the Britsh in 1760 it had a population of 5,000, all of whom lived in present-day Vieux Montréal. As a result of the British conquest, and the subsequent cession of Canada to Britain in 1763, there was a large exodus of French nobility and military officers back to France. At the same time there was a large influx of immigrants from Scotland, who quickly became prominent in the burgeoning fur trade. The occupation of Montreal by the Americans under General Montgomery, which lasted for seven months during the winter and spring of 1775–76, made very little impact on the city, although the American Revolution itself did affect Montreal by prompting thousands of Loyalists to flee the new republic and re-settle there.

In 1783 a new enterprise was set up — the Northwest Trading Company — by a partnership of Montreal's leading fur traders. This consolidated Montreal's pre-eminence in the fur trade and made possible the large-scale export of furs to Europe. The importance of the fur trade gradually diminished after 1821, when the Northwest Trading Company was merged with its

more powerful rival, the Hudson Bay Company, but the economic boom continued with other industries beginning to flourish. It was also the early part of the nineteenth century that saw the arrival of a large wave of European Jewish immigrants, who brought with them skills crucial to Montreal's development as a major business and financial center. Thus, by the time the city was incorporated in 1832 it was already a significant force in Canadian life; by the time of Confederation in 1867 it was the most important city in Canada.

plex, was built. With the exception of a short spell in the early 1960s, Drapeau continued in office until the mid-1980s, a remarkable span of 30 years during which he literally changed the face of the city with spectacular shopping complexes like Place Ville Marie, the stunning array of buildings and structures associated with EXPO '67, the magnificent cultural and performing arts center, Place des Arts, and many other less obvious examples of his determination to beautify and modernize the city. If Montreal today is one of the three best cities in the world in

Its importance and growth continued into the twentieth century, although in the period between the two world wars it acquired a rather unsavory reputation as "Sin City". Illegal gambling, prostitution, and gangesterism all thrived under the protection of corrupt authorities. This slide into decadence came to an abrupt end, however, in 1954 with the election of Jean Drapeau as mayor. Corruption among city officials was weeded out, hoodlums were prosecuted, brothels and gambling houses were closed down. At the same time there was extensive redevelopment and renovation of derelict areas, a modern subway system was installed, and the ambitious Place Ville Marie, a downtown underground shopping com-

which to live, it is due in no small measure to the fact that Jean Drapeau lived in it.

GENERAL INFORMATION

All kinds of information, guides, and maps are available from Tourisme Québec in Quebec City (see above). The toll-free telephone number for Tourisme Québec throughout North America is (800) 363-7777. The Montreal office is in the Maison du tourisme, centre Infotouriste, 1001 rue du Square-Dorchester, at the corner of Metcalf and Square-Dorchester, ℂ (514) 873-2015. There is also an information kiosk at 2 Place Ville Marie, near University and Cathcart Streets, and two smaller Infotouriste offices at Dorval

Airport and at 173 rue Notre Dame Est in Vieux Montréal. The Greater Montreal Convention and Tourism Bureau is at 1010 rue Ste-Catherine Ouest, Suite 410, Montreal H3B 1G2, ((514) 871-1595 or 871-2015.

WHAT TO SEE AND DO

Vieux Montréal

Vieux Montréal, or the Old Town, is bounded by rue Berri, rue St-Antoine, rue McGill, and the waterfront, and until the nineteenth century all of Montreal was contained within this area. By the 1960s, no longer the city's center, the Old Town had fallen into disuse and disrepair, so the government stepped in and declared it an historic area, whereupon a program of restoration and renovation of its attractive older buildings begun. It is now alive and well, bustling with restaurants, bars, shops, galleries, outdoor cafés, and street entertainment. The best way to see the historic Old Town is to wander around on foot along its narrow streets and beautiful squares. Vieux Montréal is served by two Metro stations: Place d'Armes and Champs-de-Mars.

The delightful **Place Jacques Cartier** is a large cobbled square lined with old houses, restaurants, cafés, and craft shops. In the summer tourists and Montrealers alike are drawn here by the outdoor cafés, the colorful craft and flower markets, and the street performers. At the north end of the square a **statue of Lord Nelson** stands on top of a high column erected in 1809 to honor his victory at Trafalgar. This might be a good time to pick up some information from the Tourist Information Bureau situated at the Notre-Dame end of the square and browse through it while soaking up the atmosphere and some refreshment at one of the cafés here. Running along the south side of the square is the **rue St-Paul**, a lively main street which is filled with fashionable shops and restaurants.

Just across from the square on rue Notre-Dame stands the **Hôtel de Ville** (City Hall), a dignified Second Empire-style building, and just west of it is the domed **Old Courthouse** building. Facing the Hôtel de Ville on the corner of Notre-Dame and St-Claude is the elegant **Château de Ramezay**, which dates from 1705. Originally the home of the

French governors, it was subsequently used for a variety of purposes, its most recent incarnation being that of a museum where you can see period furnishings, costumes, artifacts, and displays on the history of the city and of the Château itself. It is at 280 Notre-Dame Est, (((514) 861-3708, and is open daily except Mondays.

One block east of here running between Notre-Dame and St-Paul is **rue Bonsecours**, a beautiful little street which is well worth a visit. The **Maison du Calvet** stands here, an attractive French Colonial house which

dates from 1725 and has been furnished with antiques. At the bottom of the road stands the lovely church of **Notre-Dame-de-Bonsecours**, known as the Sailors' Chapel, which stood at the waterside until the land was reclaimed. The original church was built here in 1657 by Marguerite Bourgeois, the founder of an order of teaching nuns, then rebuilt in 1678 and again in 1772. It has a quaint and interesting interior where model ships, votive offerings from sailors, hang from the ceiling and in its small museum the life of the founder is depicted in a curious series of tableaux made with dolls.

OPPOSITE: The Château de Ramezay, now a museum. ABOVE: The Place Jacques Cartier, with its statue of Lord Nelson in the background.

Walk up the church tower for some good views of the Old Town and the harbor.

If you feel like wandering by the water's edge, south of Place Jacques Cartier you'll find **Le Vieux Port**, a redevelopment of the old port area where there are parks, restaurants and cafés, and in the summer months cruises, exhibitions, and free open-air entertainments of all kinds and for all ages. Browsers or those with a nose for a bargain might be interested in sniffing around the **flea market** here.

A few blocks west of Place Jacques Cartier along rue Notre-Dame is the **Place d'Armes**, which was the site of a battle between the settlers and the Iroquois in 1644. The French victory is commemorated by a statue of Sieur de Maisonneuve which stands in the center of the square. Looking to the north side of the square you'll see the **Banque de Montréal**, a dignified Classical building with a stately columned portico. It houses a small and quite interesting banking museum which you can visit between 10 am and 4 pm on weekdays. At the south end of the square tucked away behind old stone walls is Montreal's oldest building, the **Seminary of St-Sulpice**, which dates from 1685. You can't explore this fine old building because it is still used by Sulpician monks and not open to the public.

Next to the seminary is the vast **Notre Dame Basilica**, a twin-towered neo-Gothic structure built in 1829. The huge and richly decorated interior contains some very fine carving, a splendidly ornate main altar, and there's a small museum which outlines the history of the church. The church (℡ 514/849-1070) is open daily and offers guided tours; the museum (℡ 514/842-2925) is open at weekends only.

At the nearby **Montreal History Centre** housed in the old fire station at 335 Place d'Youville, ℡ (514) 845-4236, the history of the city is described in a series of audio-visual displays. The last show begins at 3.30 pm; the Centre is closed on Mondays. Just around the corner, the **Musée Fortin** at 118 rue St-Pierre, ℡ (514) 845-6108, houses the works of Marc-Aurkle Fortin (1888–1970), a Quebecois landscape painter, and also temporary exhibitions of the work of other local artists. The museum is closed Mondays.

Just across from the History Centre stands **Les Écuries d'Youville**, a group of early nineteenth-century warehouse and factory buildings enclosed by old stone walls. The buildings have been renovated and function as offices and shops, and there are some pleasant restaurants here. The attractive courtyard provides a peaceful haven for tired sightseers.

Downtown

The downtown district of Montreal, bordered by Atwater, St-Denis, St-Antoine, and Sherbrooke, has quite a different character. In the 1960s steel and glass skyscrapers, high-rise hotels, and complexes began to appear here. This sweeping modernization was also happening below ground with the

development of Montreal's **Underground City**, a huge network of shopping and business centers, cinemas, and restaurants with access to hotels, railway stations, and many other facilities. Whether or not you like the idea of shopping malls, going about your business without having to be out-doors can be quite an appealing prospect in the winter rain and snow. Walkways link such complexes as **Place Bonaventure**, **Place du Canada**, and **Place Ville Marie**, while others are a Metro ride away.

The center of this system and the first complex to have been built is the **Place Ville Marie** (often referred to as the PVM). Above the ground the square is dominated by the 45-story **Royal Bank Tower**, a remarkable cruciform structure designed by architect I.M.Pei and now one of Montreal's most famous landmarks.

It could be said that **Dominion Square** is the heart of Montreal, and with tour buses and calèches waiting here, it's a good place to start your explorations. But before taking off, look around the square. On one side stands the **Sun Life Building**, a great gray wedding cake of a place which was Mont-real's first skyscraper and once Canada's largest building. Facing it stands the **Bank of Commerce**, a slick, glass skyscraper, and the **Château Champlain** hotel, another vast modern structure sometimes referred to as "the cheese-grater" because of its semi-circular windows. At the southern end of the

Montreal's skyline.

square along the blvd René Lévesque (formerly known as blvd Dorchester) **Marie-Reine-du-Monde** (Mary Queen of the World Cathedral), a scaled-down copy of St Peter's in Rome, stands valiantly in the midst of the modern giants.

Eastwards along blvd René Lévesque past the PVM, turn left on to University Street and two blocks along at rue Ste-Catherine you'll find **Christ Church Cathedral**, a fine Gothic-style church dating from the 1850s. **Rue Ste-Catherine** is Montreal's main shopping street, and west of the cathe-

dral you'll find the major department stores. Further west along Ste-Catherine on and around **Crescent** and **Bishop Streets** is Montreal's center of chic. Once a seedy run-down area, the Victorian buildings have been restored and now house exclusive and trendy boutiques, cafés, and restaurants.

For a cultural interlude, go eastwards along rue Ste-Catherine to the **Place des Arts**, ((514) 842-2112, an arts complex for theater, opera, ballet, music, and art. If you haven't had enough of shopping malls by this time there's an underground link from Place des Arts to the nearby **Complexe Desjardins**, an enclosed mall which extends above and below ground level. For a completely different kind of shopping, south of

here near Place d'Armes Metro and centered around rue de la Gauchetière is Montreal's **Chinatown**.

On the north side of rue Sherbrooke, where it intersects with University, stands the famous **McGill University**, where you might like to wander around the pleasant green campus which lies at the foot of Mont Royal. Facing the campus on the south side of Sherbrooke is **McCord Museum**, 690 Sherbrooke Ouest, ((514) 392-7100, which traces the history of Montreal and Canada as a whole through collections of artifacts, art, costume, displays, and a massive photographic collection.

Continuing westwards, Canada's oldest museum, the **Musée des beaux-arts** at 1379 Sherbrooke Ouest, ((514) 285-1600, houses an art collection that spans all ages and all parts of the world, so whatever your taste you'll find something to please you here. As you might expect, it has a large collection of Canadian art; European art movements are also well represented. Inuit sculptures, African masks, and pre-Columbian figures are among the permanent exhibits and the museum also hosts major international exhibitions. The museum is open daily except Mondays and holidays.

If you're interested in architecture, you might like to visit one of Montreal's more recent institutions, Le **Centre Canadien d'Architecture**, which is on blvd René Lévesque at rue Fort, ((514) 939-7000, an architectural museum and research center, with exhibition halls open to the public and a bookstore.

Outside Downtown

Centered around the **rue St-Denis** is Montreal's **Latin Quarter**. St-Denis is filled with colorful cafés, restaurants, nightclubs, bars, interesting shops, and art galleries: it's an area that's big on atmosphere and easy on the pocket. It's a haunt of the students from the **Université du Québec**, which is located here, and fittingly it's where the annual jazz festival is held. Proceeding northwards, one block beyond the intersection with Sherbrooke you'll find **Square St-Louis** on the left, an attractive square of beautiful Victorian houses looking on to a small park, and it is home to many writers, artists, and musicians. At the western end of the square runs **rue Prince Arthur**, a lively street which offers ethnic food, shops, and street entertainment.

For some more ethnic flavors, turn off Prince Arthur at **blvd St-Laurent**, an immigrant neighborhood which you may find refreshingly ungentrified. It's a busy area of shops, bars, cafés, delis, and restaurants. There's a real mix of cultures and you can sample the food of Eastern Europe, the Middle East, Italy, Greece, Spain and other countries. Incidentally, St-Laurent, also

brought here. How you get to the park depends on your mood: you can go there by calèche, drive most of the way there by car, or walk from Peel, du Parc, or Drummond Streets. The **Chalet** offers refreshments and stunning views from its terrace and to the east stands a large metal cross, illuminated at night and visible from all over the city, commemorating the wooden one that Sieur de Maisonneuve placed there in 1643.

You might like to make a pilgrimage to the **Oratoire St-Joseph** (St. Joseph's Oratory) situated on the northwest slope of

known as "The Main", was once the dividing line between the French- and English-speaking communities, and although this is no longer strictly true, there are still hints of this cultural split. It remains the east-west dividing line for street numbers.

One of Montreal's most stunning features is, of course, the mountain which dominates the cityscape, **Mont Royal**. The **Parc du Mont Royal** is the city's finest park and was skillfully planned by the architect of New York's Central Park, Frederick Law Olmstead. In the summer it's a popular place for walking, jogging, picnicking, riding, sitting, sunbathing, and for just taking in the views of the city below. In winter, skates, sleighs, skis and snowshoes are

Mont Royal. In 1904 a monk called Brother André, who was said to have great healing powers, raised a chapel to St. Joseph here where he worked tirelessly to treat the sick. A large domed basilica, visible for miles around, was built here in 1960 and the original chapel still stands. Inside the basilica is a museum dedicated to Brother André; abandoned crutches and wheelchairs bear witness to his powers. The Oratory, at 3800 Queen Mary Road, is open daily and can be reached by taking the Metro to Côte des Neiges or Snowdon stations.

Celebrating in stone: The huddled masses OPPOSITE, and the home of the Mass ABOVE, Montreal's Mary Queen of the World Cathedral.

During your visit to the Latin Quarter, you might like to combine a trip to the **Parc Lafontaine** off Sherbrooke Est between ave du Parc-La Fontaine and ave Papineau (nearest Metro: Sherbrooke). It's an ideal place to do a spot of rowing, take a swim in one of the public pools, stroll around the French- and English-style gardens or have a picnic while enjoying one of the free open-air entertainments that often go on here. In summer there's a children's zoo here where the animals are housed in fanciful storybook settings. The park is open from mid-May to the end of September.

Further along Sherbrooke, on the eastern edge of the city, is **Parc Maisonneuve** where you'll find the **Olympic Park** which was built for the 1976 Summer Olympics (although not completed until 1987). This huge and vastly expensive complex is bold and striking in its design; the centerpiece is the gigantic **Olympic Stadium** which can seat 80,000 and is overlooked by a striking tilted tower designed for winching the retractable roof. The **Vélodrome** is another stunning structure, and the **Aquatic Centre** has six pools of different kinds. You can go up the tilted tower by cable car to the observation deck and enjoy views of the complex and up to 80 km (50 miles) beyond if weather conditions permit. To get there you can take the Metro to Viau or Pie IX. There are guided tours of the complex in both French and English which allow you to go inside the buildings. For information call ((514) 252-4737.

For a completely different experience, next to the Olympic Park you'll find the **Jardin Botanique** (Botanical Garden), one of the world's largest, where over an area of 180 acres about 26,000 species of plants from all around the world are displayed in a series of gardens and greenhouses. The summer is undoubtedly the time to see the gardens at their spectacular best, but in winter the visitor can escape into the exotic atmospheres of the greenhouses. The truly celestial **Japanese Garden** is a must. A small train will take you on a guided tour of the gardens. It's at 4101 Sherbrooke Est, ((514) 872-1400, and the nearest Metro is Pie IX. It's open daily and admission to the gardens is free but there is a charge for the conservatories.

In the St. Lawrence River, facing the Old Town is the **Île Ste-Hélène**, an island which was enlarged using landfill during the 1960s. Ste-Hélène and the completely man-made neighboring **Île Notre-Dame** were the setting for the international exhibition, EXPO '67. After the fair closed the pavilions became permanent exhibition halls and this complex, known as **Man and His World**, hosts numerous entertaining events and exhibitions during the summer. For more strenuous entertainment there's **La Ronde**, Île Ste-Hélène's enormous amusement park, with the world's second highest roller coaster and all the shows, rides, and thrills needed to keep the shrieks and the laughter going. It's open daily 11 am to midnight from late May until the end of August, ((514) 872-6222. To keep the adrenalin pumping you can go and stare at some sharks in the neighboring **Aquarium**, and many other varieties of aquatic life besides, including seals and penguins. It's open daily, but with shorter opening hours off-season. For information call (514) 872-4656.

Under Jacques Cartier Bridge you can see the Old Fort built by the British in 1822 and containing the **David M. Stewart Museum** where military uniforms, equipment, and maps are on display. In the summer there's color and action in the fort with military parades and mock battles. The fort and museum are open daily but closed on Mondays during the winter months. For information call (514) 861-6701. Île Ste-Hélène can be reached by Metro to Île Ste-Hélène Station or by Victoria or Jacques Cartier Bridges.

Sports

Baseball fans can watch the Expos play at the magnificent Olympic Stadium at the Olympic Park on ave Pierre-de-Coubertin. The nearest Metro station is Viau and you can telephone (514) 253-3434 for information. **Hockey** devotees flock to the Forum at 2313 Ste-Catherine Ouest, ((514) 932-6131, where the Canadiens play their National Hockey League opponents from October to April, but tickets can be difficult to get. Every August the Player's Challenge **tennis** tournament is played at Jarry Tennis

Montreal's Botanical Garden is among the world's largest — and best.

Stadium, rue Jarry and blvd St-Laurent, ((514) 273-1515.

Also in August, professional **cyclists** compete in the **Grand Prix Cycliste des Amériques** which takes them on a 224-km course through the streets of Montreal and up on Mont Royal ((514/879-1027 for details) and **La Classique Cycliste Canadian Tire** takes place in June, one of the most popular cycling events in the world. There's **Formula One racing** each June when the Grand Prix Molson du Canada takes place at the Gilles-Villeneuve Track on Île Notre-

Dame, ((514) 392-0000, and for **racing** of the four-legged variety go to the Hippodrome Blue Bonnets Racetrack, 7440 blvd Dacarie, ((514) 739-2741, where there's harness racing all year round on Mondays, Wednesdays and Friday at 7.30 pm and on Sundays at 1.30 pm.

There are several public **golf** courses within a short drive of downtown. Route 20 West will take you to Golf Dorval at 2000 rue Reverchon, Dorval, ((514) 631-6624, where there's a 36-hole course, and further west along Route 20 is the Fresh Meadows Golf Club at 505 ave du Golf, Beaconsfield, ((514) 697-4036, where there's a nine-holer. At Club de golf de Laprairie, 75 blvd Taschereau, Laprairie, off Route 10 East, ((514) 659-1908, there's an 18-hole course.

Golf Municipal de Montréal, ((514) 872-1143, is near the Viau Metro station on blvd Viau, and has a nine-hole course.

Tennis players have literally hundreds of courts to choose from and should ring Montreal Sports and Leisure, ((514) 872-6211 for information. The Parc Mont-Royal is a popular spot for **jogging** and **cycling**; there are also over 20 cycling paths running through Montreal. There are many indoor and outdoor **swimming** pools in the city (again contact Montreal Sports and Leisure for details), but the place to go has to be Olympic Park, ((514) 252-4622, where there are five pools open to the public.

Jet boating over the Lachine rapids is an exhilarating experience and very popular with younger people. Excursions leave Victoria Pier in the Old Port five times a day May to September.

There are over 170 **skating** rinks in Montreal, the majority of which are outdoor and the biggest of which is the Olympic Rowing Basin on Île Notre-Dame. The parks are very popular with skaters. Winter also brings cross-country and downhill **skiing**, **tobogganing** and **snowshoeing** to the parks and some of the very best skiing is to be had north of the city in the Laurentians.

Shopping

Montrealers are passionate about shopping and there are overwhelming numbers of boutiques, shopping malls, and department stores catering for every need or whim. Montreal is Canada's fashion center and is well known for its high fashion and top quality clothing outlets. It is also a good place to shop for Inuit art and other Canadian crafts. The **Canadian Guild of Crafts** at 2025 Peel Street, ((514) 849-6091, has a particularly good selection, with knowledgeable staff to offer advice.

Opening hours are generally 9:30 or 10 am to 6 pm with later closing hours, usually until 9 pm, on Thursdays and Fridays and a slightly earlier closing time of about 5 pm on Saturdays. Shops in Underground City often have the later closing time of 9 pm Monday to Friday. If you're determined to shop until you drop, then quite a few shops are open in Vieux Montréal on Sundays. A couple of tips: don't spend U.S. dollars in the stores — change them in the bank where you'll get a substantially better rate — and do get hold of the Tourist Bureau's free *Shopping, Restaurants and Nightlife Guide*, which is very useful for planning your shopping trip.

The main shopping street is **rue Ste-Catherine**, which is the most centrally located. At Ste-Catherine Ouest you'll find major department stores such as Simpson's, Ogilvy's, Eaton's, and La Baie, where you'll find just about everything. However, the most exclusive fashion-only store, Holt-Renfrew, is at 1300 Sherbrooke Ouest.

Also along **Sherbrooke Ouest**, in the area around the Musée des beaux-arts, you'll find antiques shops, galleries, and craft shops. Between Sherbrooke and Ste-Catherine in the **rue Crescent** attractive Victorian buildings house chic and exclusive boutiques, art galleries, and antique shops, as well as cafés and bars where you can take a break.

In **Vieux Montréal** there are plenty of tacky souvenir shops but it also has its share of boutiques, antique and craft shops, especially around **rue St-Paul**, **St-Amble**, and **St-Jacques**. **Notre-Dame Ouest** between Guy and Atwater is the main antiques area, and antique hounds should also sift through the piles in the large flea market, **Marché aux Puces**, which is on Quai King Edward in the Vieux Port and open daily. There are all kinds of second-hand or older goods here: jewelry, furniture, clothes, you name it. Even if you don't find the priceless antique you were hoping for, you'll have good fun and a few laughs looking for it.

Montreal has its **Chinatown** situated along and around rue de la Gauchetière between rue Jeanne-Mance and blvd St-Laurent. Over in the Latin Quarter, **rue St-Denis** has an academic chic about it with its bookstores, art galleries, and trendy boutiques. West of St-Denis at the lower end of the **blvd St-Laurent** the street is lined with ethnic food stores and shops of all countries, and it's a good area for inexpensive clothes shops. As you move north beyond Mont Royal the character of the street changes and becomes seriously chic with shops that sell high-fashion clothing and home furnishings.

Underground City offers miles of shopping of all kinds and links the big shopping complexes such as **Place Bonaventure**, **Complexe Desjardins**, **Les Cours Mont-Royal**, and **Place Ville Marie**, to name. but a few. There's just about everything you need here and a lot more. In the bitter winter weather or on the hottest days many are glad to dive into this air-conditioned environment.

Nightlife

Montreal has long had a well-deserved reputation for scintillating nightlife, with a

choice of entertainment that ranges from the highbrow to the downright tacky and there are masses of bars and clubs to choose from. You'll find listings in the *Montreal Gazette* and in booklets you can pick up at Tourist Information points.

The world-famous **Orchestre Symphonique de Montréal** play at Salle Wilfrid-Pelletier at the Place des Arts when they're not on tour or playing at one of the city's other venues. For further information call ((514) 842-3402. The **Orchestre Métropolitain du Grand Montréal**, ((514) 598-0870,

OPPOSITE: Looking down from the tower of the lovely Notre-Dame-de-Bonsecours.
ABOVE: Nightlife on sleazy street.

an orchestra of younger musicians, plays at **Théâtre Maisonneuve**, also in the Place des Arts. Classical music can also be heard at the **Théâtre Port Royal** in the Place des Arts and **Pollack Hall** at McGill University, ((514) 398-4547. Opera fans will be interested to know that the **Opéra de Montréal**, ((514) 521-5577, stages four or five operas each year at Salle Wilfrid-Pelletier.

Balletomanes can see the excellent **Grands Ballets Canadiens,** ((514) 849-8681, at the Salle Wilfrid-Pelletier when they're not touring, the popular **Les Ballets Jazz de**

held in August. English-language films show in many cinemas such as the **Seville** at 2155 Ste-Catherine Ouest, ((514) 932-1139, the **Rialto** at 5723 ave du Parc, ((514) 274-3550, and **Cinéma V**, 5560 Sherbrooke Ouest, ((514) 489-5559. For an unusual cinematic experience there's the **IMAX Cinema** down at the Old Port, ((514) 496-IMAX, where the cinema screen is seven stories high.

The big-name pop and rock concerts take place at the **Forum**, ((514) 932-2582. The **Spectrum de Montréal**, ((514) 861-5851, is

Montréal, ((514) 875-9640, and several other thriving contemporary dance troupes.

There are around a dozen theaters in the city and most productions are in French, but the **Centaur Theatre** in the Old Town, ((514) 288-3161, is the foremost English-language theater company. Each summer the 10-day **Just For Laughs Festival** is held in concert halls and outdoor places all over the city. Call (514) 845-3155 for details. At other times there's the **Comedy Nest** at 1234 Bishop, ((514) 395-8118, where you can be entertained, or not, by stand-up comics.

There's plenty to keep movie-goers happy, especially as Montreal hosts several film festivals every year, the most famous being the **Montreal World Film Festival**

quite large and hosts all kinds of shows, while the smaller **Club Soda,** ((514) 270-7848, is a well-established venue for a variety of rock bands, including international acts.

For jazz on a summer's day there's the two-week **Montreal International Jazz Festival** which takes place both in and out of doors. Call (514) 288-5363 for details. Montreal does like its jazz and one of the favorite spots is **L'Air du Temps** in the Old Town at 191 rue St-Paul, ((514) 842-2003, which is a small and friendly place. Downtown you could go to **Biddles** at 2060 Aylmer, ((514) 842-8656, and chew on a spare rib or a chicken leg while you enjoy the sounds, or go to the popular **Le Bijou** at 300 Lemoyne, ((514) 288-5508, which has a bluesy tinge.

WHERE TO STAY

Luxury

There aren't many needs not catered for in the **Bonaventure Hilton International**, 1 Place Bonaventure, Montreal H3G 1Z5, ((514) 878-2332, toll-free (800) HILTONS. Centrally situated in the upper portion of a skyscraper, with a shopping mall, restaurants, and Metro below, a rooftop swimming pool for year-round use, two and a half acres of gardens, a health club and the usual Hilton high standards, you could want for little more. The 37-floor **Le Centre Sheraton** at 1201 blvd René Lévesque, Montreal H3B 2L7, ((514) 878-2000, toll-free (800) 325-3535, is conveniently situated for the smart shops and restaurants of the rue Crescent area. The hotel has several bars of its own, a nightclub, restaurant, full health club facilities and a very smart, modern interior. The top five floors contain the most luxurious suites and rooms and have extra-special service.

Close to Dominion Square, **Le Château Champlain**, 1 Place du Canada, Montreal H3B 4C9, ((514) 878-9000, toll-free (800) 828-7447, is a tall and unmistakable building known as the "cheese grater". It has restaurants and entertainments and the rooms are airy and very well equipped. **La Reine Elizabeth** at 900 blvd René Lévesque, Montreal H3B 4A5, ((514) 861-3511, toll-free (800) 268-9143, is the city's largest hotel and you can rely on the service being excellent. It holds several restaurants including the famous Beaver Club.

Les Quatre Saisons is prestigiously located at 1050 rue Sherbrooke Ouest, Montreal H3A 2R6, ((514) 284-1110, toll-free (800) 332-3442, and is one of the very best hotels Montreal has to offer. The service is impeccable, the elegant rooms are equipped with just about everything you could want, and if it isn't there then it can probably be arranged. Its rival is the nearby **Ritz-Carlton** at 1228 rue Sherbrooke Ouest, Montreal H3G 1H6, ((514) 842-4212, toll-free (800) 223-9868. Established in 1912, this hotel has catered for the whims of many of the rich and famous over the years. The rooms are elegant and spacious, the service is everything you could wish it to be, and afternoon tea in the garden is a tradition.

The **Delta Montréal** at 450 Sherbrooke Ouest, Montreal H3A 2T4, ((514) 286-1986, toll-free (800) 268-1133, is a high-rise tower with smart, spacious, well-appointed rooms. It has superb fitness facilities which include indoor and outdoor pools, squash courts and gym, and there's a well-planned supervised activity center for children.

Mid-range

One of Montreal's most charming downtown hotels is the **Château Versailles** at 1659 rue Sherbrooke Ouest, Montreal H3H 1E3,

((514) 933-3611, toll-free (800) 361-7199, which now fills four lovely old stone houses and offers 70 comfortable, well-equipped rooms with bathrooms and warm, friendly service. Slightly further west in a residential area of downtown near the Forum sports and concert arena, **Manoir le Moyne** at 2100 blvd de Maisonneuve Ouest, Montreal H3H 1K6, ((514) 931-8861, is a suite-only hotel. With its pools and saunas, restaurant and self-contained apartments, it creates the home-from-home environment that is popular with 'families or those who plan long stays. Similar in concept but more cen-

OPPOSITE: Dining al fresco on the rue Prince Arthur. ABOVE: A facade in the Place Jacques Cartier.

trally situated is the **Hôtel l'Appartement Inn Montréal** at 455 rue Sherbrooke Ouest, Montreal H3A 1B7, ((514) 284-3634, which has 125 apartments, of varying sizes, and guests have use of a swimming pool, sauna, and laundry facilities.

Ideally placed for the restaurants and nightlife of the Latin Quarter, the **Hôtel Holiday Inn le Richelieu** at 505 rue Sherbrooke Est, Montreal H4T 1S7, ((514) 842-8581, toll-free (800) HOLIDAY, has 320 rooms and good facilities including an indoor pool. People certainly don't stay at

the **Hôtel de l'Institut** for the look of the place but they do stay there for the service, convenient location, and good value. Students of the Institute of Tourism and Hotel Management train here and are determined to please. The rooms are comfortable, the hotel looks across to Square St-Louis and it's on top of Sherbrooke Metro station at 3535 rue St-Denis, Montreal H2X 3P1, ((514) 282-5120. Close to rue St-Denis and to Old Town is the **Hôtel Lord Berri** at 1199 rue Berri, Montreal H2L 4C6, ((514) 845-9236, toll-free (800) 363-0363, where the rooms have comforts such as mini-bars and in-room movies, some floors are set aside for non-smokers, and there's a bright and busy sidewalk café.

Inexpensive

Just off Sherbrooke, **Manoir Ambrose** at 3422 rue Stanley, Montreal H3A 1R8, ((514) 288-6922, offers an assortment of 22 accom-modations in an attractive old building near the heart of downtown. There's a pleasantly bohemian air about the **Hôtel Château Napoléon** near the fashionable rue Crescent at 1030 McKay, Montreal, ((514) 861-1500, which has 61 pleasant rooms, all with bathroom and TV.

Near St-Denis the **Hôtel Bon Accueil** at 1601 rue St-Hubert, Montreal H2L 3Z1, ((514) 527-9655, has 20 rooms all with bathroom and TV and offers very good value, as does the nearby **Hôtel Le Breton** at 1609 rue St-Hubert, Montreal H2L 3Z1, ((514) 524-7273, which has 13 rooms, seven of which have bathrooms and all have TV. Just south of Sherbrooke Est is the clean and cozy **Castel St-Denis** at 2099 rue St-Denis, Montreal H2X 3K8, ((514) 288-6922, which has 14 rooms.

There's plenty of **Bed & Breakfast** ac-commodation in Montreal, ranging from basic to luxurious, and several agencies to help you find something to suit your needs. Write to or phone the following agencies: Downtown Bed & Breakfast Network, 3485 rue Laval, Montreal H2X 3C8, ((514) 289-9749; Bed & Breakfast de Chez Nous, 5386 rue Brodeur, Montreal H4A 1J3, ((514) 287-9653; and Relais Montréal Hospitalita, 3977 rue Laval, Montreal H2W 2H9, ((514) 287-9653.

There's a **YMCA** downtown at 1450 Stanley Street, Montreal H3A 2W6, ((514) 849-8393, a **YWCA** at 1355 blvd René Lévesque Ouest, Montreal H3G 1T3, ((514) 866-9941, and the **Auberge de jeunesse internationale de Montréal** at 3541 Aylmer Street, Montreal H2X 2B9, ((514)843-3317. Also in downtown **McGill University**, ((514) 398-6367, **Collège Français**, ((514) 495-2581, and **Concordia University**, ((514) 848-4756, all offer accommodation at low prices.

For details of **campsites** contact the Quebec Department of Tourism, Fish and Game at 150 blvd St-Cyrille Est, Montreal G1R 4Y1. There are some situated on the South Shore and Southwest of Montreal and also in Basses-Laurentides.

WHERE TO EAT

Eating out is another favorite pastime of Montrealers, so there's an abundance of

ABOVE: An old bar in Old Montreal.
OPPOSITE: Place Jacques Cartier.

restaurants and bistros. French and French Canadian cuisine predominates but there are many ethnic varieties to choose from. Quite a large proportion of the restaurants also allow you to bring your own wine, so check this out in advance.

Expensive

The **Beaver Club** was a club formed by the early fur traders which by the last century had evolved into a gentlemen's club. It survives as a restaurant in the Hôtel Reine Elizabeth at 900 blvd René Lévesque Ouest,

((514) 861-3511, where its origins are very much in evidence with the pelts and mementos hung about the walls and in its formal atmosphere. The cuisine is French, both classic and nouvelle, and the service is superb. More excellent French food is served at **Les Chênets** at 2075 Bishop Street, ((514) 844-1842, one of Montreal's priciest restaurants where warm, glowing colors set the scene. **Le Café de Paris** at the Ritz-Carlton Hotel, 1228 Sherbrooke Street, ((514) 844-4212, is classical in its cuisine and its elegant decor, and strains of piano music accompany your superb meal. Its venerable wine cellar provides an excellent list of wines ranging in price from moderate to very, very expensive.

The interior of **Le Lutétia** at 1430 rue de la Montaigne, ((514) 288-5656, is an explosion of ornate decorative styles, baroque in the broadest sense and an ideal place for romantic *dîner à deux*. The excellent menu offers classic and nouvelle cuisines and the

wine list is of a similarly high standard. Moving eastwards, **Les Mignardises** at 2035–2037 rue St-Denis, ((514) 842-1151, is probably Montreal's best and most expensive dining spot. This is a small, elegant French restaurant where both the service and the food are quite simply perfect.

Ardent carnivores will think they have died and gone to heaven in **Moishe's** at 3961 blvd St-Laurent, ((514) 845-1696, a steakhouse of the highest order. The meat is expertly prepared and aged in the restaurant's own cold rooms and steaks are grilled over wood.

In Vieux Montréal, **Zhivago** at 419 rue St-Pierre, ((514) 284-0333, has all the trappings of old Russia with its gypsy singers, draperies, and private dining compartments. This extravagance extends to the cuisine, which is Russian in spirit if not strictly authentic.

Perfectly prepared fresh seafood is served in **Chez Delmo**, at 211 Notre-Dame Ouest, ((514) 849-4601, in comfortable, old-fashioned surroundings. There are oyster bars at the front of the restaurant, popular for informal lunchtime dining. At **La Marée**, 404 Place Jacques-Cartier, ((514) 861-8126, in the beautiful surroundings and intimate atmosphere of an eighteenth-century house the seafood is also cooked to perfection and served with delicious sauces.

Moderate

For French cuisine there's **Le Vent Vert** at 2105 rue de la Montagne, ((514) 842-2482, where the food is very good and prepared with imagination and flair. **L'Express** at 3927 rue St-Denis, ((514) 845-5333, is the place to see and be seen. It is a crowded, noisy bistro and the food and the wine list are excellent. In Vieux Montréal **Restaurant Jacques Cartier** at 254 rue St-Paul Est, ((514) 398-0932, is a quiet spot where the food is flavorsome and interesting and the service friendly and efficient.

For good Greek food, **Milos** at 5357 ave du Parc, ((514) 272-3522, is an excellent choice. You select the ingredients of your meal from the fresh seafood, meat and vegetables that are displayed. One of the best Indian restaurants around is **Le Taj** at 2077 rue Stanley, ((514) 845-9015, where the menu is North Indian and includes tandoori dishes.

Montreal street scene.

Light Italian dishes feature in fashionable **Prego**, 5142 blvd St-Laurent, ((514) 271-3234, while at **Restaurant Vespucci**, 124 Prince Arthur Est, ((514) 843-4784, the lengthy menu is more traditionally Italian.

Katsura at 2170 rue de la Montagne, ((514) 849-1172, provides elegant and tranquil Japanese surroundings and a menu that includes all the sushi dishes. You can book a private tatami room for dining in traditional Japanese manner and there's also the option of the restaurant's sushi bar.

To sample Quebecois food you should go to the **Auberge le Vieux Saint-Gabriel** at 426 rue St-Gabriel, ((514) 878-3561, an old and interesting building in Vieux Montréal which is said to be North America's oldest restaurant. Also in the Old Town, **Les Filles du Roy**, 415 rue Bonsecours, ((514) 849-3535, gears itself to the tourist trade with the restaurant and staff dressed up in traditional Quebecois manner. The food isn't memorable here but it's all done with great enthusiasm.

Inexpensive

The largest and busiest Chinese restaurant is the **Cathay Restaurant** in Chinatown at 73 rue de la Gauchetière Ouest, ((514) 866-4016, where dim sum is served in the afternoons. Nearby the **Café Jardin de Jade** at 57 rue de la Gauchetière, ((514) 861-4941, also offers very good value.

Montreal has some excellent delis where smoked meat served in or with rye bread and pickle is the classic fare. **Ben's** at 990 blvd Maisonneuve, **Schwartz's** at 3895 blvd St-Laurent, and **Dunn's**, which never closes, at 892 rue Ste-Catherine all have their devoted customers.

For hamburgers, **La Paryse** at 302 Ontario Est, ((514) 842-2042, is the best place in town, where they make them with good ground beef and lashings of everything to satisfy the largest appetites.

There's hearty Polish food and ridiculously low prices in the **Mazurka** at 64 rue Prince Arthur Est, ((514) 845-3539, and so it's not surprising that the place is always busy. **Laurier BBQ** at 381 ave Laurier Ouest, ((514) 273-3671, is something of an institution where traditional Quebecois food is

served and French-Canadian families gather.

HOW TO GET THERE

Almost all of the world's major airlines fly into Montreal. Flights from South America and the Caribbean, Europe, Africa, and Asia are handled by Aéroport Mirabel, 55 km (34 miles) northwest of the city. Generally speaking, the ride into the city should take about 45 minutes and cost about $60 by taxi. Flights from Canadian, American, and Mexican cities are handled by Aéroport de Dorval, 22 km (14 miles) southwest of the city. The ride into the city ordinarily takes about 20 to 25 minutes and costs about $25 by taxi. Aerocar Buses (514/397-9999) have a regular shuttle service between both airports and the Queen Elizabeth Hotel, and between the airports themselves, at a very reasonable price.

Montreal is also connected to all the major cities in Canada by the VIA Rail network's intercity trains which arrive at the Gare Centrale (514/871-1331) under the Queen Elizabeth Hotel at the corner of boulevard René Lévesque and rue Mansfield. The station is connected underground to the Bonaventure station of the Metro and the Windsor railway station for the local commuter trains. If you are coming by train from the U.S., Amtrak (call toll-free 800/872-7245) has one train from Chicago to Montreal, via Detroit and Ottawa, and two East Coast trains: the excellent, reservations-only *Montrealer* which begins in Washington, D.C. and goes via New York City overnight to Montreal, and the *Adirondack*, which goes every morning from Grand Central Station in New York.

Greyhound (212/593-2000) has regular bus service to Montreal from cites all over North America, while Voyageur (514/842-2281) operates buses from many points within Quebec and Ontario.

Motorists will want to take the Trans-Canada Highway (Route 20) from the Maritimes, and either the TCH or Route 40 from Quebec City. From Toronto you will take Route 401. From the U.S. there are three principal routes: I-87 through New York State, which becomes Route 15 at the

Canadian border; I-89 from Boston through New Hampshire and Vermont, becoming Route 133 at the border; and I-91 from New Haven, Connecticut through western Massachusetts and Vermont, which becomes Route 55 at the border before joining Route 10 into Montreal.

GASPÉ PENINSULA

Not far from Montreal, yet a world away, is the Gaspé Peninsula. Jutting out into the Gulf of St. Lawrence like a clenched fist, the peninsula is an ancient landmass bounded on the north by the vast estuary of the St. Lawrence River and on the south by the Baie des Chaleurs ("Bay of Warmth"). Rising out of the heavily-forested interior are the Chic-Choc Mountains, a continuation of the Appalachian chain, with peaks of over 1,220 m (4,000 ft) above sea level, the highest in the province. Some of the world's best moose and deer hunting, as well as salmon fishing, are to be found in the uplands and river valleys of these mountains. The wild, boulder-strewn north coast, from Matane around to Percé, has some of the most dramatic scenery in Canada, punctuated at frequent intervals by tiny fishing villages. The gentler, warmer, less precipitous coastline of the south shore, though still dotted with little fishing villages, has most of the peninsula's farms and small industries.

But what is so striking about the Gaspé, apart from its stunning scenery, is its overwhelming sense of isolation. Not only is it geographically somewhat isolated from the rest of the country, but the little villages themselves are isolated from each other, even when they are only a few kilometers apart. And the villagers all seem isolated from the twentieth century, preferring to go about their business — usually as fishermen, but sometimes as merchants and craftsmen — in exactly the way that generations of their forefathers did. It is this simplicity, this stubborn respect for tradition, that makes the Gaspé an enchanting as well as scenic place to visit.

The twentieth century arrives, modestly, in the Gaspé.

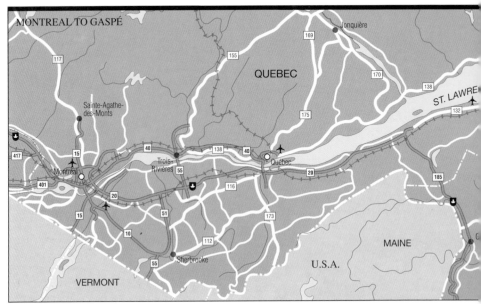

BACKGROUND

The first European visitors to the Gaspé were the Vikings in the eleventh century, followed four centuries later by the Basque fishermen who had discovered the rich fishing grounds of the Gulf of St. Lawrence. Then in 1534 Jacques Cartier — who else? — landed at the present site of the city of Gaspé, where, in the presence of a small band of bewildered Micmac Indians, he erected a tall wooden cross on a hill overlooking the bay and claimed the area for France. He named it Gaspéche, from the Indian word Gaspeg, meaning "land's end". It wasn't until the early seventeenth century that French fishermen began arriving and establishing little coastal villages which, despite the harsh and primitive conditions, survived thanks to the rich harvest from the sea. More villages were settled in the mid-eighteenth century by Acadians deported by the British from Nova Scotia. At about the same time, English settlers began establishng farming communities along the south coast, which were then augmented by the arrival of Loyalists in the aftermath of the American Revolution.

And then… , it's as if time stood still. A few waves, or ripples, of immigrants arrived from Scotland and Ireland, but nothing much changed. The pattern of village life

was set: cling to the coast, and the sea will provide. And the formula worked. The sea has provided not only fish in abundance, but in the eighteenth and nineteenth centuries it provided bonus extras in the form of shipwrecks along the Gaspé's rocky northern coastline. In fact, entire villages were founded by the survivors of shipwrecks with the stores and equipment they salvaged from their wrecked vessels. And in cases where there were no survivors, the residents of existing villages would bury the dead sailors and then help themselves to the sunken cargo.

There are no longer any shipwrecks or roaming tribes of Indians, or primitive outdoor plumbing, but in many essential respects the Gaspé today remains untouched — and therefore unspoiled — by the modern world.

GENERAL INFORMATION

Apart from the wealth of information you can get from the provincial tourist information offices, there is more specific information available from the Gaspé Tourist Association, which has offices at 357 route de la Mer, Sainte-Flavie, Quebec G07 1L0, ((418) 775-2223, and a mailing address at P.O. Box 810, Carleton, Quebec G0C 1J0, ((514) 873-2015 (collect calls accepted).

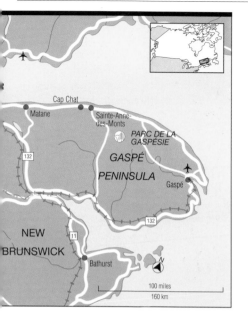

WHAT TO SEE AND DO

As you make your way eastwards across the north coast of the Gaspé you really shouldn't pass through **Grand Métis** without stopping to see the magnificent **Jardins de Métis**. When Elsie Reford inherited her uncle's estate near Grand Métis in 1919 she used her remarkable horticultural talents to create this series of beautifully landscaped settings for a vast variety of shrubs, perennials, and annuals, and her achievement is all the more remarkable because many of the species are found nowhere else this far north. Her home, the elegant Victorian Villa Reford, still stands in the park and is now a museum with a restaurant and shop. You can visit the park between June and mid-September, when it's open daily, ((418) 775-2221.

Continuing eastwards on Route 132 you'll come to **Matane**, a fishing town well-known for its salmon and shrimp, so it stands to reason that it's a good place to stop for a bite or to buy your fish and bite on it elsewhere. Starting in June Atlantic salmon swim up the Matane River to their spawning grounds. The dam here has a specially constructed passage through which the salmon swim and there's an observatory by the dam where you can listen to taped information

as you watch them struggle by. South of Matane a little way and just off Route 195, the **Matane Wildlife Preserve** is a good place to pitch your tent and do some canoeing, boating, or fishing, or just to take a hike. For information call ((418) 562-3700.

Back along Route 132, **Cap Chat** offers keen fishermen lots of opportunities. The lakes are brimming with trout, the river teems with salmon, and some of the locals will take you cod fishing at an hourly rate.

The next village is **Sainte-Anne-des-Monts**, and from it Route 299 will take you south into the **Parc de la Gaspésie**, a magnificent wilderness of some 200 hectares (500 acres) which encompasses lakes, forests, and the wildlife reserve in the Chic-Choc Mountains. Moose, caribou, deer, and a few black bears roam here, the landscape is rich and varied, and Arctic fauna still flourishes on the upper reaches of the mountains. Mont Jacques Cartier is the tallest peak, and if you can take the cold, the wet, and the hike, the views are breathtaking. The park is laced with hiking trails and roads, there's some good fishing and during winter it's popular for cross-country skiing. About 40 km (25 miles) from Ste-Anne-des-Monts along Route 299 is the **Gîte du Mont-Albert**, a lodge from which all trails begin, and where you'll find accommodation, campsites, a restaurant, an information point and a nature center. For further information you can telephone (418) 763-3039.

You can return to the coastal road at **Mont-St-Pierre**, a little village sheltering in a beautiful bay. It's one of the top Canadian spots for **hang-gliding** and if you fancy trying it yourself, a hang-gliding school operates there between June and August. There's also a two-week hang-gliding festival, **La Fête du Vol Libre**, held here each summer.

The northeastern tip of the peninsula that juts out into the gulf forms the **Parc National Forillon**, 238 sq km (92 sq miles) of spectacular coastline and forest where wildlife abounds. The northern side is characterized by dramatically sheer limestone cliffs, pebble beaches, and impressive headlands from which seals and occasionally whales can be sighted. There is a rich and remarkable variety of flora, and among the many forms of wildlife you may find moose, lynx, and black bears. The park offers a wealth of activities for you to choose from: there are guided tours, nature walks, hiking trails, boat trips to seal colonies, an island bird sanctuary and trips for whale-watching, scuba-diving, or fishing — plus beaches to relax on when you've done all those things. In winter there are trails for cross-country skiing and snowshoeing.

At Rivière-au-Renard Route 197 takes you south along the western side of the park to Gaspé, but you should follow Route 132 if you want to see the magnificent northern

other than its historical significance, for it was here in 1534 that Jacques Cartier first landed on North American soil and claimed it in the name of the King of France, an event commemorated with a **monument** that depicts in bas-relief scenes of Cartier's journey. Near the monument and overlooking the bay stands the **Musée de la Gaspésie** where you can spend a pleasant hour learning about the peninsula's history. Fishermen should take note that three Atlantic salmon rivers run into the sea here, and it's possible to fish them by prior arrangement with the

coastline at this point. Route 132 brings you along the coast to the old village of **Cap-des-Rosiers**, the site of many shipwrecks, and you can visit Canada's tallest **lighthouse** which dates from 1858, open from June to August, ((418) 892-5613, or learn more about the park at the interpretive center. Some privately-owned boats offer deep-sea fishing trips and cruises with the sanction of the park authorities. From here the Route 132 brings you to the south side of the **Forillon Park**, where the coastline along the Baie de Gaspé is softer and there are sandy beaches.

The port of **Gaspé** is the industrial and administrative center of the peninsula. It doesn't have a great deal to offer the tourist

government office which strictly controls the fishing. Other than this, there's nothing to keep you here.

The fishing village of **Percé** is a small and pleasant place set against a mountainous backdrop, but it is renowned for the strangeness and splendor of its geological landscape. Cliffs rise steeply from the sea, but nothing quite prepares you for the sight of the famous **Percé Rock**. Connected by a narrow strip of sand to Mont Joli, this majestic reddish-gold limestone rock is 427 m (1,400 ft) long, nearly 91 m (300 ft) high and is pierced by a natural hole at its eastern end, from which the name Percé ("pierced") originates. Beside it stands a pillar of stone, all that is left of a second arch that collapsed in the nineteenth century. At low tide you can walk out to the rock and wonder at it from close quarters, but if the tide is in you can take a path that leads to a cave close by it.

Mont Ste-Anne affords some wonderful views of the area, including the Rock, and despite a height of 320 m (1,050 ft) it is not a difficult walk if you follow the trail near the church. Another trail, the Route des Failles, takes you to **la Grande Crevasse**, a dramatic split in the rock to the west of Mont Ste-Anne.

Continuing southeast along Route 132, the south coast of the Gaspé assumes a very different character to that of the north. The coastline is low, the beaches are sandy, and some of the land is farmed. During the American revolution many Loyalists fled to this area and many of the towns as a result bear English names.

A little north of the town of Port Daniel, **Port Daniel Park** is a good spot for trout and salmon fishing, while further west the little town of **Bonaventure** sits in a pleasant bay. Its **Musée Historique Acadien** at 97 Port-

Boat trips run from the wharf to the **Île Bonaventure**, an island which is now a bird sanctuary, home to various species of seabirds and an enormous colony of over 50,000 gannets. You can either be content to circle the island or you can disembark and catch another ferry back. Go armed with binoculars and walking shoes; a hat may also be a good idea.

Attracting tourists as it does, the town is busy by Gaspésian standards, and there are souvenir and craft shops, cafés, and some excellent dining. From June to August the **Percé Wildlife Interpretation Center** on the route d'Irlande, ((418) 782-2240, is open daily and there are several small museums scattered around the town.

Royal Avenue, ((418) 534-2550, features period furniture and old domestic appliances. At the attractive town of Carleton, it's worth a walk or bus ride to the top of **Mont St-Joseph** for a panoramic view of the south coast of the Gaspé and of the shore of New Brunswick across the Baie des Chaleurs.

At the **Parc de Miguasha** the museum is devoted to the study of fossils, and specimens from the area are supplied to other museums around the world. You can take a look at the cliffs where the fossils are found and also see the laboratory processes used to separate them from the rock. Further

OPPOSITE and ABOVE: Bird-watchers and watched birds flock to the Île Bonaventure.

along Route 132, at Restigouche the final naval battle between the French and English was fought in 1760, and this is commemorated in the **Battle of Restigouche Historic Park** at Pointe-à-la-Croix. An interpretive center (open mid-June to early September) has among its exhibits parts of the *Machault*, the French warship sunk during the battle.

Matapédia is an attractive little village at the confluence of the Matapédia and Restigouche rivers, both of which are full of salmon. From here Route 132 goes north to

Ste-Flavie on the northern shore, a distance of roughly 160 km (100 miles). This is a very scenic route which takes you through the Matapédia valley with its pine-covered hills and tucked-away villages, so allow yourself time to enjoy it.

WHERE TO STAY

At **Matane**, the elegant **Hôtel des Gouverneurs** at 250 ave du Phare Est, Matane G4W 3N4, ((418) 566-2651, is part of the luxury hotel chain and has good facilities including swimming pool, fitness room, and a good restaurant. There are 72 rooms, many of which offer pleasant sea views, and the prices range from the lower end of moderate to the lower end of expensive. The **Motel Inter-Rives**, 1550 ave du Phare Ouest, Matane G4W 3N4, ((418) 562-6433, also has 72 rooms and offers similar facilities at moderate prices. **Motel la Vigie**, further along at 1600 ave du Phare Ouest, Matane G4W 3M6, ((418) 562-3664, is a moderately-priced 32-room hotel near the

dock, and the **Hôtel-Motel Belle Plage** at 1210 rue Matane-sur-Mer, Matane G4W 3M6, ((418) 562-2323, is reasonably good and inexpensive. For information on **campsites** at the Matane Wildlife Preserve call (418) 562-3700.

On the beach at **Cap Chat** the **Cabines Goemons sur Mer**, 195 rue Notre-Dame Est, Cap Chat G0J 2G0, ((418) 786-2291, provides inexpensive self-catering accommodation. At Ste-Anne-des-Monts, both the 72-room **Motel à la Brunante** at 94 blvd Ste-Anne Ouest, St-Anne-des-Monts G0E 2G0, ((418) 763-3366, and the smaller, slightly more expensive **Motel Monaco des Monts**, 90 blvd Ste Anne Ouest, St-Anne-des-Monts G0E 2G0, ((418) 763-3321, toll-free (800) 361-6162, offer comfortable accommodation and reasonably good dining facilities at prices which are inexpensive to moderate. The **Hotel Beaurivage** at 100 ave Première Ouest, C.P. 1358. G0C 2G0, ((418) 763-2224, offers inexpensive accommodation and has a very good restaurant.

In the **Parc de la Gaspésie**, the **Gîte du Mont Albert**, P.O. Box 1150, Parc de la Gaspésie G0E 2G0, ((418) 763-2285, offers accommodation either in the lodge itself or the chalets around it. The rooms are pretty basic, but none the less pleasant for that. With the peaceful setting, fresh mountain air, views of Mont Albert, and a crackling fire in the grate, who's complaining? Prices here range from inexpensive to moderate and reservations are essential. Camping is also available here.

At **Mont-St-Pierre**, the **Motel au Délice**, 100 rue Prudent-Cloutier, Mont-St-Pierre G0E 1V0, ((418) 797-2850, has 17 comfortable rooms with bathrooms and is probably the best accommodation on offer, while the **Motel Mont-St-Pierre**, 60 rue Prudent-Cloutier, Mont-St-Pierre G0E 1V0, ((418) 797-2202, has the advantage of a restaurant; both are inexpensive. In Forillon Park there are some well-equipped **campsites**, and on the south coast of the Forillon peninsula there's a **youth hostel** at Cap aux Os. At Cap-des-Rosiers the **Hôtel-Motel le Pharillon** at 1293 blvd Cap-des-Rosiers, Cap-des-Rosiers G0E 1E0, ((418) 892-5641, has 38 inexpensive rooms with TV and kitchenettes, and there's a restaurant.

At **Gaspé** you'll find one of the best hotels on the peninsula: the **Auberge des Commandants**, 178 rue de la Reine, Gaspé G0C 1R0, ((418) 368-3355. All 44 rooms are air-conditioned with TV and the prices are moderate. At Percé the best choice has to be the **Hôtel-Motel La Normandie** at 221 Route 132 Ouest, Percé G0C 2L0, ((418) 782-2112, toll-free (800) 463-0820. In this attractive wooden building, well-situated for views of the sea and the Percé Rock, there are 45 pleasant rooms all with private bath and TV, a sitting area, a restaurant, and

Moving to the **south shore** of the peninsula, at Bonaventure there are a couple of quite good motels: the **Motel Bourdages** at 118 ave Grand-Pré, Bonaventure G0C 1E0, ((418)534-2053, and the **Motel de la Plage** at 136 ave Port-Royal, Bonaventure G0C 1E0, ((418) 534-2934, both of which are inexpensive. At Carleton the two best places to stay are the moderately-priced **Motel Baie Bleue** at 1746 blvd Perron, Carleton G0C 1J0, ((418) 364-3355, toll-free (800) 463-9099, which offers 95 accommodations, an outdoor heated swimming pool and a good

guests have the use of a gym. Prices range from inexpensive to moderate, depending on the view. The similarly-priced **Motel les Trois Sœurs Pavillon le Revif** at 77-B Route 132, Percé G0C 2L0, ((418) 782-2183, toll-free (800) 361-6162, is also very comfortable and the service is good. At 222 Route des Failles, Percé G0C 2L0, ((418) 782-2852, the **Auberge du Gargantua & Motel** has 11 inexpensive accommodations with great views of the Rock and probably the best restaurant in the Gaspé, and there's an old-fashioned charm about the **Maison Avenue House** at 38 ave de l'Eglise, Percé G0C 2L0, ((418) 782-2954, where five simple and clean rooms are offered at inexpensive rates.

restaurant, and the **Manoir Belle Plage** at 474 blvd Perron, Carleton G0C 1J0, ((418) 364-3388, also with restaurant and with prices ranging from moderate to expensive.

WHERE TO EAT

It is hardly surprising that the menus of Gaspésian cafés and restaurants are swimming with seafood that is well-prepared and inexpensively priced. Cod tongues in batter are a Gaspésian specialty and have a surprisingly subtle flavor. As the Gaspé is such

OPPOSITE: A house in the fishing village of Percé. ABOVE: The famous Percé Rock stands sentry at the water's edge.

an outdoor place, there's always the option of buying your smoked fish from one of the many excellent fisheries and having a picnic somewhere along the way.

At the center of **Matis Park**, the Villa Reford has a busy restaurant where you can taste some traditional Canadian fare. In Matane there's a good and moderately-priced restaurant at the **Hôtel-Motel Belle Plage**, where you can sit watching the river flow, and good dining at similar prices can be found at the restaurant at the **Hôtel des Gouverneurs**.

At **Ste Anne-des-Monts** it's again a case of looking to the hotels, with the best restaurant being at the **Hôtel Beaurivage**, and another reasonably good one in **Motel Monaco des Monts**. Before leaving the town, you might want to gather the makings of a picnic for your trip to the Parc de la Gaspésie, in which case you can buy some smoked fish down by the dock.

In the **Parc de la Gaspésie** itself there's a real treat in store at the restaurant in the **Gîte du Mont Albert**, situated on Route 299, ((418) 763-3039. The highly acclaimed restaurant specializes in classic French cuisine and also regional dishes. Students from the Québec Institute of Tourism and Hotel Management serve here as part of their training and are very anxious to please. Prices are moderate and reservations are essential.

At **Mont-St-Pierre** the restaurant at the **Motel St-Pierre** serves good, inexpensive food, and before you enter the Forillon National Park there are plenty of pit stops. Once you're out of the wilderness, Percé offers an array of eateries.

Gastronomic delights await you in Percé's **Restaurant d'Auberge du Gargantua**, 22 Route des Failles, ((418) 782-2852. Beautifully situated with a fine view of the Percé Rock, the restaurant specializes in French cuisine, seafood, Gaspésian dishes, and a sinful array of desserts. Prices here fall within the moderate category but are the most expensive in the area. Still, a meal here is a real must. The restaurant at the **Hôtel-Motel La Normandie** offers very good dining in attractive surroundings and with good views of that Rock. **Hôtel-Motel Bleu-Blanc-Rouge**, 104 Route 132, ((418) 782-2142, specializes in seafood and provides a

snug atmosphere in which to enjoy it. At the wharfside, the **Maison du Pêcheur**, Place du Quai, ((418) 782-5331, is also very good, moderately-priced, and serves excellent lobster. Its location makes it an interesting spot at lunchtime and its large windows afford views of you-know-what.

At **Carleton**, the good and moderately priced restaurant at the **Motel Baie Bleue** is probably the best spot to dine, while at Matapédia it's at the **Hôtel-Motel Restigouche** in the rue du Saumon, ((418) 865-2155.

HOW TO GET THERE

VIA Rail serves Matane, Gaspé, Percé, and points along the south shore, but the only way to get there and get the most out of being there is to go by car. From Montreal or Quebec City, the Trans-Canada Highway (Route 20) goes to Rivière-du-Loup, from where the coastal highway, Route 132, does a complete loop of the peninsula. From New Brunswick, Routes 11 and 17 converge on Campbellton at the Quebec border, where you cross over and pick up Route 132.

OPPOSITE: The lighthouse at La Martre.
ABOVE: A fisherman at Rivière-du-Renard, north of the port of Gaspé.

Ontario

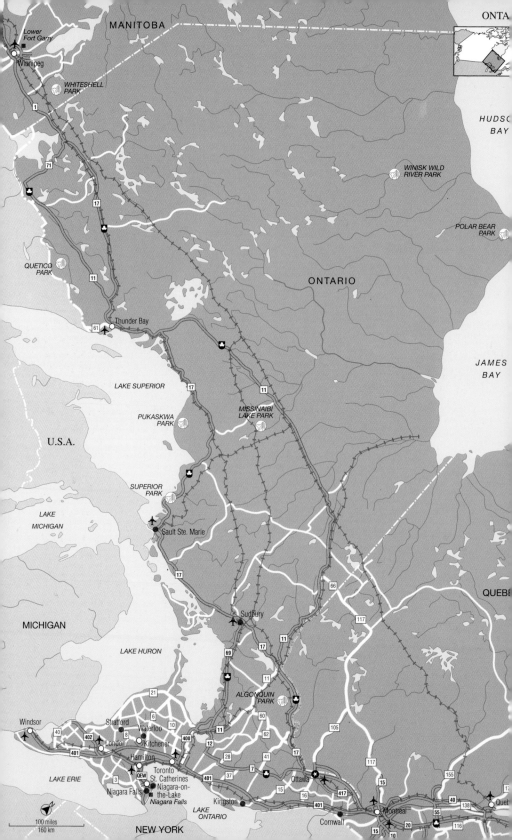

ONTARIO is easily the richest, most populous, and most visited province in Canada. With a population of nine million, it is home to a third of all Canadians. It has more mineral resources than any other province. It has some of the most fertile farmland in the country, along with the longest frost-free season in which to cultivate it. It has the country's industrial heartland, which produces half of all of Canada's manufactured goods. It has the country's capital, Ottawa, as well as its largest city, Toronto. And it has approximately 400,000 freshwater lakes, covering some 200,000 sq km (70,000 sq miles). It has, in a word, everything.

Orginally a part of the French colony of New France, and then of the British colony of Canada, it became a separate province in 1791 when the Constitutional Act divided the colony into the predominantly French-settled Lower Canada (Quebec) and the Loyalist-dominated Upper Canada (Ontario). Its first capital was Niagara-on-the-Lake, but in 1793 Toronto was selected to be the capital and was promptly renamed York. In 1813 York came under attack from the invading Americans and was burned to the ground. (A year later the British retaliated by burning, or at least blackening, the White House.) When York was rebuilt it expanded rapidly, helped by a tide of immigration from Britain and Europe, and in 1834 was incorporated as a city, reverting to its original Indian name of Toronto.

When the British North America Act of 1867 created the Dominion of Canada, the former Upper Canada joined the Confederation as the new province of Ontario, a name derived from an Iroquois word variously translated as "shining waters" and "high rocks standing near the waters" and is thought to refer to Niagara Falls. Ottawa became the capital of the newly confederated Canada, with Toronto remaining the provinical capital. Since then Ontario has gone from strength to strength, becoming during the twentieth century the economic center of the nation as well as the cultural center for English-speaking Canadians.

Although Ontario is Canada's second largest province, after Quebec, with an area of 1,068,587 sq km (413,000 sq miles), its industrial and commercial pre-eminence is due almost entirely to that chipped-arrow-head-shaped peninsula that begins at Toronto and extends southwest to the point where it pokes into Detroit. This is Canada's machine room. But that is not all. Low-lying and lapped by three of the Great Lakes (Ontario, Erie, and Huron), it is blessed with extremely rich soil, making it an agricultural center as well. Add to all this Toronto's dominance as a commercial and banking center, and you can see why the province prospers.

OTTAWA

In almost every sense, Ottawa is the ideal capital city. It is imposing: its neo-Gothic government buildings are set high on a bluff overlooking the Ottawa River. It is beautiful: its many official buildings and its many handsome residential neighborhoods share the city with numerous parks, lakes and open spaces, all surrounded by a four-kilometer-wide greenbelt and overhung by clear, unpolluted air. It is cultured: its six national museums and stunning National Arts Centre are only the "official" end of a cultural spectrum that is splendidly varied and impressive. It is cosmopolitan: it is the most compeletely bilingual city in Canada, and it boasts some of the best hotels and restaurants. And it is fun: the whole reason for Ottawa's existence, the Rideau Canal that sweeps through the heart of the city, is a summer-long haven for boating and canoeing enthusiasts, while in winter it becomes the world's longest skating rink.

Thus inventorying all the attractions of this paragon among the world's capitals, it comes as a shock to recall that only 150 years ago this was a rough-and-ready, brawling backwoods village where French lumberjacks and Irish construction workers regularly and drunkenly fought with each other. In those days it was known as Bytown, after the man who built the canal, but in 1855 it changed its name to Ottawa when Queen Victoria chose it to be the capital of the short-lived United Province of Canada, thus making it the natural choice as national capital when the Confederation came into being ten years later.

It was a widely unpopular choice, and a long time passed before Canadians stopped referring scornfully to "Westminster-in-the-Wilderness". Nevertheless, the people of Ottawa immediately set about erecting buildings worthy of a national capital, and — perhaps equally important — set about changing their image. If they were successful in the former pursuit, they were too successful in the latter. For almost a century Ottawa was noted for its sobriety, propriety, dignity, and decorum — in other words, for being numbingly boring. Then in the 1960s

settlement at the confluence of the Ottawa, Rideau, and Gatineau Rivers, which he rightly considered an ideal spot from which to ship timber to Quebec. In 1826 the settlers were joined by Colonel John By and a group of Royal Engineers, accompanied by a small army of mostly Irish laborers, who had been sent by the Duke of Wellington to build a canal. After the War of 1812 Wellington had been concerned that a long stretch of the St. Lawrence was within easy reach of American guns, so he decided on the construction of an alternative waterway from

the city suddenly seemed to get its second wind. Wonderful new buildings went up, the city's cultural life was reinvigorated, the entertainment scene expanded, recreational facilities proliferated — it was as if the city had decided, all of a sudden, to start enjoying itself.

The result has been, as four million tourists a year will attest, a city where visitors certainly find it easy to enjoy themselves.

BACKGROUND

There was nobody here but a few Outaouaic Indians, after whom the place was named, when Philemon Wright arrived from New England in 1800. He established a small

the Ottawa River to Lake Ontario. The project, which was completed in 1832, resulted in a 200-km (125-mile) system of canals, rivers, locks, dams, and lakes stretching from Bytown, as the village had come to be known, to Kingston, Ontario. It was called the Rideau Canal.

By the mid-1830s Bytown had a thriving industry producing and shipping squared timber, thus confirming Philemon Wright's judgment in establishing a settlement here. But it was another aspect of Bytown's situation that led to its becoming the capital of Canada. Distressed by the bitter rivalry between the larger cities of Upper and Lower Canada over which should be chosen as the capital of the new United Province of

Canada, Queen Victoria in 1855 selected Bytown because it was situated on the border between the two provinces. Having been thus honored, the people of Bytown changed its name to Ottawa and began preparing this one-industry (timber) town to handle a second industry: government.

Today, the 835,000 inhabitants of the city once derided as "Westminster-in-the-Wilderness" can gloat over the fact that, unlike the citizens of most capitals, they live near the seat of political power yet within a short drive of genuine, beautiful wilderness. It has proven a happy combination.

GENERAL INFORMATION

Ontario Travel publishes a whole series of useful guides which are available free if you dial (800) ONTARIO, or write to Ontario Travel, Queen's Park, Toronto M7A 2R9. Canada's Capital Visitor and Convention Bureau has a Visitor Information Centre in the National Arts Centre, 65 Elgin Street at Confederation Square in Ottawa, ((613) 237-5158, while the City of Ottawa Information Centre is in the Frelman Mall on Rideau Street, ((613) 564-1415. For information about Hull, just across the river in Quebec, there is a Hull Information Kiosk in the Maison du Citoyen, 25 Laurier Street, Hull, ((819) 778-2222.

WHAT TO SEE AND DO

Sights

The best way of sightseeing in Ottawa is on foot, as the major attractions are all within easy walking distance of one another. However, you may like to take a ride on one of the double-decker sightseeing buses which leave from Confederation Square frequently in the summer months.

Undoubtedly the main sight is **Parliament Hill**, the very heart of Ottawa and a good place to start your tour. Here, high above the Ottawa River, stand some splendid sandstone structures capped with green copper roofs, a neo-Gothic extravagance of towers and pinnacles. A huge fire in 1916 destroyed most of the original buildings and they were rebuilt a few years later with the addition of the soaring 92-m (302-ft)

high **Peace Tower** at the center, a monument to Canadians who died in the First World War. Take a trip up the tower (there is an elevator) for some excellent views over Ottawa. The **Parliament Buildings** or Centre Block house the Senate and House of Commons, and free tours are conducted daily at half-hour intervals (for details (613/996-0896). When Parliament is in session you can sit in the public galleries to watch. The **East and West Blocks** are offices closed to the public but you can visit the **Parliamentary Library**, the one place

that escaped the fire of 1916, a polygonal domed building with an impressive, panelled interior.

From late June to late August the **Changing of the Guard** takes place daily at 10 am on the lawns in front of the Parliament Buildings. With the military music, colorful uniforms and magnificent backdrop it's quite a spectacle. Every evening there's a **son et lumière** show on Parliament Hill.

To the east lies the **Rideau Canal**, which stretches 200 km (125 miles) between Ottawa and Kingston and is now used purely for recreational purposes. Lined by gardens and trees, it's a lovely place in summer to walk along or to go boating on, while in the winter skaters glide over it. In early February it's the center of the winter festival known as **Winterlude**.

Looking across eastwards from the Parliament Buildings you'll see the **National Gallery of Canada** at Sussex Drive, ((613)

OPPOSITE: The Parliament Buildings in Ottawa. ABOVE: An exhibit in the National Gallery.

990-1985, a stunning new glass structure designed by Moshe Safdie which overlooks the Ottawa River. Filled with natural light, the gallery contains one of the best collections of Canadian art anywhere as well as examples of the work of many of the world's greatest artists. It also contains a large and impressive international photographic collection. It is open daily during the summer with free admission on Thursdays. Close by stands the **Canadian War Museum** at 330 Sussex Drive, ℂ (613) 992-2774, with exhibits which trace Canada's military his-

tory; one exciting display with sound effects simulates life in the trenches.

Across Alexandria Bridge from the National Gallery and facing Parliament Hill stands the **Canadian Museum of Civilization** at 100 Laurier Street in Hull, ℂ (819) 994-0840. This enormous new building contains such exhibits as a west coast Indian village, a rain forest, an igloo, and an IMAX and OMNIMAX theater. The emphasis is on Canadian culture and on visitor participation.

The **National Museum of Natural Sciences** at McLeod and Metcalfe Streets, ℂ (613) 996-3102, is housed in an historic

Victorian building. As its name suggests, it is concerned with the formation of the earth and its life forms. There's a dinosaur section which rarely fails to be popular with children. Open daily in summer.

The **National Museum of Science and Technology** at 1867 blvd St-Laurent, ℂ (613) 991-3046, with its hands-on displays is popular with both children and adults. There are some magnificent old steam engines, vintage cars, machinery, and samples of all kinds of technology, including the Apollo 7 space capsule. The fun is that you can touch and test many of the exhibits. Open daily during the summer months, admission free.

Moving northwards a little, the **National Aviation Museum** at Rockcliffe Airport off blvd St-Laurent, ℂ (613) 998-4566, has an extensive collection of over 100 aircraft that trace the history of aviation from the beginning of this century to the present day. Open daily in the summer months, admission free.

At The Driveway and Carling Avenue is one of the city's loveliest parks, the 12,000-acre **Central Experimental Park**, ℂ (613) 995-5222. With its fields, beautiful gardens and Arboretum, Agricultural Museum, animals and horse-drawn wagon tours, it's a very pleasant and relaxing place to spend some time. Admission is free.

The wilder parkland of **Gatineau Park** is only a couple of miles northwest of the city center. It has 88,000 acres of woodlands, lakes, and hills, where black bears, moose, white-tailed deer, and raccoons are among the wildlife that roam. It's an ideal place for fishing, boating, swimming, camping, hiking, and picnicking, and **Moorside**, an historic house on the parkway, is a delightful spot for lunch or dinner. For information call (613) 992-5473.

Sports

You can see the Ottawa Rough Riders of the Canadian **Football** League play at Lansdowne Park in the Civic Centre, ℂ (613) 563-4551, and **soccer** fans can watch the Ottawa Intrepid playing their Canadian Soccer League opponents at the Terry Fox Stadium on Riverside Drive during May to October, ℂ (613) 722-7774. From July to November

ABOVE: "The world's longest skating rink" — the Rideau Canal in winter. OPPOSITE: A street entertainer in Ottawa's Byward Market.

there's **harness racing** at the Rideau-Carleton Raceway, ((613) 822-2211. Strange as it may seem in this hockey-mad country, there is no professional ice hockey team.

Ottawa has two public 18-hole **golf** courses: the Champlain on Aylmer Road, ((613) 777-0449, and the Capital Golf Course on Route 31, ((613) 521-2612. Also there are more than 30 private clubs with greens fees. **Tennis** enthusiasts will be pleased to know that there are free courts throughout the city; for information call the city recreation department at (819) 648-3222. For those who

enjoy the excitement of **whitewater rafting** and those who have never tried it before but would like to, there are several companies running one- or two-day trips, such as River Run, ((613) 646-2501, and Equinox Adventures, ((819) 648-2241. There are several places where you can rent **boats**, **canoes**, and **paddleboats** along the Rideau Canal, such as Dow's Lake Pavilion, 1001 Queen Elizabeth Drive, ((613) 232-1001, and Hog's Back Marina between Riverside Drive and Route 16, ((613) 733-5065.

In winter there's **skiing** close to town in the Gatineau Hills. The nearest spot is Camp Fortune along Route 5. It has five day lodges, 19 trails, night skiing, rentals, a ski school and ski shop. Mont Cascades on

Route 307 outside Cantley, ((819) 827-0301, has two lodges and 10 trails, and about 29 km (18 miles) from Ottawa on Route 366 near Wakefield is Edelweiss Valley, ((819) 459-2328, which has 18 runs, a ski school, night skiing, and also **skating** and **sleigh riding**.

Shopping

One of Ottawa's principal shopping areas is the **Rideau Centre** at 50 Rideau Street, which covers an area of 14 acres and is built on three levels. It contains a convention center, a 475-room luxury hotel, 18 restaurants, three cinemas, a shopping complex with over 220 stores, and is topped with a two-hectare (five-acre) park. Another major shopping center is the **Sparks Street Mall**, an outdoor mall on Sparks Street between Elgin and Lyon Streets which has the distinction of being Canada's first pedestrianized street. Over this five-block area you'll find boutiques, department stores, sidewalk cafés, and historic buildings interspersed with rock gardens, sculptures, and fountains. Shoppers can enjoy the diversions offered by street entertainers and open-air displays.

Close by, over the Rideau Canal, is the **Byward Market**, a down-to-earth farmers' market which has been going since 1830. Farmers have now been joined here by local artists and craftspeople whose wares are on display in the old Market Building. Specialty food stores and restaurants have also sprung up here. The market is open daily from May to October. It's located between Clarence and George Streets.

Nightlife

It has to be said that you don't go to Ottawa for the nightlife. The city after dark has changed for the better in recent years, but the best show in town is probably the nightly **son et lumière** on Parliament Hill.

There's a wide variety of programs at the **National Arts Centre**, where there's a 2,300-seat opera auditorium, a 950-seat theater, the smaller Studio for experimental works, and the Atelier which seats only 150. You can choose from dance and variety shows, operas, and ballets. The Centre has its own National Arts Centre Orchestra and bilingual theatrical company. For information about what's on call (613) 966-5051; to make reservations call (613) 755-1111.

You can listen to some rock music at **Barrymore's**, 323 Bank Street, ((613) 238-5842, and at the very popular **Grand Central**, 141 George Street, ((613) 233-1435. Big band music plays on Friday and Saturday nights at the **Penguin Café**, 292 Elgin Street, and there's jazz at **Friends and Company**, 221 Rideau Street, on Tuesday nights. You'll find jazz on Sunday afternoons and at other times upstairs at the **Rainbow Bistro**, 76 Murray Street, ((613) 594-5123, and blues at the **Downstairs Club**, 207 Rideau Street. You can hear folk and country music playing at the **Bank Café**, 294 Bank Street, and there's more country twanging at the **Gilmour**, 363 Bank Street. **Patty's Place** at 1070 Bank Street is a pleasant and friendly Irish pub where folk music plays from Wednesday to Saturday.

WHERE TO STAY

Luxury

The renowned **Château Laurier** at 1 Rideau Street, Ottawa K1N 8S7, ((613) 232-6411, is a beautiful castle-like building which opened in 1912 and whose guests have included the rich, the famous, and the royal. Situated at the bottom of Parliament Hill on Confederation Square, many of its 500 rooms and suites offer beautiful views. Among its facilities are an indoor swimming pool, the smart Canadian Grill restaurant and the elegant Zoe's Lounge. It's the flagship of the Canadian National hotel chain and its high standards and comfortable elegance make it still the place to stay. Also close to Parliament Hill is the **Skyline** at 101 Lyon Street, Ottawa K1R 5T9, ((613) 237-3600, which has undergone extensive renovation and offers over 400 rooms with good facilities. There's an indoor pool and two popular restaurants, the Henry VIII and Le Trianon.

At the **Four Seasons**, 150 Albert Street, Ottawa K1P 5G2, ((613) 238-1500, there's every modern convenience and comfort, personal service and the most expensive rooms in town. Built in the 1960s, this 17-floor hotel offers 236 attractive rooms and just about every service you could

require. It has an indoor swimming pool, sauna and whirlpool, a wine bar and its own restaurant, the elegant Carleton Room.

Connected to the Rideau Centre, the 24-floor **Westin** at 11 Colonel By Drive, Ottawa K1N 9H4, ((613) 560-7000, overlooks the Rideau canal. It has 475 tastefully decorated rooms, squash courts, gym, indoor pool, sauna, and restaurants. The **Radisson**, at 100 Lyon Street, Ottawa K1P 5R7, ((613) 237-3600, is another modern high-rise hotel with nearly 500 large and well-equipped rooms, a fitness club, indoor swimming pool, a piano bar, café, and the revolving La Ronde restaurant with great views of the city and the river.

The **Hôtel-Plaza de la Chaudière** at 2 rue Montcalm, Hull J8X 4B4, ((819) 778-3880, is a European-style hotel, elegant and very well equipped with modern conveniences. It has a very grand reception area, a beautiful restaurant called Le Châteauneuf, and its sumptuous decor extends throughout its 240 rooms.

Mid-range

The **Beacon Arms** at 88 Albert Street, Ottawa K1P 5E9, ((613) 235-1413, has recently renewed its decor and its popularity. It has 154 rooms and, considering its proximity to Parliament Hill, it is very reasonably priced. Staying close to Parliament Hill, the **Lord Elgin** at 100 Elgin Street, Ottawa K1P 5K8, ((613) 253-3333, offers extremely good value. Built in 1940, this stately stone building has 315 rooms and there's a Scottish style expressed in the decor and in the excellent choice of whiskies at the bar.

The **Hotel Roxborough** at 123 Metcalfe Street, Ottawa K1P 5L9, ((613) 237-5171, toll-free (800) 263-4298, is very centrally located. Its relative intimacy (there are only 150 rooms), cozy piano bar, French restaurant, and nice complimentary touches such as newspapers delivered to the room, shoeshine service and continental breakfast, make it an excellent choice. The **Park Lane Hotel** at 111 Cooper Street, Ottawa K2P 2L5, ((613) 238-1331, is also very conveniently situated and offers 235 smart and comfortable rooms which include some self-catering suites.

The **Cartier Place Hotel**, 180 Cooper Street, Ottawa K2P 2L5, ((613) 236-5000, has

130 comfortable and well-equipped apartments of differing sizes with maid service and dry cleaning included in the cost. Facilities include an indoor swimming pool, sauna, gym, and a restaurant. Under-14s stay free of charge in their parents' room. The **Minto Place Suite Hotel** at 187 Lyon Street, Ottawa K1R 7Y4, ((613) 232-2200, has 418 suites of varying sizes with all conveniences, very well-equipped kitchens and comfortable living rooms. With its special weekend rates, children under 18 allowed to stay free of charge, and being literally on top of shops and restaurants, it's a good choice for families.

Inexpensive

There's a booklet listing budget accommodation which is available from Canada's Capital Visitor and Convention Bureau (see GENERAL INFORMATION), and you could also contact Ottawa Area Bed & Breakfast, P.O. Box 4848, Station E, Ottawa K1S 5J1.

Some of the best value downtown is found at the **YM-YWCA**, 180 Argyle Street, Ottawa K2P 1B7, ((613) 237-1320, where there are 268 double and single rooms with air conditioning, telephone, and some with private bath. Guests have use of an indoor pool, squash courts, gym, library, and laundry. Also downtown there's Swiss-style accommodation at **Gasthaus Switzerland**, 89 Daly Avenue, Ottawa K1N 6E6, ((613) 237-0335, where there are 22 rooms, some with private bath. On Rideau Street the **Townhouse Motor Hotel** at N° 319, ((613) 236-0151, and the **Parkway Motor Hotel** at N° 475, ((613) 232-3781, are both good value, and near the canal **McGee's Inn** at 185 Daly Street, ((613) 237-6089 is a large Victorian house offering 14 rooms, some with private bath .

At the high end of inexpensive the **Talisman Motor Inn** is to the west of the town center at 1376 Carling Avenue, Ottawa K1Z 7L5, ((613) 722-7601, toll-free (800) 267-4166. It stands in Oriental-style grounds and offers 300 attractive rooms with balconies and use of an outdoor swimming pool.

There are two **Journey's End Motels** east and west of Ottawa which have the clean, modern, and agreeable accommodation that one has come to expect of this chain. The one to the east of the city is at 1252

Michael Street, Ottawa K1J 7T1, ((613) 744-2900 and the one at the west end is at 222 Hearst Way, Kanété, Ottawa K2L 3A2, ((613) 592-2200.

East of downtown the **Concorde Motel** at 333 Montreal Road, Vanier, Ottawa K1L 6B4, ((613) 745-2112, has 36 comfortable and well-appointed rooms with TV, an outdoor swimming pool, and a piano bar, while at the **Butler Motor Hotel**, 112 Montreal Road, Ottawa K1L 6E6, ((613) 746-4641, there are 94 air-conditioned rooms with TV, a pool, patio, dining room, and bar.

WHERE TO EAT

Expensive

In the Westboro district of Ottawa, I would recommend the **Opus Bistro** at 1331 Wellington Street, ((613) 722-9549. This small restaurant is elegant in its simplicity and the menu features much of the best of contemporary cuisine. Open Tuesday to Saturday for dinner only. At **Chez Jean Pierre**, 210 Somerset Street, ((613) 235-9711, owner/chef Jean Pierre Muller produces superb French dishes at expectedly high prices. Closed Sundays and Mondays. **Le**

Thirst-quenching, Ottawa-style.

Jardin at 127 York Street, ((613) 238-1828, is known for its reliably high quality. There is a French emphasis both in the menu and the decor. It is in a nineteenth-century house with a particularly beautiful upstairs dining room. Open daily for dinner only.

In Hull the **Café Henri Burger** at 69 rue Laurier, ((819) 777-5646, which first opened in the 1920s has undergone a recent renovation and continues to enjoy a well-deserved reputation for high quality. There's French cuisine at **Oncle Tom**, 138 rue Wellington, Hull, ((819) 771-1689, in a Victorian setting with a very intimate atmosphere. And it's worth the short drive into the Gatineau Hills to enjoy the beautiful setting and the superb French food at **L'Orée du Bois**, Kingsmere Road, Old Chelsea, ((819) 827-0332.

Moderate

The Italian restaurant **Mama Teresa** at 300 Somerset Street West, ((613) 236-3023, is something of an institution. It's popular and crowded; the food, particularly the pasta, is very good and the atmosphere is friendly. Italy meets California on the menu at the **Bay Street Bistro**, 160 Bay Street, ((613) 234-1111, and the result is very palatable and very popular. Open daily. For Indian food try the smart and popular **Haveli** at 87 George Street, Market Mall, ((613) 230-3566, or the excellent **Sitar**, 417A Rideau Street, ((613) 230-2222, which is open daily. **Silk Roads** at 300 Sparks Street Mall, ((613) 236-4352, is an interesting Afghan restaurant which is open daily.

The **Place Next Door**, 320 Rideau Street, ((613) 232-1741, is one of Ottawa's favorite spots. It has a homey, friendly atmosphere, and delicious steaks, ribs, and seafood. There's a distinctly English feel about **Friday's Roast Beef House**, 150 Elgin Street, ((613) 237-5353, where steaks and ribs again predominate in a very Victorian setting. Canadian food and Canadian wines are to be had at **Le Café**, in the National Arts Centre on the Canal, ((613) 594-5127. It's a pleasant spot for any meal of the day and stays open quite late Monday to Saturday.

Inexpensive

The **Elephant and Castle**, 10 Rideau Street, ((613) 234-5544, is a popular and central meeting place where pub-style food is served, and it's open all day every day. One of the best Chinese restaurants in town is the **Golden Dragon**, 176 Rideau Street, ((613) 237-2333, which has a large menu, plenty of seating and dim sum is served Saturday and Sunday lunchtimes. **Nate's** at 316 Rideau Street, ((613) 236-9696, is a well-known and well-worn Jewish deli that is a reliable source of good, cheap food from morning until late, late into the night.

There are several good eateries in the Byward Market area, including **The Ritz**, 15 Clarence Street, ((613) 234-3499, one of a chain of Italian pizzerias you'll find scattered around Ottawa, **Café Bohemian**, 89 Clarence Street, ((613) 238-7182, which has quite a lot of Greek food on the menu, and the **Khyber Pass**, 271 Dalhousie Street, ((613) 235-0881, where some very good Afghan food is served. You can go back in time to the 1950s at **Zak's Diner** at 14 Byward Market, ((613) 233-0433, where there's lots of vinyl, chrome, and fifties music on the jukebox. **Hurley's Roadhouse** at 73 York Street, ((613) 230-9347, is also a lively and popular place that does basic food such as burgers and steaks.

HOW TO GET THERE

Ottawa is served by many international carriers in addition to Air Canada and Canadian Airlines International. The airport is conveniently located just south of the city, only about 20 minutes from downtown. Buses as well as taxis are available for transport. VIA Rail has several trains daily to and from Toronto and Montreal. For information in Ottawa call (613) 238-4706; for reservations, (613) 238-8289.

Voyageur Colonial, ((613) 238-5900, operates a bus service that links Ottawa with other Canadian cities. If you are traveling by car, the Trans-Canada Highway (Route 417) is the principal east-west highway into and out of Ottawa. Approaching from the south you will want to take Route 16, which crosses the border at Ogdensburg, New York, and also connects with Route 401, the main Toronto–Montreal highway.

TOP: Byward Market. BOTTOM: The start of the bed race during the Winterlude festival.

SOUTHWEST OF OTTAWA

If you were an inhabitant of an area that had a dazzling, sophisticated city and a major world capital — say, Montreal and Ottawa — at one end, and a sprawling, wealthy metropolis — say, Toronto — at the other, you would probably feel that somehow the twentieth century had skipped over you. And in the case of that area extending southwest of Ottawa, you would have every reason to feel that way. But it so happens that this is just the way the people of this part of Ontario like it, especially in Kingston and Quinte's Isle, where they have been at pains to preserve the character and quiet dignity of an earlier age.

KINGSTON

Strategically sited where Lake Ontario meets the St. Lawrence River, this was an important Indian trading center long before the French fur traders arrived in the first half of the seventeenth century. Although the French immediately coveted the spot as an ideal location from which to trade with the Indians, constant fighting between the Iroquois and the Hurons prevented them from establishing a trading post until 1673 when a lull in the hostilities allowed Louis de Buade, Comte de Frontenac, to establish a fortified settlement here. Fort Frontenac, as it was known, survived for almost a century before falling to a force of British-American troops in advance of the Treaty of Paris which in 1763 ceded control of all of Canada to Britain. Like so many other towns and cities near the border with the eastern United States, it was resettled in the 1780s by self-exiled Loyalists, who gave it the name Kingston. Rapidly becoming a key British naval base and home to a large shipyard, Kingston survived the War of 1812 unscathed, and went on to enjoy two significant boosts to its economy: in 1832, when it became the southern terminus of the newly-completed Rideau Canal, and again in 1841, when it became, briefly, the capital of both Upper and Lower Canada. Already a prospering military center, Kingston soon became an important

academic center with the founding of Queen's University.

In the 150 years since then Kingston has remained remarkably unchanged in several respects. Although now a thriving city of over 60,000 people, it has remained true to the original: even today there are few buildings more than two or three stories tall, and Kingston's main street in the latter part of the eighteenth century, Brock Street, is still an important commercial thoroughfare and still has some of the same stores it had two centuries ago. Likewise, Kingston has retained its strong military connections: the Royal Military College, the National Defence College, and the Canadian Army Staff College are all located here. But most noticeably, it has preserved — and in many

instances restored — not only its graceful gray limestone public buildings from the nineteenth century but also its many fine Victorian private residences. Add to all this the parks, the attractive waterfront, and the colorful open-air markets, and you have a throughly delightful place to visit.

Finally, Kingston has also retained its strategic importance. Although it no longer figures in Canadian naval strategy, it occupies a crucial place in many tourists' travel strategy because it lies, conveniently, almost exactly half-way between Montreal and Toronto. And, equally conveniently, it is ideally placed for boat excursions on Lake Ontario and sightseeing trips to the Thousand Islands region.

QUINTE'S ISLE

Surrounded by the waters of Lake Ontario, Quinte's Isle is a pastoral idyll floating offshore. It, too, was settled by Loyalists, but instead of establishing the sort of commercial, industrial, cultural, and military centers that their fellow exiles created elsewhere, these Loyalists decided to take advantage of the island's position and rich soil to make it a quiet farming paradise. As a result, today it produces more vegetables and fruit than almost any other area of comparable size in Ontario — a lot of which is grown by descendants of the original

Kingston: an oasis of Victorian serenity.

settlers. The island is dotted with roadside stands selling fresh produce.

It is also increasingly dotted with art galleries and craft shops, as many artists and craftspeople have come here to get away from the rigors and distractions of life on the other shore. The great Canadian artist D.R. Dawson, for example, has now settled here in the town of Picton, having lived for years on a Greek island. Inevitably, too, the island has begun to undergo the experience of being "discovered", and consequently now has facilities and developments geared to

pleted in 1836 to defend the naval dockyard at Point Frederick from attack. Part of the fort has reconstructed barracks, kitchens, and officers' quarters, and shows what life was like for the nineteenth-century guardsmen. The specially trained Fort Henry Guard perform military drills daily; in July and August there's the color and music of the spectacular Ceremonial Retreat on Mondays, Wednesdays, and Saturdays at 7:30 pm. The Fort is east of the city off Route 2 and has an Information Centre, ((613) 542-7388.

the tourist trade. But it remains largely unspoiled — and thoroughly pleasant.

GENERAL INFORMATION

The Kingston Tourist and Visitors' Bureau is at 209 Ontario Street, Kingston K7L 2Z1, ((613) 548-4415, and the Quinte's Isle Tourist Association is at 116 Main Street, Picton K0K 2T0, ((613) 476-2421.

WHAT TO SEE AND DO

Kingston

The stout and forbidding **Fort Henry** glowers over Kingston from a high hilltop. This massive fortification was com-

Across Navy Bay from Fort Henry on Point Frederick stands the **Royal Military College** and in its grounds a Martello tower houses the **Royal Military College Museum**. There are some displays on the history of the college and, somewhat bewilderingly, the small arms collection of General Porfirio Diaz, the President of Mexico from 1886 to 1912.

The **City Hall** at 264 Ontario Street was built in 1843 when Kingston was capital of the United Province of Canada, and this grand domed building is one of the country's finest examples of classical architecture. During the summer there are guided tours Monday-Saturday. In front of the City Hall **Confederation Park** stretches down to the water's edge and is the site of concerts and other open-air events in the summer. Behind City Hall on King Street three times a week there's an open-air market and an antiques market on Sundays.

Moving eastwards along the waterfront, the **Marine Museum of the Great Lakes** at 55 Ontario Street is devoted to the history of shipping on the Lakes from the seventeeth century to the present day, including the history of shipbuilding in the area. Among the exhibits is a 3,000-ton icebreaker called the *Alexander Henry*. The

museum is open daily from mid-April to mid-December.

Continuing eastwards, the **Pump House Steam Museum** at 23 Ontario Street, ((613) 546-4696, is housed within the restored Kingston Pumping Station and its exhibits include steam engines, models, and the huge steam pumps themselves which have been restored to working order. Nearby in Macdonald Park is another Martello tower known as the **Murney Tower**, part of the defenses built in 1846. It now houses a museum devoted to the history of the area as well as reconstructed soldiers' quarters. It's open from mid-May to early September.

A lovely nineteenth-century house is the setting for the **Agnes Etherington Art**

Centre at University Avenue by Queen's University, ((613) 545-2190. The wide-ranging collection includes Canadian, African, and European art, antiques, and the house itself is furnished in period style. Admission is free and the house is open Tuesday to Sunday.

Bellevue House at 35 Centre Street, ((613) 542-3858, is an extravagant green and white Tuscan-style villa set in attractive grounds. It was built in 1840 by a wealthy merchant and its elaborate appearance earned it the nicknames "Pekoe Pagoda" and "Tea Caddy Castle". During 1848–49 it was home to Canada's first prime minister, John A. Macdonald, and the interior has been restored and furnished to that period with some Macdonald memorabilia displayed. The house is open daily to the public.

East of Kingston in the St. Lawrence River lie the **Thousand Islands**, which in fact number more than 1,000, ranging in size from quite large to a mere few meters. Some are forested and verdant, and the houses on them range from humble to palatial. This beautiful 80-km (50-mile) stretch of the St. Lawrence has long been a very popular holiday spot and there are quite a number of cruises and tours of the islands in operation. **Wolfe Island** is the largest of the Thousand Islands, and if you take a free trip on the car ferry to it you can enjoy some good views of Kingston and some of the islands. For tours from Kingston contact the Island Queen Showboat, ((613) 549-5544, Thousand Islands Cruises, ((613) 549-1123 or the catamaran Sea Fox II, ((613) 384-7899.

The **St. Lawrence Islands National Park** encompasses 17 of the islands and part of the mainland at Mallorytown Landing where the park has its Visitor Centre. The center is open daily from mid-May to mid-October and has an Interpretive Centre, a campground, and a water-taxi that runs from here to the islands, where there are some more campsites. While you're here, take a look at the wreck of the *HMS Radcliffe*, a gunboat that saw action in the 1812 war and is kept in a shelter close to the Interpretive Centre.

OPPOSITE: Muster ceremony at Kingston's Fort Henry. ABOVE: Bellevue House in Kingston remains rooted in the mid-nineteenth century.

For some more of the outdoor life, the nearby, **Frontenac Provincial Park** offers untouched wilderness in Canadian Shield country where you can hike, canoe or, when the weather's right, cross-country ski. The Trail Centre is a few miles to the north of Sydenham along County Road.

For more canoeing and boating you can go down the historic **Rideau Canal** which connects Kingston to Ottawa. You can take a pleasant boat trip along the system or even hire a houseboat and enjoy the parks and towns that line the route.

Quinte's Isle

Quinte's Isle is a restful place and a drive around the island along its quiet roads and through its old settlements makes a very pleasant day's outing. It is also a recreational spot with the flatness of the land making it a popular cycling spot, while the waters offer sailing and fishing opportunities.

The small town of **Picton** is the largest in the area and the hub of the island. It's an attractive, quiet town with some interesting old buildings and a deepwater harbor. You can pick up maps and guides in the tourist office here and take a look at some of the many crafts that are produced here. Each summer it's the center of a music festival called **Quinte Summer Music**, in which top Canadian performers participate. Elsewhere in the island, **Bloomfield** is a settlement which dates from the early nineteenth century and is a good place for crafts, pottery, and antiques. **Consecon** is a small and picturesque village with a millpond and some delightful views over the water.

East of Picton Route 33 brings you to the **Lake on the Mountain**, a small lake 60 m (200 ft) above Lake Ontario. Its origins are unknown, but legend has it that the lake is fed from Niagara Falls. This lovely spot is well worth a stop for the spectacular views over Lake Ontario.

West of Picton lie **Sandbanks and North Beach Provincial Parks,** ideal for picnicking, sailing and swimming. Sandbanks is a huge sandbar that extends across a bay and has freshwater dunes that reach up to 24 m (80 ft) in height. North Beach is good for swimming, windsurfing, and sailing; there's also a place that rents out equipment and gives lessons. For information on the parks you can contact the Sandbanks Provincial Park, RR1, Picton K0K 2T0, ((613) 476-2575.

The **Ameliasburgh Historical Museum** lies just over six kilometers (four miles) west of Route 62 on County Road, and among its exhibits are a restored steam engine, a weaver's cottage, a nineteenth-century church and some pioneer buildings, complete with furnishings, tools and artifacts appropriate to the period. It is open daily Victoria Day to Labor Day, and weekends to Thanksgiving.

WHERE TO STAY

Kingston
MID-RANGE

Close to the City Hall, the **Queen's Inn** at 125 Brock Street, Kingston K7L 1S1, ((613) 546-0429, is an attractive old stone building which has 17 pleasant rooms. Particularly good for families, the **Seven Oaks Motor Inn** at 2331 Princess Street, Kingston K7M 3G1, ((613) 546-3655, has 40 accommodations set in acres of land with a very large swimming pool: it offers excellent value.

Nearer the waterfront, the **Belvedere Hotel** at 141 King Street East, Kingston K7L 2Y9, ((613) 548-1565, is an elegant older building, with charming and individually decorated rooms, each with telephone and TV. The **Prince George Hotel** at 200 Ontario Street, Kingston K7L 2Y9, ((613) 549-5440, is a beautiful early nineteenth-century building offering 24 rooms with views over the lake. Further along, **Confederation Place** at 237 Ontario Street, ((613) 549-6300, is a modern hotel that overlooks the harbor and has 100 comfortable rooms, an outdoor swimming pool, and a restaurant.

The **Hochelaga Inn** at 24 Sydenham Street South, Kingston K7L 3G9, ((613) 549-5534, is an attractive early nineteenth-century house with 23 well-equipped rooms, handsomely decorated with period pieces. Near Fort Henry the **Highland Motel**, RR2, Kingston K7L 5H6, ((613) 546-3121, offers 45 rooms and facilities that include tennis courts and an outdoor pool.

INEXPENSIVE

For **Bed & Breakfast** accommodation in the Kingston area you can contact the following agencies: Kingston Area Bed & Breakfast Association, P.O. Box 37, Kingston K7L 4V6, ℂ (613) 542-0214, or Mrs Ruth MacLachlan, 10 Westview Road, Kingston, ℂ (613) 542-0214. For really unusual B & B accommodation you could stay aboard the icebreaker Alexander Henry that is docked at the Marine Museum at 55 Ontario Street, ℂ (613) 542-2261. You can stay in what were once the crew's quarters or at extra cost in the Captain's cabin.

There's also the possibility of **farm accommodation** outside Kingston itself. Hollow Tree Farm at RR1, Yarker K0K 3N0, ℂ (613) 377-6793 is a nineteenth-century farmhouse set in 50 hectares (125 acres) of farmland some 25 km (16 miles) northwest of Kingston. For details and a brochure write to Maurice and Daphne Lalonde at the farm. Nineteen kilometers east of Kingston and close to the St. Lawrence River is Leanhaven Farm, owned by Jean and Ross McLean. It is at RR3, Route 2, Gananoque K7G 2V5, ℂ (613) 382-2698.

There's a **campground** along the waterfront at Lake Ontario Park, which is not far from the city center and has very good facilities. There's another on Wolfe Island and several on the islands of the St Lawrence Islands National Park.

Quinte's Isle
MID-RANGE
At the high end of the medium-priced hostelries, the **Isiah Tubbs Resort** at RR1, West Lake Road, Picton K0K 2T0, ℂ (613) 393-5694, offers a wide variety of very attractive and comfortable acommodation: rooms or suites in the restored inn, lodges, or seasonal cabins, all with excellent facilities. Standing in 12 hectares (30 acres) of land by West Lake, the resort offers its own recreational facilities in addition to those afforded by its location.

If you enjoy messing about in the water you might be particularly interested in staying at the **Tip of the Bay Motel** at 35 Bridge Street, Picton K0K 2T0, ℂ (613) 476-2156. It overlooks Picton Bay, has its own docking facilities, and offers fishing packages. The **Merrill Inn** at 343 Main Street East, P.O. Box 2310, Picton, K0K 2T0, ℂ (613) 476-7451, is a charming hotel dating from

the 1870s. Each of the 15 rooms is individually decorated with antiques but is also furnished with modern conveniences. Guests have the use of an attractive sitting room and a pleasant sun porch.

INEXPENSIVE
Tara Hall at 146 Main Street, Wellington K0K 2L0, ℂ (613) 399-2801, is a lovely landmark house with beautiful decorative detail throughout and three guest rooms. In Bloomfield, **Mallory House** at RR1, Box 10, Bloomfield K0K 1G0, ℂ (613) 393-3458, offers some of the most charming accommodation on the island. This early nineteenth-century farmhouse set in attractive grounds has three guestrooms and is comfortably and cozily decorated throughout with old furnishings. The **Bloomfield Inn** at 29 Stanley Street West, P.O. Box 16, Bloomfield K0K 1G0, ℂ (613) 393-3301, has nine rooms and one of the best restaurants in the area.

For **farm accommodation** there's **Woodville Farm**, a modern home overlooking the Bay of Quinte about eight km (five miles) north of Picton run by Catherine and Glen Flake, RR2, Picton K0K 2T0, ℂ (613) 476-5462. **Burowood Jersey Farm** is a dairy farm 10 km (six miles) south of Picton, near Sandbanks Provincial Park and is owned by Les and Jean Burrows, RR1, Cherry Valley K0K 1P0, ℂ (613) 476-2069.

For a list/brochure of **Bed & Breakfast** accommodation contact Bed & Breakfast Independents of Prince Edward County, Box 443, Wellington K0K 3L0, ℂ (613) 399-3085.

There are four popular **campsites** at Sandbanks Provincial Park, details of which can be obtained by contacting the Superintendent, Sandbanks Provincial Park, RR1, Picton K0K 2T0, ℂ (613) 476-2575. There are also several private campsites nearby.

WHERE TO EAT

Kingston
MODERATE
One of Kingston's best-known dining spots is the **Firehall Restaurant** at 251 Ontario Street, ℂ (613) 384-3551, an old fire station that dates from 1840, where regional dishes are served in attractive and unusual surroundings. Upstairs is the Pumpers lounge

bar, and in the Greenhouse room you can enjoy the harbor view amid plants and stained glass. West of the town, **Clark's by the Bay** at 4085 Bath Road, ((613) 384-3551, serves some delicious dishes in a cozy atmosphere, and the table d'hote is an excellent choice. Open Tuesday to Saturday evenings only.

For good Italian food go to **Gencarelli** at 629 Princess Street, ((613) 542-7976, where you can eat out on the pleasant rooftop terrace in the warm weather. It's open daily for lunch and dinner.

INEXPENSIVE

The other well-known Kingston restaurant is **Chez Piggy** at 68 Princess Street, ((613) 549-7673, set in a restored livery stable that was built in 1810. The interior is attractive and warm, and the small menu features some interesting dishes. It is open for dinner and lunch from Tuesday to Saturday, and for Sunday brunch.

The **Kingston Brewing Company** at 34 Clarence Street, ((613) 542-4978, serves basic bar food amid the tanks in which their own very commendable beer and lager is brewed. Seafood and burgers are the specialties at the **Canoe Club** in the Prince George Hotel, 200 Ontario Street, ((613) 384-3551, and there's some good vegetarian food on offer at the **Sunflower Restaurant**, 20 Montreal Street.

Quinte's Isle

There's an old-fashioned coziness about the **Waring House Restaurant** which is in an 1835 stone house located just west of Picton on RR8, ((613) 476-7367. It specializes in

European cuisine. Its breads and pastries are home baked, and the dining room exudes warmth quite literally with its open fireplace and wooden floor. Prices are moderate and reservations are needed for weekends and summer months. It's open Tuesday to Friday for lunch and dinner. Also in Picton, the **Wheelhouse View Cafe** just by the Adolphustown Ferry is a good spot for inexpensive eating.

At Consecon, there's a country pub atmosphere in **The Sword**, RR1, ((613) 392-2143, where Cajun dishes feature as specialties among other good and moderately priced dishes, and there is an exceptionally good wine list. It's open daily Tuesday to Sunday.

There's fine dining in a Victorian setting at **Angéline's Restaurant** in the Bloomfield Inn, 29 Stanley Street West, Bloomfield, ((613) 393-3301. It's an attractive old house with a warm and welcoming interior and there's the option of dining out on the lawn in the fine weather. The chef's specialties include freshwater fish and pheasant, and his Austrian origins are in evidence when his wonderful pastries are served for afternoon tea. The restaurant is open daily for lunch and dinner in July and August, and Thursday to Monday the rest of the year. Reservations are essential for dinner. Moderately priced.

The **Maples Restaurant**, P.O. Box 62, Bloomfield, ((613) 393-3316, is a friendly and popular restaurant which specializes in inexpensively priced home-style cooking with a European flavor. From April to Thanksgiving it's open daily, and from Thanksgiving to January it's open Wednesdays to Sundays.

HOW TO GET THERE

Most people arrive in Kingston by car. Situated on Route 401 midway between Montreal and Toronto, it is an easy morning's (or afternoon's) drive from either city — and even quicker to reach from Ottawa or Syracuse, New York. It is also well-served by buses, with at least eight daily to and from Montreal, Ottawa, and Toronto. Schedules and fares are available from Voyageur, ((613) 548-7738. There is a ferry from Glenora to Adolphustown on Quinte's Isle which takes about 15 minutes and runs every quarter of an hour during the summer.

TORONTO

However hard one struggles to be open-minded, one cannot help but arrive in a new place with certain preconceived ideas about what one will find there. In the case of Toronto, I arrived thinking of Peter Ustinov's wonderful description of it as "New

of corruption, poverty, violence, filth, noise, despair, homelessness, meanness, indifference, incompetence, and crime — concrete jungles, in other words. Toronto does have a lot of concrete, of course, but it also has over 200 verdant parks. It does have a lot of shiny new skyscrapers, but it also has many lovingly preserved old buildings. It is certainly growing at a rapid pace, but its growth is carefully controlled so that adequate provision is made for housing in any develoment involving new office space. It is large, but it has excellent public transport, including a

York run by the Swiss." But what I hadn't counted on, when chuckling at the humorous implications of the remark, was its amazing accuracy. Toronto's buildings are not just tall, they do indeed scrape the sky; its crime rate is not just low, it's the lowest of any major city in North America; its streets are not just clean, I actually saw two city workers outside my hotel scrubbing a municipal litter bin with soap and water — in the rain!

With a metropolitan population of around three million and an urban area of some 650 sq km (250 sq miles), Toronto stands (and sprawls) as a gleaming, humming rebuttal to those who argue that big cities must inevitably become breeding grounds

sparkling and efficient subway system. Its schools are good, its cultural amenities are first-rate, its services are efficient, its streets are not only clean but safe, and its citizens are orderly and polite. No wonder people flock to live here.

While the spirit of the city is symbolized by the soaring CN Tower, its enterprising character is represented by the world's largest subterranean city — 12 blocks of shops, restaurants, cinemas, and cafés underground. And while it was once best known for its suffocating sense of propriety — for

OPPOSITE: The statue of John A. Macdonald, Canada's first prime minister, in Kingston.
ABOVE: Toronto's skyline.

many years it had "blue laws" restricting drinking, and was derisively as referred to as "Toronto the Good" — it is now a lively recreational, cultural, and entertainment center (it has more theaters than any city in North America except New York). But perhaps the best measure of the extent to which Toronto has managed to achieve just the right balance between the old and the new, between dynamism and tradition, is the fact that it strikes American visitors as a British city while to Europeans it seems very American. Which probably makes it the most *Canadian* city in Canada.

BACKGROUND

Ironically, considering it is now Canada's largest city, Toronto got off to a very slow start. The Huron Indians, who named the site (it means "meeting place"), saw the spot merely as the first (or last) link in a land chain connecting Lake Huron with Lake Ontario, as did the early French fur traders. In the first half of the eighteenth century the French decided that it might be worth building a fort there to protect their traders, but it was destroyed during the Seven Years' War. After the war the victorious British showed no interest in developing the site until 1793, when the Lieutenant Governor, John Graves Simcoe, decided to establish a town there. Soon thereafter it became the capital of Upper Canada in place of Niagara-on-the-Lake, which was thought to be too dangerously close to the American border. It was renamed York after George II's son, the Duke of York.

York's early days as a capital were inauspicious, to say the least. Its few dirt streets resembled linear bogs, earning the town the unflattering name of "Muddy York". Nor was its image much improved by the fact that one of its earliest industries was livestock slaughtering, which led to the sobriquet "Hogtown". Then in 1813 an American force attacked the town and burnt down every building of any size. But if its first 20 years were unpromising, York's next 20 years were marked by such economic and population growth that in 1834 it was incorporated as a city and given back its original name, Toronto.

For better or worse, economic and political power in Toronto — indeed in the province as a whole — was held almost exclusively by an elite group of wealthy businessmen. Known as the Family Compact, this small "club" exercised such power that its influence extended far beyond the boundaries of government and commerce to have a determining impact on every aspect of life in Toronto. Because these men were Anglophilic as well as Anglophone, Toronto became English in character as well as language. Because they were puritanical as well as philistine, it became "Toronto the Good", most righteous of cities, and most boring. And while its population expanded rapidly throughout the remainder of the nineteenth century — thanks largely to the arrival of Scots fleeing the Highland Clearances and Irish fleeing the Potato Famine — its horizons didn't expand much until after World War II, when a tidal wave of immigrants from all over the world enlarged and enlivened the city, transforming it from a dull gray zone of strictly-enforced virtue into the ethnically diverse, vibrant, cosmopolitan city that today graces the north shore of Lake Ontario.

GENERAL INFORMATION

For comprehensive information on Ontario as a whole as well as its capital city, contact Ontario Travel, Queen's Park, Toronto M7A 2R9, ((416) 965-4008, toll-free (800) ONTARIO, or visit its Information Centre on Level 2 below Eaton's store in the Eaton Centre on Yonge Street. For information on Toronto itself get in touch with the Metropolitan Toronto Convention and Visitors Association, Queen's Quay Terminal, P.O. Box 126, 207 Queen's Quay West, Toronto M5J 1A7, ((416) 368-9821, toll-free (800) 387-2999. The MTCVA also operates two year-round information booths — one at the southwest corner of Yonge and Dundas Streets and one at the Foreign Exchange Centre of the Scotia Plaza as well as seasonal information kiosks at the Royal Ontario Museum, at the Metro Zoo, at the CN Tower, beside the Hilton Harbour Castle Hotel, and outside the Royal Bank.

WHAT TO SEE AND DO

The Waterfront Area

The most conspicuous feature of the Toronto skyline is the **CN Tower**, a tall, slim concrete structure that resembles a giant needle. Ostensibly a transmitter mast, this tower stands 554 m (1,815 ft) high, making it the world's tallest free-standing structure. It contains a revolving restaurant, a disco, and an indoor and outdoor observation platform. A glass elevator on the outside of the building will take you to the "Sky Pod" two-thirds of the way up the tower, and those with a real head for heights can go on to a higher observation deck with curved glass windows laying the most spectacular

and giddy view of the city literally at your feet. If you have a problem with heights, this is definitely not for you. The tower is at 301 Front Street West, ((416) 360-8500, and is open daily. At the base of the tower you can take a "Tour of the Universe", a simulated futuristic space-shuttle trip including check-in through the spaceport. It's all done quite convincingly and is great fun. Open daily.

Close by on Front Street is the remarkable **Skydome**, ((416) 341-3663, a domed sports stadium with an ingeniously designed 86-m (282-ft) high retractable roof. It is home to the Canadian football team the Argonauts and the baseball Blue Jays. It seats up to 60,000 spectators, depending on the game or event, and has the world's

The stretch of waterfront between Bay and Bathurst Streets is a developing urban park providing shopping, recreation, and cultural events, and is known as **Harbourfront**. It was once an area of dilapidated wharfs, warehouses, and factories, which the federal government took over and through extensive building and refurbishment created an area of marinas, restaurants, cafés, shops, cinemas, and housing. Indeed, some believe that the construction work has now gone too far and that too many condominiums are spoiling the area. At the **York Quay Centre** there's an art gallery and theater, and close by is a large **antiques market**, while at the **Queen's Quay Terminal** there are shops, offices, and the Premiere Dance Theatre. At **Pier 4** there are sailing schools and equipment stores and at **Spadina Quay** you can visit the **Canadian Railway Museum**, ((416) 297-1464, open June to October.

Moving westwards you can find out about some of Toronto's most dramatic history at **Fort York** on Garrison Road, ((416) 392-6907. The fort was first built in 1793 to defend the town, and when in 1813 the Americans captured the city the fort's magazine was blown up by the retreating British, killing 300 Americans and 150 British. It was rebuilt in 1816 and was restored earlier this century. It offers the visitor a good picture of the life of the British soldier in the early nineteenth century, with its furnished officers' and soldiers' quarters, and military drills performed by authentically uniformed men during the summer months. The nearest subway station is Bathurst.

largest scoreboard. There's a restaurant with a huge seating capacity and a 364-room hotel with 70 of the rooms overlooking the playing field. On one famous occasion the presence of these hotel windows resulted in a serious distraction from a baseball game. During a 1990 game between Toronto and Seattle, a man and a woman in one of the rooms became extremely intimate in full view of the crowd. In the words of the hotel manager, "the people, for their own particular reason, wanted to perform in front of 40,000 fans." As a result, new hotel rules forbid "activities not considered appropriate in public". Tours of the stadium are conducted between 9 am and 6 pm, when there's no clash with events.

Continuing west along the waterfront, at Exhibition Place you'll find the **Marine Museum of Upper Canada**, ((416) 392-6827, which traces the history of shipping and trade in the area. During the summer the **Ned Hanlan**, a restored 1932 tugboat, is open to the public. Also at Exhibition Place, hockey fans can make their pilgrimage to the **Hockey Hall of Fame**, ((416) 595-1345. It is open daily.

Built on three artificial islands on the Lake, **Ontario Place**, 955 Lake Shore

The Skydome in Toronto.

Boulevard West, ((416) 965-7711, is an indoor-outdoor entertainment complex. Futuristic pod-like structures on tall steel legs house theaters where shows and films on Ontario can be seen. In a large geodesic theater known as the **Cinesphere**, IMAX films are shown on an 18-m (60-ft) high screen. The **Forum** is an outdoor concert hall used for all kinds of musical entertainment; the **Canadian National Ballet** make appearances here. The **Children's Village** is a well-designed, supervised play area. And all age groups enjoy a visit to the *HMS Haida*, a

Canadian destroyer used in World War II and the Korean War, which is moored in a marina. Ontario Place is open daily from mid-May to mid-September.

You can take a boat trip out to the **Toronto Islands** from Ontario Place and also from the dock at the foot of Bay Street near the Harbour Castle Hotel. This collection of small islands off the downtown waterfront offer recreational possibilities such as swimming, fishing, boating and cycling and are a popular retreat from the summer heat for Torontonians and visitors alike. **Hanlan's Point** has tennis courts and a

pleasant beach, **Ward's Island** is good for swimming, but the most popular is **Centre Island** with its children's farm, playgrounds and rides. For further information ring Metro Parks, ((416) 392-8184.

Downtown

Toronto's King and Bay Street area is its financial center and here you'll find the **Toronto Stock Exchange** at First Canadian Place, ((416) 947-4676, where you can watch the action on the trading floor from a gallery or take a tour of the building. Of the bank towers the most striking is the **Royal Bank Plaza** with its two triangular towers of gold reflecting glass. It is situated at Front and Bay Streets. A true cathedral of commerce, it contains an international art collection which includes a vast sculpture by Jesùs Soto composed of 8,600 aluminum tubes.

The **City Hall** in Nathan Phillips Square, ((416) 392-7341, is a highly acclaimed piece of modern architecture in front of which stands a Henry Moore sculpture, known locally as The Archer. A couple of blocks east of the City Hall stands **Mackenzie House**, 82 Bond Street, ((416) 392-6915, a Victorian town house which was the home of William Lyon Mackenzie, Toronto's first mayor and leader of the 1837 rebellion. Following the rebellion he lived in exile in the U.S. and when he was able to return to the city his friends gave him this house. Now restored and furnished in mid-nineteenth century style, the house has displays telling the story of his life. The nearest subway stop is Dundas.

To the east of City Hall, the **Art Gallery of Ontario** at 317 Dundas Street West, ((416) 977-0414, houses one of the country's most important art collections. The **Henry Moore Sculpture Centre**, with over 300 exhibits, has the largest public collection of Moore's works in the world. The **European Collection** covers movements in art from the seventeenth century through to the early twentieth century, while three galleries are devoted to the comprehensive **Canadian Collection**. Adjoining the modern Art Gallery building is a beautiful Georgian brick house known as **The Grange**. This was once the home of the prominent Boulton family, which later became the first home of the Art

ABOVE: Toronto's Old City Hall.
OPPOSITE: The entrance to the Canadian National Exhibition building.

Ontario

Gallery and has now been restored to the elegance of an 1830s residence. The Gallery and The Grange are open daily mid-June to August, and closed on Mondays during the rest of the year. The nearest subway stops are St. Patrick and Dundas.

Queen's Park Area

Moving slightly north to the area around Queen's Park, you'll find the **Royal Ontario Museum** at 100 Queen's Park, ((416) 586-5549, Canada's largest public museum and one of its most wide-ranging, as it covers art, archaeology, and the natural sciences. Among its most famous features are its Chinese art treasures, its Ming Tomb, the Dinosaur Gallery, a huge replica of a bat cave complete with special effects, and the popular hands-on Discovery Gallery. Open daily. Other branches of the museum are the **McLaughlin Planetarium**, next to the ROM, ((416) 536-5736, the **Sigmund Samuel Building** at 14 Queen's Park Crescent West, ((416) 586-5549, which houses a large collection of Canadiana, including room settings and folk art, and the **George R. Gardiner Museum of Ceramic Art** at 11 Queen's Park, ((416) 593-9300, which includes extensive collections of Pre-Columbian pottery, Italian Maiolica, English Delftware, and eighteenth-century European porcelain.

Near the museum in Queen's Park stands the **Provincial Parliament Building**, ((416) 965-4028, a Romanesque pink sandstone building dating from the late nineteenth century. You can attend parliamentary sittings when the house is in session.

Neighborhoods

Toronto's immigrant communities have been encouraged to maintain their cultural individuality, and the result is a rich and colorful ethnic patchwork. For example, at Dundas Street East is one of two large Chinatown communities; the other is along Dundas Street West. There's a big Italian community at St. Clair Avenue West and Dufferin Street which is rumored to have more Italians than Florence, and along Gerrard Street East you'll find Little India. Between Pape and Woodbine Streets bouzouki music can be heard in the Greek district

known as "the Danforth". Between Bathurst and Spadina Streets south of College Street is the lively open-air **Kensington Market**, with its distinctly Portuguese accent.

Some of Toronto's other neighborhoods are characterized by lifestyle or income rather than by nationality, such as the genteel **Forest Hill** area or the wealthy **Rosedale** area. The **Beaches** area, situated along Queen Street East at Woodbine, has a touch of California about it. It's largely a professional neighborhood with a beach and lakeside parkland, a two-mile long Boardwalk

and a core of cafés, shops, and restaurants. The area bordered by Parliament Street, the Don River, Danforth Avenue and Gerrard Street is known as **Cabbagetown**. Originally built to provide housing for factory workers, it was a run-down slum area by the 1960s but then underwent extensive renovation to become a very pleasant residential and commercial district.

Queen Street West is Toronto's equivalent of London's King's Road with its trendy boutiques, galleries, clubs, bistros, restaurants and bars concentrated on the section of Queen Street West lying between University Avenue and Bathurst Street. Close to the College of Art, the street has developed a certain bohemian air and it's great fun to wander around. Moving from the hip to the seriously chic, **Bloor/Yorkville** is the smartest part of town. The area — bounded by Charles Street, Davenport Road, Yonge Street, and Avenue Road — was once a downbeat, dilapidated hippie hangout, but after renovation it is now filled with art galleries, cafés, restaurants, and the chicest of shops.

There's an altogether different kind of atmosphere around **Mirvish Village** at Markham Street south of Bloor, where entrepreneur Eddie Mirvish has his flagship

built it between 1905 and 1911 for $3.5 million, and with its cellars, towers, secret passageways, and stables it's rather like a set for an old Hollywood movie. Its wood panelling, marble swimming pool, massive ballroom, and marble-floored conservatory with stained glass dome are examples of the unfettered extravagance with which the castle was built and which eventually reduced Sir Henry to surrender his glorious dream palace to the city in payment of back taxes. It is open daily to the public. The nearest subway station is Dupont.

store, the brash and breezy "Honest Ed's". With the money Ed has made he has become a well-known patron of the arts and he was responsible for the rejuvenation of this block of pleasant Victorian buildings containing restaurants, bars, and shops selling antiques, books, and art.

Outside Downtown

The eccentrically splendid **Casa Loma** sits atop a hill at 1 Austin Terrace, ((416) 923-1171, commanding views over the city. This 98-room, baronial-style mansion was the folly of Sir Henry Pellatt, a financier, who

At **High Park** on Queen Street West you can play a game of tennis, enjoy the gardens and picnic grounds, go fishing or boating, take the children to the zoo, and on a summer's day see some Shakespeare in the open air. It is the city's largest park and at its center is **Colborne Lodge**, a lovely Regency villa bequeathed to the city by its architect/owner John George Howard. This elegant home is open daily to the public and contains some watercolors of Toronto painted by Howard himself. He was also an engineer and his house boasts the first indoor flush toilet in Ontario. To get there take the Metro to High Park.

For wildlife watchers and those who just enjoy a peaceful retreat, the **Tommy**

ABOVE: People and pigeons share a lunch break. OPPOSITE: The Toronto Blue Jays, baseball's 1992 World Series Champions, playing in the Skydome.

Thompson Park (also known as the Leslie Street Spit) might be the place to go. Landfill from building sites created the spit that extends out into the lake and unexpectedly the wildlife literally flocked to it. It is now a sanctuary for birds such as gulls, geese, herons, swans, and ducks, and foxes and rabbits keep on arriving. It is open to the public only at weekends and is situated south of the junction of Leslie Street and Queen Street East.

About 11 km (seven miles) north of downtown in the Don River Ravine stands

Excursions

To see what life was like in rural Ontario during the nineteenth century, take a trip to the **Black Creek Pioneer Village**, which is 29 km (18 miles) northwest of downtown at 1000 Murray Ross Parkway, ((416) 661-6610. This recreated village includes a blacksmith's shop, a mill, and a general store, all run by costumed villagers who will also demonstrate their crafts and skills. Sometimes a special event such as a wedding is enacted. Open daily from mid-March to December 31.

the splendid **Ontario Science Centre**. Another of architect Raymond Moriyama's triumphs, the museum integrates beautifully with its environment and its series of buildings are linked by enclosed escalators and ramps which allow the visitor to enjoy stunning views. Moriyama's respect for the natural beauty of the site is rumored to have extended to penalty clauses in building contracts for each tree destroyed. This hugely popular museum presents science and technology in a way that encourages viewer participation and demonstrates its everyday relevance. Allow plenty of time to look around, and remember that it gets very busy at weekends. The museum is open daily and is at 770 Don Mills Road, ((416) 429-0193.

Not far away is a huge theme park known as **Canada's Wonderland** at 7725 Jane Street in Concord, ((416) 832-2205, about 32 km (20 miles) northwest of downtown. Over an area of 370 acres there are various theme areas offering rides, shows, roller coasters, water slides, shops, and a lot of shrieking and whooping. It's open daily from June to September.

The **Metro Toronto Zoo** is situated in the Rouge River valley, 40 km (25 miles) northeast of downtown on Meadowvale Road, ((416) 392-5900. Here the natural habitats have been recreated to allow the animals greater freedom. Around the zoo an area of untouched land provides the setting for North American wildlife and can only be visited by monorail. A Zoomobile will take you around the zoo if you don't feel like walking, and in the winter there's the special option of following a cross-country skiing trail. Open daily and with longer hours in the summer months.

A visit to the **McMichael Canadian Art Collection** at Islington Avenue, Kleinberg, ((416) 893-1121, about 40 km (25 miles) north of the city, makes a very pleasant outing. The most important collection of the works of the Canadian painters known as the Group of Seven is housed here. These painters were a revolutionary force in Canadian art, the first to produce uniquely Canadian painting inspired by the unspoiled beauty of the northern Ontario landscape. Also represented here are Inuit and Indian art. The gallery is a lovely log and stone building with a high pitched roof; and there are windows throughout giving views of the beautiful countryside that inspired the paintings within.

Sports

The spectacular Skydome stadium is the home of the Blue Jays **baseball** team, ((416) 595-0077, and from June to early November the Argonauts **Canadian football** team ((416/595-1131) also plays here. From October to April **ice hockey** fans worship at the Maple Leaf Gardens, 60 Carlton Street, ((416) 977-1641, where the Toronto Maple Leafs play, but tickets are very difficult to come by. There's thoroughbred **horse racing** at the Woodbine Racetrack, Rexdale Boulevard at Route 427, Etobicoke, ((416) 675-6110, where in the summer the famous Queen's Plate is run and in October the Rothman's International. There is thoroughbred and harness racing all year at the Greenwood Race Track, 1669 Queen Street East, ((416) 698-3131. If you're a **golf** lover then you might be interested to know that Glen Abbey in Oakville, ((416) 844-1800, is where the Canadian Open is played.

For those who want to be participants, Toronto offers great opportunites for all kinds of sports. If you call ((416) 964-8655, Sports Ontario can supply you with details, while Metro Parks, ((416) 392-8184, have details on swimming pools, beaches, golf courses, and tennis courts.

Bicyclists will find plenty of trails around the parks, and there's no shortage of places renting out cycles. **Fishing** enthusiasts should bear in mind that the pollution in Lake Ontario means they have to be very careful about eating anything caught there, but each year the Great Salmon Hunt attracts anglers to try their luck at landing the biggest salmon. To find out about **yachting, sailing** and **windsurfing** you should contact the Canadian Yachting Association at 333 River Road, K1L 8B9 or the Ontario Sailing Association, ((416) 495-4240. **Swim-**

mers can choose from a large number of public and private pools, or beaches in the Toronto Islands. Call Metro Parks, ((416) 392-8184, for details.

There are several **golf** courses where the visitor can play in and around Toronto; you can get information on courses that are open to the public from Ontario Travel, ((416) 965-4008. **Tennis** players are also well catered for with plenty of public and private courts, details of which are available from the Metropolitan Parks Department and the Canadian Tennis Association, Toronto Office, 25 Imperial Street, ((416) 488-5076.

Toronto has over 100 natural and manmade **skating rinks**, both indoor and outdoor, so you're never far from one. **Cross-**

country skiing is a favourite Torontonian pastime, and there are downhill and cross-country trails throughout the city, some of which go out on to the lake.

Shopping

Toronto caters to just about every shopper's needs and budget. It's a good place to buy Canadian crafts and Canadian-made quality clothing, not because these goods are particularly cheap here but because the quality is particularly good. Shop opening hours tend to be from 9 or 10 am to 6 pm

from The Atrium at Bay Street down to Union Station and has over 1,000 shops as well as many other facilities. It connects with major hotels, offices and seven subway stations, providing a welcome escape from the bitter winter weather and the humidity of hot summer days.

In the **Bloor/Yorkville** district on and around Bloor Street, Yorkville Avenue, Hazelton Avenue and Cumberland Street, are Toronto's most exclusive and chic shops. Here you'll find such names as Chanel, Cartier, Hermès, and Louis Vuitton. There

from Monday to Saturday, often with a late night on Thursdays, although shops in the Underground City tend to stay open until 9 pm from Monday to Friday. You'll even find some shops open on Sundays down at the Harbourfront.

Stretching from Dundas Street to Queen Street along Yonge Street is the **Eaton Centre**, one of the world's largest shopping centers. Enclosed within by a huge glass and steel arched roof, with its beautiful sculpted flock of geese over the shops, people come here to admire as well as shop. It houses over 300 shops, many eateries, and two of Canada's biggest department stores — Eaton's and Simpsons. The Centre links with Toronto's **Underground City**, which runs

are shopping malls such as the Holt Renfew Centre, the Manulife Centre and Hazelton Lanes, and attractive old houses containing art galleries, boutiques, and cafés. There's a different kind of chic on **Queen Street West** between John Street and Spadina Avenue, where there's a more arty flavor. Here you'll find bookshops, record shops, trendy and not-so-trendy clothes shops, galleries and health shops.

South of Bloor Street on Markham Street in **Mirvish Village** it's impossible to miss **Honest Ed's**. Walking around this huge bargain store with its lights and signs can

Upmarket and downmarket shopping in Toronto. OPPOSITE: Eaton Centre. ABOVE: Shops on Yonge Street.

be an overwhelming experience, but there are some good buys to be found here. North of here, near the Art Gallery of Ontario, is **Village on the Grange**, on McCaul Street, ℂ (416) 598-1414, a shopping complex of about 60 stores. It's a particularly good place to look for a gift that's out of the ordinary. **Kensington Market**, bordered by Bathurst Street, Spadina Avenue, Dundas and College Streets, has a bazaar atmosphere with all kinds of cheap goods and foods.

Over at the Harbourfront, **Queen's Quay Terminal** at the bottom of York Street is a warehouse that has been converted to hold novelty shops and boutiques, and close by at Queen's Quay West, ℂ (416) 340-8377, you'll find the **Harbourfront Antique Market** where there are over 100 stalls selling all manner of objects.

Nightlife

Toronto is a lively place after dark and offers a very wide choice of entertainment. For details of what's on, you can check the listings in the *Toronto Star* on Friday, the *Globe and Mail* on Saturday and the monthly *Toronto Life* magazine. Tickets for a range of plays, shows, and concerts can be arranged through **Ticketmaster**, ℂ (416) 872-1111, and half-price tickets for many of these entertainments are available on the day, for cash, from **Five Star Tickets**, ℂ (416) 596-8211.

Toronto has a large, lively and varied **theater scene**. The **Royal Alexandré Theatre** at 260 King Street West, ℂ (416) 593-4211, stages Broadway and London and Canadian productions, and has been beautifully restored to its turn-of-the-century splendor. The **Elgin and Winter Garden Theatres** at 189 Yonge Street, ℂ (416) 872-5555, present musicals and drama. The larger Elgin theater has been restored to the gilt and grandeur of the Edwardian era, and upstairs the Winter Garden is a smaller theater, whimsically decorated to look like an English garden. At the **St. Lawrence Centre for the Arts**, 27 Front Street East, ℂ (416) 366-7723, classics and Canadian plays are among the works performed by Toronto rep companies, and at the **O'Keefe Centre**, 1 Front Street East, ℂ (416) 393-7469, you can see musicals and Broadway shows. For more innovative

theater there's the **Théâtre Passe Muraille**, 16 Ryerson Avenue, ℂ (416) 363-2416, and the **Poor Alex Theatre**, 296 Brunswick Avenue, ℂ (416) 927-8998, one of Toronto's foremost theaters in this line. At the **Tarragon Theatre**, 30 Bridgman Avenue, ℂ (416) 531-1827, Canadian works are usually performed.

The **Canadian Opera Company** is based at the O'Keefe Centre, 1 Front Street East, ℂ (416) 363-6671, where it presents a program of seven operas during the period from September to June. The highly acclaimed **National Ballet of Canada**, 157 King Street East, ℂ (416) 362-1041, is also based at the O'Keefe Centre and also make summer appearances at Ontario Place in the open-air theater. The **Première Dance Theatre** at 207 Queen's Quay West, ℂ (416) 973-4000, performs both classical and modern works.

The **Toronto Symphony Orchestra**, ℂ (416) 593-7769, has its home at the **Roy Thomson Hall**, 60 Simcoe St, ℂ (416) 598-4822, and plays here from September to June and at **Ontario Place** in July and August. The Roy Thomson Hall is also home to the **Toronto Mendelssohn Choir**, ℂ (416) 598-0422, and it attracts top names in music of all kinds. There's symphonic music at the **Massey Hall** at 178 Victoria Street, ℂ (416) 363-7301, and chamber music and recitals at the **St. Lawrence Centre**, 27 Front Street East, ℂ (416) 366-7723.

Cinema lovers will appreciate the wonderful **Cinéplex** in the Eaton Centre, ℂ (416) 593-4535, where there are 17 cinemas. At the **Ontario Film Institute** in the Ontario Science Centre, 770 Don Mills Road, ℂ (416) 429-0454, retrospectives and new international films are shown. There are also several repertory cinemas around Toronto.

Toronto's oldest **jazz** venue is **George's Spaghetti House** at 290 Dundas Street East, ℂ (416) 923-9887, where you can see local bands perform. **Chick n' Deli**, 744 Mount Pleasant Road, ℂ (416) 489-3313, is a hot spot at the moment and the elegant **Café des Copains**, 48 Wellington Street East, ℂ (416) 869-0148, has jazz downstairs. There's rhythm and blues at **Club Bluenote**, 128 Pears Avenue, ℂ (416) 924-8244; **Albert's Hall**, Brunswick House, 481 Bloor Street West, ℂ (416) 964-2242, also has blues and New Orleans jazz. The **Top O' The Senator** upstairs at the Senator restaurant, 253 Victoria Street, ((416) 364-7517, is one of the foremost jazz venues, with a reputation for presenting exciting new talent. You can also hear jazz at the **Roy Thomson Hall** and the **Massey Hall** (see above for details).

The big **rock** venue is **El Mocambo**, 464 Spadina Avenue, ((416) 961-2558, where many top bands have played over the years. Rock and country music plays at the **Birchmount Tavern**, 462 Birchmount Road, ((416) 698-4115. And there's reggae and Latin music at **Bamboo**, 312 Queen Street West, ((416) 593-5771.

that attract the young crowds are the large **Copa**, 21 Scollard Street, ((416) 922-6500, and **Down Towne Brown's**, 49 Front Street East, ((416) 367-4949. **Berlin** at 2335 Yonge Street, ((416) 489-7777, is a dressier place which attracts a slightly older and more affluent crowd, and **Sparkles** is perched high up in the CN Tower at 301 Front Street, ((416) 360-8500. Early rock and roll often features in the otherwise modern **De Soto's**, 759 Mount Pleasant Road, ((416) 480-0222, while the old rock and rollers really come out of the woodwork

There are several places where you can watch **cabaret** acts, such as **Second City**, 110 Lombard Street, ((416) 863-1111, a nightclub with a comedy revue that has produced some very talented comedians. There's stand-up comedy at **Yuk-Yuk's Komedy Kabaret**, 1280 Bay Street, ((416) 967-6425, and drag acts at **An Evening at La Cage**, 279 Yonge Street, ((416) 364-5200. For more conventional cabaret entertainment there's the glamorous **Imperial Room** at the Royal York Hotel, 100 Front Street West, ((416) 368-6175, a supper club which attracts big-name entertainers.

Dance clubs here, as everywhere else, change with frequency and you need to check the listings for details. Among those

downstairs at **Studebakers**, 150 Pell Street, ((416) 597-7960.

WHERE TO STAY

Accommodation in Toronto can become quite scarce at the peak of the summer season, so if you plan to come around this time of year reservations are recommended well in advance. Accommodation Toronto, ((416) 596-7117, can help you find the right accommodation and in addition provides a free booking service. Discounts are usually offered over weekends and senior citizens

Buildings old and new jostle for airspace above the streets of Toronto.

will usually find themselves entitled to a discount of up to 15 percent.

Luxury

Close to the downtown theater district the **King Edward** at 37 King Street East, Toronto M5C 1E9, ((416) 863-9700, is a truly grand hotel. Built in 1903, its turn-of-the-century splendor, its columns, marble, polished wood, and beautiful ceilings make it worth a visit even if you can't afford to stay. The rooms are beautiful, spacious, and well-equipped, and there's 24-hour room service. It has some of the finest dining in the city and a lovely lounge which offers afternoon tea and cocktails.

There's luxury of a more modern kind at the twin-towered **Harbour Castle Westin**, 1 Harbour Square, Toronto M4J 1A6, ((416) 869-1600, situated at the lakeside. There are nearly a thousand comfortable and well-equipped rooms with views of either the lake or the skyline, and its excellent facilities include a health club and spa. It has some good restaurants including the revolving Lighthouse restaurant, and a free shuttle service will take you downtown.

Next to the CN Tower, **L'Hôtel**, 225 Front Street West, Toronto M5V 2X3, ((416) 597-1400, toll-free (800) 268-9420, is ideally suited for business people. All 587 rooms and suites are spacious, there are computer ports and workdesks in the rooms, and you can work off the stress and strain in the hotel health club. Opposite Union Station stands the **Royal York**, 100 Front Street West, M5K 1E3, ((416) 368-2511, one of Toronto's best known hotels. It has a total of 1,438 rooms, which tend to be a little on the small side, but it has excellent facilities with two floors for conventions, over a dozen restaurants, shops, a fitness club, the famous Imperial Room nightclub and all kinds of other services.

Moving midtown near Queen's Park, the **Sutton Place Hotel Kempinski** at 955 Bay Street, Toronto M5S 2A2, ((416) 924-9221, maintains extremely high standards. Its 282 rooms are furnished in elegant French style and have the usual array of facilities. The Sanssouci dining room is known for its superb food and its decor; Alexandré's Piano Bar is the smart spot to lunch. The **Windsor Arms Hotel**, 22 St. Thomas

Street, Toronto M5S 2B9, ((416) 979-2341, is a characterful, ivy-covered Victorian building, which opened in 1928 as an apartment hotel, and now offers 81 rooms and suites beautifully decorated with antiques. There's an air of tranquility about this hotel, the service is smooth and correct and it has four highly-rated restaurants. Moderately-priced rooms are also available.

In Yorkville, the high-rise **Four Seasons Hotel** at 21 Avenue Road, Toronto M5R 2G1, ((416) 964-0411, toll-free (800) 332-3442, is part of the excellent chain of the same name and manages even to surpass the expected high standards. There are 381 attractive and very comfortable rooms, many of which offer excellent views of the city, and there are business facilities, a health club, swimming pool, restaurants, and attentive service. Fitness and sports fanatics will love the **Four Seasons Inn on the Park**, located northeast of downtown near the Ontario Science Centre at 1100 Eglinton Avenue East, Toronto M3C 1H8, ((416) 444-2561, toll-free (800) 268-6282. It is beautifully positioned above a ravine and is set in 200 hectares (500 acres) of land. The rooms are not terribly special but the services are all you'd expect from the Four Seasons chain and it has swimming pools of different kinds, a fitness center, tennis courts, squash and racquetball courts, aerobics classes, and there's horse riding in the grounds. There are supervised activities for children throughout the day, and there's even a resident plastic surgeon.

Mid-range

Conveniently located in downtown, the **Delta Chelsea**, 33 Gerrard Street West, Toronto M5G 1Z4, ((416) 595-1975, is a very busy hotel with 1,600 modern rooms, some with kitchen facilities. It has four restaurants, a supervised children's play area, swimming pool, and health club. If you're planning a cultural binge, the **Hotel Victoria** at 56 Yonge Street, ((416) 363-1666, might be of particular interest as it's very close to both the O'Keefe and St. Lawrence Centres. There are 42 small, modern rooms with private bath, access to a nearby health club, a dining room, lounge and bar, and an elegant reception area. Very good value.

Located behind City Hall, the **Holiday Inn Downtown**, 89 Chestnut Street, Toronto M5G 1R1, ((416) 977-0707, toll-free (800) HOLIDAY, has the usual Holiday Inn facilities and its 715 large and comfortable rooms are very well-equipped with some welcome extra conveniences. There are indoor and outdoor pools, a fitness room, sauna, a restaurant and some pleasant bars. Close to the Eaton Centre is the **Hotel Ibis**, 240 Jarvis Street, Toronto M5B 2B8, ((416) 593-9400, part of a European chain of hotels. It's not terribly prepossessing from the outside, but there are 294 pleasant and comfortable rooms with good amenities. The **Primrose Hotel** at 111 Carlton Street, Toronto M5B 2G3, ((416)977-8000, toll-free (800) 268-8082, is conveniently placed for shopping and entertainment, and offers 338 large, pleasant rooms with individual climate control. It has an outdoor swimming pool, a sauna, a Viennese-style coffee shop and offers evening entertainment in the One Eleven lounge. It is an excellent bargain, and partly for that reason is a big favorite with conferees and conventioneers.

The centrally situated **Brownstone**, 15 Charles Street East, Toronto M4Y 1S1, ((416) 924-7381, toll-free (800) 263-8967, is a delightful place with friendly service and 108 spacious rooms with minibar. It has a good restaurant, a piano bar, and a patio for warm summer days.

About ten miles outside the city, **The Guild Inn**, 201 Guildwood Parkway, Scarborough M1E 1P6, ((416) 261-3331, offers a beautiful and very unusual setting. In 1932 this manorial building housed the Guild of All Arts with its art and craft workshops, and its popularity brought about the need for guest rooms and attracted many famous guests. Spread over the 36-hectare (90-acre) grounds are important architectural fragments salvaged from old Toronto buildings pulled down to make way for new developments. Included in the collection is the marble facade from the Imperial Bank of Canada, several columns, and a sign from Toronto's old firehall. The hotel has a good dining room, a veranda where you can take cocktails, an outdoor swimming pool and tennis court. Prices range from moderate to expensive.

Inexpensive

At the upper end of the inexpensive range, **Bond Place**, 65 Dundas Street East, ((416) 362-6061, is convenient for the Eaton Centre and has 285 smallish but well-appointed rooms with climate control and TV. The **Strathcona** at 60 York Street, Toronto M5J 1S8, ((416) 363-3321, is an older hotel, centrally located opposite the Royal York and offering excellent value. There are 200 rooms with private bath and TV, and the hotel has a restaurant, bar, and coffee shop. Also centrally placed is the **Quality Inn** at 300 Jarvis Street, ((416) 977-4823, which is part of a hotel chain and offers 96 rooms, some of which are self-catering units.

The **Karabanow Guest House** at 9 Spadina Avenue, Toronto M5R 2S9, ((416) 923-4004, is recommended by the Hotel Association and is situated close to the Royal Ontario Museum; the **Burkin Guest House**, 322 Palmerston Boulevard, Toronto M6G 2N6, ((416) 920-7842, is an older house with clean and attractively furnished rooms.

For lists of **Bed & Breakfast** accommodation you can contact Ashleigh Heritage Homes, Box 235, Postal Station E, Toronto M6H 4E2, ((416) 535-4000, who specialize in family homes of architectural interest or homes with gardens. Send SAE for brochure. Toronto Bed & Breakfast, 253 College Street, P.O. Box 269, Toronto M5T 1R5, ((416) 588-8800, will supply a brochure free of charge, and Metropolitan Bed & Breakfast at 615 Mount Pleasant Road, Suite 269, Toronto M4S 3C5, ((416) 964-2566 will supply lists. The Downtown Toronto Association of Bed & Breakfast Guesthouses, P.O. Box 190, Station B, Toronto M5T 2W1, ((416) 977-6841, will supply a brochure of renovated Victorian houses all in downtown and all nonsmoking, run in the main by people who are active in the arts.

There are several **campgrounds** within 40 km (25 miles) of the city, but none within metropolitan Toronto. One of the closer ones is the Toronto West KOA Kampground, P.O. Box 198, Campbellville L0P 1B0, ((416) 854-2495. For further information on campgrounds write to or ring Ontario Travel, Queen's Park, Toronto M7A 2E5, ((416) 965-4008.

WHERE TO EAT

Expensive

At **Julien,** 387 King Street, ((416) 596-6738, classic French dishes are simply and beautifully presented in a pretty, tranquil setting, and with excellent service. It is open Monday to Friday for lunch and dinner and for dinner only on Saturday. **Winston's,** 104 Adelaide Street West, ((416) 363-1627, serves haute cuisine in a grand setting of murals and art nouveau. It's a prestigious

dining spot which attracts many Establishment figures, and the food, wine list and service are superb.

Fenton's at 2 Gloucester Street, ((416) 961-8485, is renowned for its creative continental cuisine, flair, and its lovely surroundings. There are three dining areas: the cozy Fenton's Front Room, the very popular and delightful Fenton's Garden, and the intimate bistroesque, and less expensive Restaurant. It's a very popular spot for Sunday brunch. Continental food with a French and nouvelle accent is served in the elegant and expensive **Scaramouche**, 1 Benvenuto Place, ((416) 961-8011. The food is of the highest quality, the desserts are legendary, the restaurant offers a wonderful view of the city, and the atmosphere is formal.

Located in a beautiful old town house, **La Scala**, 1121 Bay Street, ((416) 964-7100, offers fine Italian dining in an opulent setting of chandeliers, red velvet, and statues. The restaurant is open for lunch and dinner Tuesday to Friday and for dinner only on Monday and Saturday. There's also a cock-

tail lounge. Eclectic North American cooking is to be had at **North 44°**, 2537 Yonge Street, ((416) 487-4897, in attractive surroundings of burnished metal and stone. Among the delights here are such dishes as fried oysters over jalapeño cream, underroasted lamb, and special desserts; there's an exceptionally good wine list.

Arguably the best steaks in town are to be had at **Barberians**, 7 Elm Street, ((416) 597-0335, where the precisely prepared item arrives untouched by fashionable cuisine. The atmosphere is friendly with early Canadian decor and Canadian paintings adorning the walls. The **Tom Jones Steakhouse**, 17 Leader Lane, ((416) 366-6583, is an old inn decorated in warm Old English style where the steaks are simply and beautifully prepared and accompanied with steamed and sautéed vegetables. The menu also features seafood specialties and the emphasis is on traditional fare. Open throughout the day Monday to Friday and for dinner only Saturday and Sunday. A piano bar upstairs serves cocktails.

Moderate

At the intimate and attractive at **Le Bistingo**, 349 Queen Street West, ((416) 598-3490, French food is prepared with great skill, and at **Bistro 990**, 990 Bay Street, ((416) 921-9990, there's more excellent French cuisine simply prepared and a good selection of wines. The place has the look of a grand wine cellar with arches and unusual pictures lining the walls. There's a homey atmosphere at **Jake's Restaurant**, 406 Dupont Street, ((416) 961-8341, where international dishes are prepared with an individual touch and vegetarians are very well catered for.

More international cuisine is served at the small and friendly **Berkeley Café**, 141 Berkeley Street, ((416) 594-6663, with the main influences coming from Thailand and the Philippines, where the dishes vary from mildly spicy to hot. There are some very nice wines available by the glass. **Bangkok Garden**, 18 Elm Street, ((416) 977-6748, is a very good and popular Thai restaurant, where the waiters are extremely helpful and the setting is somewhat exotic. The tiny **Seri Batik** at 784 Broadway Avenue, ((416) 463-3663, serves Thai-Malaysian-Indonesian dishes, and the sauces and satays are particularly good.

Katsura at the Prince Hotel, 900 York Mills Road, ((416) 444-2511, is an excellent Japanese restaurant which serves traditional Japanese food, teppanyaki, and sushi. **Tanaka** in the Holiday Inn at 370 King Street West, ((416) 599-3868, contains three Japanese restaurants, including a traditional tatami room and a sushi bar. There's a wide variety of Indian dishes at **Cuisine of India**, 5222 Yonge Street, ((416) 229-0377, featuring tandoori dishes and excellent homemade breads.

For a North American culinary experience, go to **Metropolis** at 838 Yonge Street, ((416) 924-4100, where you'll find such regional produce as rabbit, sausage, and lashings of maple syrup featuring on a menu that shows imagination, and some good Canadian beers are served. Some of the best seafood in town can be found at the popular **Mermaid**, 330 Dundas Street West, ((416) 597-0077, including oysters, lobster, and smoked eel. The dishes are beautifully prepared to emphasize freshness and texture.

Inexpensive
Charmer's Café at 1384 Bathurst Street, ((416) 657-1225, is a pleasant restaurant which serves American food with the emphasis on Californian and Mexican cooking, while in Mirvish Village, Ed Mirvish's restaurant **Ed's Warehouse**, 270 King Street West, ((416) 593-6676, serves straightforward food such as roast beef and steak in kitschy and fun surroundings. It is the only one of Ed's eateries to insist (surprisingly) on jacket and tie. Other Ed Mirvish restaurants in the street include **Ed's Chinese**, **Ed's Italian** and **Ed's Seafood**, and are all good value. For traditional deli fare go to **Switzers** in Chinatown at 322 Spadina Avenue, ((416) 596-6900, where Nova Scotia salmon, pastrami, bagels and blintzes are some of the specialties. There's entertainment while you dine at **The Groaning Board**, 131 Jarvis Street, ((416) 363-0265, where every evening award-winning commercials from around the world are shown. Home-style cooking is served here, half the dishes on the menu are vegetarian, and there's a huge salad bar where you can help yourself.

Various Chinese cuisines feature on the menu of **The Great Wall**, 442–444 Spadina Avenue, ((416) 961-5554. It's a big and busy restaurant offering a large range of excellent dishes at excellent prices. **Sai Woo** at 130 Dundas Street West, ((416) 977-4988, is one of the city's oldest and best-known Chinese restaurants, serving good Cantonese food in busy, basic surroundings. Dim sum is served at lunchtime on weekdays, and twice a year they hold banquets where as many as 15 courses may be served. For authentic Japanese dining, try the **Masa Dining Lounge**,

195 Richmond Street West, ((416) 977-9519, an attractive restaurant where you'll find sushi and vegetarian dishes on the menu, or **Sasaya** at 257 Eglinton Avenue West, ((416) 487-3508, which has sushi and tempura bars in addition to an extensive traditional menu.

The **Madras Durbar** at 1435 Gerrard Street East is a south Indian restaurant serving only vegetarian dishes, and the handsome **Indian Rice Factory** at 414 Dupont Street, ((416) 961-3472, offers a small but excellent menu which includes a selection of vegetarian dishes. The **Kensington Kitchen** at 124 Harbord Street, ((416) 961-3404, serves

OPPOSITE: The revolving restaurant in the CN Tower. ABOVE: Not a stopover for weight-watchers.

Middle Eastern food with particularly good appetizers and pastries, and there's Moroccan cuisine served in exotic surroundings at **The Sultan's Tent** in Yorkville at 1280 Bay Street, ((416) 961-0601, with live music and dancing.

HOW TO GET THERE

Toronto is, of course, served by all the major national airlines and virtually all the larger international airlines. Both foreign and domestic flights are handled by Lester B. Pearson International Airport, 29 km (18 miles) from downtown. The drive takes about 30-45 minutes, maybe longer in rush hour, and costs about $35 to $40 by taxi. Gray Coach Lines ((416/393-7911) operates Airport Express buses every 20 minutes between the airport and selected downtown hotels; the fare is less than $10.

VIA Rail trains from all over Canada and Amtrak trains from the U.S. arrive regularly at Toronto's Union Station ((416/366-8411) on Front Street near the Metro Toronto Convention Centre and the CN Tower. The Union stop of the subway system is in the railway station.

Greyhound, Voyageur Colonial, and Gray Coach all operate bus services into Toronto's central bus station at the corner of Bay Street and Dundas Street, near Eaton Centre. For information and schedules ring (416) 393-7911.

If you are driving from Detroit/Windsor in the west or Montreal in the east you will want Route 401. From Niagara Falls you will take the Queen Elizabeth Way, which turns into the Gardiner Expressway as it enters Toronto.

THE GOLDEN HORSESHOE

"The Golden Horseshoe", the sliver of land that arcs around from Oshawa, east of Toronto, to Niagara Falls, is so called because in addition to being horseshoe-shaped it is one of the wealthiest regions in the country. A large proportion of Canada's manufacturing industry is concentrated here, especially in and around the steel-making city of Hamilton.

If Hamilton is Canada's Pittsburgh, the Niagara peninsula is its Napa Valley: almost 80 percent of Canada's wine grapes are grown here, and at last count there were 15 wineries in the area. There is also history among the vines, for it was here that Laura Secord snuck away from the American-held village of Queenston and set out on her 30-km (19-mile) hike through the bush to warn the British of American plans for a surprise attack. Her home still stands in Queenston, as does a monument to General Isaac Brock, who died leading the first counter-attack against the Americans in the War of 1812.

But however much blood and wine may have flowed here, it's still the water that brings the tourists: Niagara Falls and Niagara-on-the-Lake, two of the most beautiful spots on earth.

GENERAL INFORMATION

For information about Hamilton contact the Hamilton-Wentworth Visitor and Convention Services, 1 James Street South, Hamilton L8P 4R5, ((416) 526-2666.

For information about Niagara-on-the-Lake contact the Niagara-on-the-Lake Chamber of Commerce, 153 King Street, P.O. Box 1043, Niagara-on-the-Lake L0S 1J0, ((416) 468-4263.

For information about Niagara Falls (*and* Niagara-on-the-Lake) get in touch with the Niagara Falls Visitor and Convention Bureau, 4673 Ontario Avenue, Suite 202, Niagara Falls L2E 3R1, ((416) 356-6061. Further information is available from the Travel Information Centre, 5355 Stanley Avenue, Niagara Falls L2E 7C2, ((416) 358-3221, or in person from the tourist offices at 5629 Falls Avenue and downtown by the Skylon Hotel.

HAMILTON

Hamilton sits in the western corner of Lake Ontario on a landlocked harbor spanned at the lakeside by a sandbar, cut through to allow ships into the port. Across this sandbar sweeps the Burlington Skyway, a section of the Queen Elizabeth Way that links Toronto with Niagara Falls. It is

Canada's steel-producing capital and its heavy industry has brought Hamilton more than its fair share of pollution. It's not all a landscape of satanic mills, however. There are some renovated old buildings and some impressive new ones, the result of new development schemes and urban renewal projects. One such development, Hamilton Place, is a large new arts center which has helped put Hamilton on the cultural map.

What to See and Do

Like Toronto's Yorkville, **Hess Village** at Hess and George Streets is a very pleasant area of renovated clapboard buildings that now house shops, restaurants, and cafés. It is a nice place for a stroll. There is plenty of activity on nearby York Boulevard where the local produce is displayed in the huge and bustling indoor **Farmer's Market** on Tuesdays, Thursdays, Fridays, and Satur-

days; and at the neighboring **Lloyd D. Jackson Square** there are some good stores to visit. A striking modern building houses the **Art Gallery** at 123 King Street, ((416) 527-6610. The Gallery has a large collection of twentieth-century Canadian and American art. The Gallery is open Tuesday to Sunday, closed on Mondays and holidays. Facing the Art Gallery is **Hamilton Place** at the corner of Main and MacNab Streets, a modern arts center with two theaters, and home to the Hamilton Philharmonic Orchestra, Opera Hamilton, and Theatre Aquarius. It also attracts famous international performers of all kinds. Call (416) 522-2994 for information or (416) 525-7710 for reservations.

Just outside the town at Dundern Park on a hill stands **Dundern Castle**, on York Boulevard, ((416) 522-5313, an impressive 36-room white stone mansion with a dignified columned portico overlooking the bay. It was built in the 1830s by Sir Allan Napier MacNab, Prime Minister of the United Provinces of Canada from 1854 to 1856. It has been furnished in the style of the 1850s and restored to its former splendor. Throughout the year there are special exhibitions here, and there's a military museum in the grounds of the castle.

A little further out of town at Routes 2 and 6, the **Royal Botanical Gardens**, ((416) 527-1158, cover 20,243 hectares (50,000 acres) of land along the lakeside. The greater part of this area is given over to natural parkland

About 32 km (20 miles) northwest of Hamilton off Route 8 is the **African Lion Safari**, ((519) 623-2620. You can take a safari tram through the various reserves where the animals roam free. Alternatively you can drive your own car through the park, bearing in mind that the baboons in the Monkey Jungle enclosure will climb all over it and remove anything they can. Convertibles are not allowed, for obvious reasons. There are many side attractions, including a scenic railway, a cruise, and a playground.

threaded with trails, but among the most stunning sights are the Rock Garden, the Rose Garden, and the gorgeous Lilac Garden in the Arboretum. It's open daily from dawn to dusk.

The **Museum of Steam and Technology** is aptly housed in the old water pumping station, south of the Queen Elizabeth Way at 900 Woodward Avenue, ((416) 549-5225. The station, built in 1859, is in itself an interesting piece of architecture; its original brass and mahogany steam pumps have been restored and can be seen in action on Sundays. Steam machinery and scale models are on show and there are displays on Hamilton's industrial history. Open daily except Saturdays.

Where to Stay

MID-RANGE

The **Sheraton Hamilton**, centrally located at 116 King Street West, Hamilton L8P 4V3, ((416) 529-5515, toll-free (800) 325-3535, has 300 modern rooms which are nicely furnished and well-equipped. Guests have use of a health club and indoor pools with an attractive poolside area. The hotel has two restaurants. There's a sense of grandeur about the **Royal Connaught** at 112 King Street East, Hamilton L8N 1A8, ((416) 527-5071, which first opened its doors in 1904. The entrance hall is lavishly decorated with

Tilling the land in Upper Canada Village, a reconstructed nineteenth-century village on the St. Lawrence River west of Cornwall.

chandeliers and columns, and the hotel's 200 rooms all have luxuriously large bathrooms. There are two restaurants and an indoor swimming pool.

INEXPENSIVE

Cheap hotel rooms are hard to come by in Hamilton, but probably the best on offer are to be found at the Town Manor Motor Hotel, **175 Main Street West,** ((416) 528-0611. **McMaster University** offers accommodation, details of which are available from McMaster University, Conference Services, 1280 Main Street West, Hamilton L8S 4K1, ((416) 525-9140 ext 4781.

For information and brochures on **Bed & Breakfast** accommodation in the area you can contact The Hamilton Chamber of Commerce, 100 King Street West, Suite 830, Hamilton L8P 1A2, ((416) 522-1151, and the Hamilton Region & Rural B & B Association, 194 Oakhill Place, Ancaster L9G 1C7, ((416) 648-0461. For **farm accommodation** there is the Chris Utter Farm situated 15 km (9 miles) east of Hamilton at RR1, Stoney Creek L8G 3X4, ((416) 662-1167; it is a fruit farm and offers a private loft with bathroom or two single rooms in the farmhouse. There's also Troybrook Farm, 25 km (16 miles) west of Hamilton at RR1, 1941 Route 5 West, Troy L0R 2B0, ((519) 647-3323, which offers accommodation in a lovely 1825 stone house.

Where to Eat

There are quite a few restaurants, ethnic and otherwise, along King Street in the town center and most of them fall within the inexpensive price range. **Le Ganges Indian Restaurant** at 234 King Street East, ((416) 523-8812, is a good spot for Indian food, with an impressive range of vegetarian dishes, and for Chinese food there's the **Hunan House Restaurant** at 273 King Street East, ((416) 529-0628. There's German-style dining in a fun atmosphere at the busy **Black Forest Inn**, 255 King Street East, ((416) 528-3538.

Shakespeare's Steak House and Tavern at 181 Main Street East, ((416) 528-0689, is decorated, as you'd expect, in Olde English style; it serves quite decent steaks at prices ranging from inexpensive to moderate. It's open Monday to Friday for lunch and dinner, and for dinner only on Saturdays. Fur-

ther along, **Pappa's Dining** at 309 Main Street East, ((416) 525-2455, with its columns, statues, and waitresses in Grecian attire, leaves you in no doubt as to the nature of the cuisine. There's a good set menu for two people available that allows you to taste lots of dishes. English fare is served at **The Winking Judge**, 25 Augusta Street, ((416) 527-1280, where such dishes as beef and Yorkshire pudding are served upstairs in the dining room, while pies and pub-style food are available throughout the day in the downstairs area.

Hess Village is a pleasant place for a bite to eat and has a few pubs and restaurants. One of its nicest spots is the elegant **Café Vienna** at 15 Hess Street South, ((416) 525-7607.

ST. CATHARINES

St. Catharines is in the heart of Ontario's wine producing and fruit growing region, and nowhere is this more evident than in the outdoor **Farmer's Market** near City Hall, where you see the abundance of the local produce. It's a popular resting place for visitors to the many festivals that the area has to offer.

What to See and Do

The 42-km (26-mile) **Welland Canal** connects Lake Ontario to the much higher Lake Erie through a series of eight locks. From nearby Port Weller it cuts through to Port Colburne on Lake Erie, allowing ocean-going ships to navigate the Great Lakes. The original canal was built in St. Catharines and at **Port Dalhousie** you can see sections of the first three canals built in 1829, 1845, and 1887, where some of the locks, warehouses and other nineteenth-century structures still stand. The present Welland Canal was completed in 1933, and there's a smart new **Welland Canal Viewing Complex** at Lock 3 where you can watch the ocean-going giants pass through the locks.

For a quick architectural sightseeing tour of the world go to the **Tivoli Miniature World**, ((416) 834-7604, situated just off Prudhomme Boulevard, Victoria Avenue exit off the QEW, close to Vineland Station. Here you can see some of the world's most famous buildings such as St. Peter's Basilica and the Eiffel Tower as well as lesser-known sites in scaled-down detailed miniatures of 1/50th actual size. Open daily from May to September.

St. Catharines hosts two annual big events. For over 100 years it has been the site of the **Royal Canadian Henley Regatta**, which in early August attracts top-class rowers from around the world and is second in size only to the famous English regatta of the same name. Then in late September there's a great party atmos-

125 comfortable rooms and its facilities include an indoor pool, sauna, and a bowling alley. There's a warm and cozy atmosphere at the **Highwayman**, 420 Ontario Street, St. Catharines L2R 5M1, ((416) 688-1646, which offers 50 rooms all with TV and private bath, and an outdoor swimming pool. The **Holiday Inn** at 2 North Service Road, St. Catharines L2N 4G9, ((416) 934-2561, toll-free (800) HOLIDAY, has 140 rooms with TV, private bath and facilities which include indoor and outdoor swimming pools, sauna, and whirlpool bath.

phere when the city hosts the **Niagara Grape and Wine Festival**, ten days of vineyard tours, concerts, dances, athletic contests, parades, and much eating and drinking.

Where to Stay

MID-RANGE

There's everything you need and more at the **Parkway Inn**, 327 Ontario Street, St. Catharines L2R 5L4, ((416) 688-2324. Conveniently situated in downtown, it has

INEXPENSIVE

Brock University offers accommodation, details of which are available through the Director of Conference Services, St. Catharines L2S 3A1, ((416) 688-5550 ext 3749. Lists of **Bed & Breakfast** accommodation are available through St. Catharines (Homestay) B&B, 17 Lantana Circle, St. Catharines L2M 4W9, ((416) 934-5913. There are a couple of **farm accommodations** outside the town: **Maaike's Homestead**, run by Maaike Dykstra, offers Dutch hospitality and home cooking in a Victorian house about 18 km (11 miles) west of St. Catharines at RR1, Beamsville L2R 1B0, ((416) 563-4335; and **Dekker's Country Home**, a nineteenth-century farmhouse run by Jake & Anne

ABOVE: Niagara-on-the-Lake.
OPPOSITE: The Inniskillen Winery outside Niagara-on-the-Lake.

Dekker 20 km (32 miles) west of St. Catharines at Sixteen Road, St. Anne's L2R 1Y0, ((416) 957-7912.

Where to Eat

There is traditional Japanese dining at a moderate price in **Isseya**, 22 James Street, ((416) 688-1141, which features sushi, tempura and teriyaki dishes. Open Tuesday to Sunday for dinner only. You'll find a pleasant spot for a light lunch or dinner at the **Wellington Court Café**, 11 Wellington Street, ((416) 682-5518. It's inexpensively priced and is open Tuesday to Saturday, and for lunch only on Mondays. You'll find several eateries in the Port Dalhousie area by the harbor and along Ontario Street.

NIAGARA-ON-THE-LAKE

Situated where the Niagara River meets Lake Ontario, delightful Niagara-on-the-Lake is one of North America's loveliest and best preserved nineteenth-century towns. It was settled by Loyalists in the late eighteenth century and, known then as Newark, became the first capital of Upper Canada in 1792. In 1813 it was completely destroyed by the Americans, was quickly rebuilt, and seems to have changed very little since that time. Its attractive situation and pretty tree-shaded streets lined with clapboard and brick houses make it a delightful stopping point during a trip to Niagara Falls.

What to See and Do

Queen Street is the town's focal point, and the only part of it that gets busy. It is one chain wide (an obsolete British measure of 20 m or 66 ft) and its lovely old buildings house bakeries, tea shops, restaurants, and shops selling all manner of goods such as crafts, jams, and confectionery. The splendid old **Niagara Apothecary Shop**, ((416) 468-3845, dates from 1866 and maintains its original walnut counters, beautifully labeled drawers, and old jars. Its medications are no longer dispensed, as the place is only a museum now, and looking at such remedies as "Dragon's Blood" or "Pink Pills for Pale People" you can't help but feel that it's probably just as well.

The town's main attraction is the annual **Shaw Festival**, which draws theatergoers from far and wide and presents top-name actors and actresses in a season of plays by George Bernard Shaw and his contemporaries. There are three theaters in the town, the main one being the **Festival Theatre**, a modern brick and glass structure with an attractive interior, at Queen's Parade and Wellington Street. The festival is held from May to October with performances daily except on Mondays. Details are available from Shaw Festival,

Box 774, Niagara-on-the-Lake L0S 1J0, ((416) 468-2172.

South on Niagara Parkway on River Road is the **Fort George Historic Park**, ((416) 469-4257. Built between 1797–99, the Fort was a major British post in the War of 1812. It was destroyed by the Americans in 1813, rebuilt in 1815, and later abandoned. It was restored in the 1930s, so that you can now visit the officers' quarters, barracks, forge, powder magazine, and see a display by the Fort George Fife and Drum Corps. The Fort is open daily from mid-May to October; tours are by appointment only during the winter. To find out some more of Niagara's history you could visit the **Niagara Historical Museum** at 43 Castlereagh Street at Davy, ((416) 468-3912, the oldest museum of its kind in Canada.

Close to Niagara-on-the-Lake are several wineries which offer tasting tours, such as the Hillebrand Estates Winery, an attractive place which would not look out of place in the French countryside. Ontario Travel will give you details of winery tours.

Where to Stay

Niagara-on-the-Lake is a small town and its hostelries can get full up in the summer, so if you plan your visit at this time of year try to book first.

One of the foremost hotels is the **Prince of Wales**, 6 Picton Street, Niagara-on-the-Lake L0S 1J0, ((416) 468-3246, a beautiful old inn with 106 rooms, including a royal suite which was once actually graced by royalty, all decorated with antique furniture and with large bathrooms. It combines Old World charm with a full range of facili-

ties, including a fitness room, an indoor pool, sauna, tennis court, restaurants, and bars. Prices are moderate to expensive. The **Pillar & Post Inn**, P.O. Box 1011, King Street and John Street, Niagara-on-the-Lake L0S 1J0, ((416) 468-2123, is another lovely hotel, with 91 rooms furnished in early colonial style, combining old-fashioned elegance with modern amenities. It has a very pleasant outdoor pool, a sauna and a whirlpool. It, too, is moderate to expensive. In contrast, the **Gate House Hotel**, 142 Queen Street, P.O. Box 1364, Niagara-on-the-Lake L0S 1J0, ((416) 468-3263, has nine rooms decorated in chic, modern Milan-style. Prices are moderate to expensive. One of the town's best hotels, the **Oban Inn**, P.O. Box 94, 160 Front Street, Niagara-on-the-Lake L0S 1J0, ((416) 468-2165, is a delightful early eighteenth-century building over-

looking the lake. It has beautiful gardens, 23 comfortable rooms with antique furniture, a piano bar, a good restaurant, and its very own ghost, so they say. Prices are moderate to expensive. The **Angel Inn** at 224 Regent Street, The Old Market Square, Niagara-on-the-Lake L0S 1J0, ((416) 468-3411, is an historic old coaching inn which dates from 1782. It has 12 rooms with canopy beds and other antique furnishings, its own dining room.

Fitness enthusiasts will love the **White Oaks Inn and Racquet Club**, just outside the town at 253 Taylor Road, RR4, Niagara-on-the-Lake L0S 1J0, ((416) 688-2550. It has 90 smart and well-equipped rooms with lots of nice touches, but the real attraction lies in amenities such as its 12 tennis courts (four outdoor and eight indoor), squash and racquetball courts, gym with Nautilus equipment, child-care facilities, cafés, and a restaurant. To make yourself feel really good, you can also treat yourself to a sauna, a sunbed, or a massage.

For details of **Bed & Breakfast** accommodation and tourist homes you can write to or ring Niagara-on-the-Lake Chamber of Commerce, Masonic Lodge, P.O. Box 1043, Niagara-on-the-Lake L0S 1J0, ((416) 468-4263.

Where to Eat

There are quite a few good restaurants in the town and generally it's a much better place for dining than Niagara Falls. The **Oban Inn** at 160 Front Street, ((416) 468-2165, has a reputation for fine dining in tasteful surroundings and is possibly the best in the area. Traditional English dishes feature on the menu, prices are moderate, and lunch and dinner are served at sittings only. The restaurant is also open for afternoon tea. There's fine European cuisine in an elegant setting at the **Prince of Wales Hotel**, 6 Picton Street, ((416) 468-3246. It's open daily for lunch and dinner, for Sunday brunch, and prices are moderate. For a more raucous dining experience, **The Buttery** at 19 Queen Street holds weekend Henry VIII banquets where old English food is served by costumed wenches and entertainment is supplied by minstrels. It's open daily and prices are moderate.

ABOVE: Entrance to The Royal George hotel in Niagara-on-the-Lake. OPPOSITE: flower nursery in the town.

The Angel at 224 Regent Street, The Old Market Square, ℂ (416) 468-3411, serves English pub food and 26 varieties of beer. The dining room serves continental food and prices are inexpensive to moderate. Open daily from lunchtime through the evening. Classic Italian food is served in chic, modern surroundings at **Restaurant Giardino** in the Gate House Hotel, 142 Queen Street, ℂ (416) 468-3263. Prices are inexpensive to moderate. **Fans** at 135 Queen Street, ℂ (416) 468-4511, is a pleasant spot where you can taste some very good, inexpensively-

priced Cantonese and Szechuan food, and at the **George III**, 61 Melville Street, ℂ (416) 468-7639, you can fill up on shrimps, burgers, chicken wings, and the like at budget prices.

NIAGARA FALLS

Midway between Lake Erie and Lake Ontario, the Niagara River hurtles over a 61-m (200-ft) cliff at a rate of 130 million liters or 34 million gallons each minute, thus creating one of the greatest wonders of the world. Divided by a small island, the Canadian Horseshoe Falls are 793 m (2,600 ft) wide and the American Falls a much smaller 305 m (1,000 ft) wide. At times over 75 percent of the water is diverted by canals to power stations on both the American and Canadian sides, resulting in a variation of the water volume depending on time of day

Two of the 12 million people who come every year to see Niagara Falls.

and year. It is said that the erosion caused by the plunging water will eventually flatten the Falls, but it is estimated that this will take about 25,000 years to happen.

Since the seventeenth century people have traveled huge distances to see the Falls and now an average of 12 million people come every year to wonder at the spectacle. No one quite knows why it has become a tradition for honeymooning couples to come here, but one legend has it that the idea caught on after Napoleon's brother brought his new bride here in 1804, riding all the way from New Orleans in a coach. Anyway, it's everything it's cracked up to be — and more. One can only echo Rupert Brooke's feelings on seeing the Falls: "I was so impressed by Niagara. I had hoped not to be, but I horribly was." So is everyone, it seems, as more Kodak film is bought here than anywhere else in the world.

What to See and Do

The downtown area is known as **Clifton Hill** and it's every bit as commercial as you'd expect, with its souvenir shops, museums, and waxworks. The **Niagara Falls Museum** at 5651 River Road contains the **Daredevil Hall of Fame**, devoted to those who dared the might of the Falls in a variety of ways, often in barrels. The museum also holds, somewhat bizarrely, a collection of Egyptian mummies.

The Falls themselves are hopelessly spectacular, however you view them. At night they are lit by rainbow-colored spotlights. In winter they are at their most amazing when the spray freezes to form wonderful natural sculptures and Canada is linked to the U.S. by ice. You can view them from **Table Rock**, the point nearest the Falls where there's a well-worn metal railing to cling to, and in **Table Rock House**, ℂ (416) 358-3268, elevators take you down to tunnels which afford views from behind the Falls. Of the many boat trips that operate, the **Maid of the Mist**, 5920 River Road, ℂ (416) 358-5781, is the most famous and affords a tremendously exciting, if damp, experience. Kitted out in hooded raincoats, you are taken to the base of the American Falls, as close as you can get to its deafening might. Trips run daily from mid-May to mid-October. The **Niagara River Boat Company** runs tours, dances and dinners aboard an old-fashioned cruise ship called the *Senator* during May to October, ((416) 468-4219/5154. For an aerial view, there are three towers, the best being the **Skylon** at Robinson Street, ((416) 356-2651, open daily. Exterior elevators carry you to the top where there's a revolving dining room, and an indoor and outdoor viewing deck. For a flying view you can take a trip in **Niagara Helicopters,** ((416) 468-4219/5154.

The **North Niagara Parkway** stretches between the Falls to Niagara-on-the-Lake, a distance of 26 km (16 miles) following the river on its way to Lake Ontario. With its parks, gardens and historic buildings and sites, it makes a delightful drive or walk. Along the way you'll find the **Great Gorge Trip** which operates daily from May to October, ((416) 356-0904, where an elevator takes you to the bottom of the gorge for a close view of the rapids in violent action. A little further along, **Niagara Spanish Aero Cars** offer cable trips over the Whirlpool Rapids for some dramatic views of the swirling water below. At **Niagara Glen**, trails lead to the river's edge and the forest offers a lovely and peaceful retreat for the weary traveler. Nearby the **Niagara Parks Commission School of Horticulture** has acres of beautiful gardens filled with shrubs and flowers maintained by students of the school. It's open daily in the summer months from dawn until dusk. A little further north is **Queenston Heights**, the original site of the Niagara Falls and the place where in 1812 the British finally defeated the American attempt to take Queenston. It's now a peaceful park and a good spot for a picnic.

Where to Stay

There are accommodation signs screaming at you everywhere around Niagara Falls. It's quite difficult to categorize accommodation in terms of price as there's a such a great fluctuation according to time of year, added to which prices seem to change according to daily demand. It really is worth bargaining for a drop in price. For help in finding accommodation you can ring (416) 356-6061.

LUXURY

The **Skyline Foxhead**, 5875 Falls Avenue, Niagara Falls L2E 6W7, ((416) 357-3090, toll-free (800) 648-7200, has a very good view of the Falls. It has 395 well-equipped rooms, some with balconies and views of the Falls. There are very good facilities, with a rooftop swimming pool, fitness facilities, and a good restaurant. Next door the **Skyline Brock**, 5685 Falls Avenue, Niagara Falls L2E 6W7, ((416) 374-4444, toll-free (800) 648-7200, is possibly the most popular place to stay. It has been in business since 1929 and there's some elegance about it. About three-quarters of the 210 rooms look towards the Falls and there's a restaurant with great views on the tenth floor. Prices vary between mid-range and the low end of the expensive range. The **Clarion Old Stone Inn** at 5425 Robinson Street, Niagara Falls L2G 7L6, ((416) 357-1234, toll-free (800) 263-8967, has 114 spacious, modern rooms although the building itself is built to look like an old-fashioned inn.

MID-RANGE

The **Skyline Village**, 5685 Falls Avenue, Niagara Falls L2E 6W7, ((416) 374-4444, toll-free (800) 648-7200, has over 200 spacious rooms and some family suites. The emphasis is definitely not on families at the **Honeymoon City Hotel**, 4943 Clifton Hill, Niagara Falls L2G 3N5, where there are 80 units, some of which are honeymoon suites with special decoration. All rooms have private bath and television, and a few have balconies. The **Best Western Your Host Motor Inn**, 5551 Murray Street, Niagara Falls L2G 2J4, ((416) 357-4330, toll-free (800) 528-1234, is quite centrally located with 247 modern rooms, some of which are suites catering for the honeymoon market with round beds and large baths. Amenities include swimming pool and sauna, a restaurant and bar.

The **Ameri-Cana** at 8444 Lundy's Lane, Niagara Falls L2H 1H4, ((416) 356-8444, offers motel accommodation set in large

OVERLEAF: The mighty Falls in majestic close-up.

grounds with tennis courts and outdoor swimming pool. It has 110 well-equipped rooms, some of which are honeymoon suites. With self-catering facilities, it's an appealing option for families. Completely different accommodation is offered at **Reese's Country Inn**, 3799 Montrose Road, Niagara Falls L2E 6S4, ((416) 357-5640, a Swiss chalet-style place, that's primarily a restaurant but with four attractive suites.

INEXPENSIVE

For details of **Bed & Breakfast** accommodation, contact Bed & Breakfast of Greater Niagara, 2631 Dorchester Road, Niagara Falls L2J 2Y9, ((416) 295-6260. **Campers** will find the Niagara Falls KOA at 8625 Lundy's Lane, Niagara Falls L2H 1H5, ((416) 354-6472, which offers very pleasant sites and good facilities. The government-owned Miller's Creek Park, P.O. Box 150, Niagara Falls L2E 6T2, ((416) 871-6557, offers privacy with generously-sized plots.

Where to Eat

MODERATE

The **Skylon Tower**, ((416) 356-2651, has the ubiquitous revolving restaurant for dining or the Summit Suite which is open for breakfast, lunch, and dinner. At **Reese's Country Inn**, 3799 Montrose Road, ((416) 357-5640, there's good international cuisine in a building which offers some lovely views of hills and gardens. Open daily for breakfast, lunch, and dinner. There's a happy country atmosphere and international cuisine at **Miller's Bistro** in the Clarion Old Stone Inn, 5425 Robinson Street, ((416) 357-1234, and you'll find good Italian food among columns and friezes at **Casa d'Oro**, 5875 Victoria Avenue, ((416) 356-5646.

INEXPENSIVE

The Niagara Parkway Commission owns the **Victoria Park Restaurant**, ((416) 356-2217, situated near the Falls, where you can dine inside or on an outdoor terrace. There's an interesting menu with some fine dishes. The Commission also runs **Queenston Heights**, which is situated exactly there, ((416) 262-4266, again offering indoor or outdoor dining, beautifully located with

some great views. **Betty's Restaurant & Tavern**, 8911 Sodom Road, ((416) 295-4436, is a very low-budget eatery where generously portioned scallops, chicken, and burgers are served all through the day.

HOW TO GET THERE

The major road linking all the towns and cities of the Golden Horseshoe, from Toronto to Niagara Falls, is the Queen Elizabeth Way. The principal American highway leading to the vicinity of the Falls, from both the southwest and the southeast, is I-90. There is hourly bus service between Toronto and Niagara Falls, and a bus twice daily between the Falls and the Prince of Wales Hotel in Niagara-on-the-Lake. There is also a regular shuttle from nearby Buffalo international Airport to the Falls. VIA Rail has three trains a day from Toronto to Niagara Falls, while Amtrak has frequent trains to Buffalo from various American cities.

SOUTHERN ONTARIO

Southern Ontario, the "land between the lakes", consists of miles and miles of gently rolling farmland laced with rivers and streams and sprinkled with charming towns and villages. Thanks to its rich alluvial soil and temperate climate, the area produces an abundance of fruit and vegetables. This means that the larger towns are genuine market towns, where you can find a mouth-watering selection of local produce. And almost anywhere you go you can find a welcoming array of inns and taverns on the English model.

Speaking of the English model, fruit and vegetables are not the only things cultivated here; so, too, is Englishness itself. The region is a cultural as well as agricultural seedbed, where the English way of life that was first planted in the eighteenth century has blossomed in the form of communities called London, Windsor, Cambridge, Essex, Waterloo, Woodstock, Blenheim, and Stratford — where the summer-long Shakespeare Festival provides a unique celebration of the Bard's work.

BACKGROUND

The Huron Indians were the first to appreciate the agricultural potential of this fertile region, but their efforts at farming the land were constantly interrupted by the belligerent, rampaging Iroquois. It wasn't until after the Anglo-French treaty in 1763 that settlers moved into the area, and not until after the American Revolution, when the Loyalists began arriving, that it acquired its distinctly British character.

GENERAL INFORMATION

For information about Kitchener, contact the Kitchener Chamber of Commerce, 67 King Street East, Kitchener N2H 6M2, ℂ (519) 576-5000.

For Waterloo, contact the Waterloo Chamber of Commerce, 5 Bridgeport Road West, Waterloo N2L 2X9, ℂ (519) 886-2440.

For London, contact the London Visitors and Convention Bureau, 300 Dufferin Avenue, London N6A 4L9, ℂ (519) 661-5000.

The first farming-based settlement was at Windsor; others followed at London and Stratford. At about the same time Germans settled in the Kitchener-Waterloo area, as did many Mennonites from Pennsylvania whose resolute pacifism during the American Revolution had made them unpopular with their American neighbors.

Today the German and Mennonite presence is still very marked around Kitchener and Waterloo, where Oktoberfest is celebrated by the German population and Mennonite quilt sales are regularly held, but the peninsula as a whole remains what it was two centuries ago: still very pretty to look at, still very British in outlook.

The tourist office in Stratford is at 38 Albert Street, ℂ (519) 271-5140, and the tourist office in Windsor is at 80 Chatham Street East, ℂ (519) 255-6530.

KITCHENER-WATERLOO

About an hour's drive from Toronto, these twin industrial cities, now amalgamated with a population of 190,000, are set in the farmlands of Southern Ontario. Over half the inhabitants are of German descent and the cities' shared German heritage gives

A Mennonite wagon in Kitchener.

the place its distinctive character. The cities were settled in 1800 by German Mennonites, a strict Protestant sect who had first settled in Pennsylvania but had been forced to leave there at the time of the American Revolution because of their pacifist beliefs. Many of their descendants continue to live in this area in Mennonite farming communities, where they faithfully adhere to rules that set them apart from the rest of the twentieth century. They do not use modern machinery, they travel in horse-drawn buggies, the men wear black suits and hats

while the women wear long dresses and small bonnets: their picturesque way of life has made them one of the area's major attractions.

What to See and Do
In early October each year people flock to the city for nine days of **Oktoberfest**, when the cities' German heritage is celebrated with German food and beer, traditional bands, dancing, sporting and cultural events in halls and tents set up around

A Terpsichorean street mural in Kitchener.

the city. The festival attracts about 600,000 people, so you need to book your accommodation well in advance. For details contact Kitchener-Waterloo Oktoberfest Inc., P.O. Box 1053, Kitchener N2G 4G1, ((519) 576-0571.

The famous Farmers' Markets attract many visitors. The **Kitchener Market** is held in a modern building at the junction of King Street East and Frederick Street. Amish and Mennonite handicrafts, cheeses, sausages, and home-baked goods are on sale early on Saturday mornings throughout the year and on Wednesday mornings from mid-May to mid-October. People come to see the farmers and families dressed in their traditional garb and with their horse-drawn buggies as much as they come to shop. Two other markets are held in Waterloo: the **County Market**, which, like the Kitchener market, is open on Saturdays throughout the year, and on Wednesday mornings from June to early October, and the **Stockyard Farmers' Market**, which is open on Thursday and Saturday mornings throughout the year.

Not far from the Kitchener market, the **Joseph Schneider Haus** at 466 Queen Street South is a German Mennonite house which has been restored to the period of the 1850s. There are special events here and demonstrations of everyday activities to complete the picture of life at that time. It's open daily from May 24 to Labor Day. To get a further idea of what life was like in the late nineteenth century, pay a visit to **Woodside** at 528 Wellington Street North in Kitchener, ((519) 742-5273, the childhood home of William Lyon Mackenzie King, who was Canada's Prime Minister earlier this century. It has been restored to the 1890s period, the time when King lived there, and displays trace his life story. It is open daily throughout the year.

Those with a healthy interest in alcohol may be interested to know that in Waterloo the old Seagram distillery barrel warehouse at 57 Erb Street West, ((519) 885-1857, now houses the **Seagram Museum**. The museum is devoted to the history and processes involved in wine and spirits production, which are explained in displays and films. Also in Waterloo, just off King Street are the pleasant campuses of the **Universities of Waterloo and Wilfrid Laurier**. The University of Waterloo has an art gallery, the Earth Sciences Museum, and the Museum of Games, and there are changing displays of various kinds at the Concourse Gallery in Laurier. Open Monday to Friday all year.

South of Kitchener at the **Doon Heritage Crossroads** some authentic pioneer buildings have been assembled and restored to re-create an early settlement. The buildings include a general store, a church, a railway station, the Gingerbread House (a late nineteenth-century building housing a collection of dolls), and a museum that has displays of Indian and early pioneer artifacts. Special events, exhibitions, and festivals are held here. It's open daily May to December and afternoons only during the rest of the year.

Where to Stay

MID-RANGE

The **Hotel Walper Terrace** at 1 King Street West, Kitchener N2G 1A1, ((519) 745-4321, is a renovated Victorian building, which has 113 attractively furnished rooms with private bath, TV, and air conditioning, and two restaurants. The more contemporary surroundings of the **Valhalla Inn**, 105 King Street East, P.O. Box 4, Kitchener N2G 3W9, ((519) 744-4141, toll-free (800) 268-2500, offer 203 attractively furnished rooms with balconies, and guests have use of an indoor swimming pool with poolside café, a sauna, a fitness center, and a bar. There's reliably good value, as usual, at the **Best Western Conestoga Inn**, 1333 Weber Street East, Kitchener N2A 1C2, ((519) 893-1234, toll-free (800) 528-1234, which has a total of 102 rooms, some of which are motel accommodations, and an indoor pool, a sauna and two restaurants. The **Holiday Inn** at 30 Fairway Road South, Kitchener N2A 2N2, ((519) 893-1211, toll-free (800) HOLIDAY, has 185 modern rooms and a good range of facilities, including indoor and outdoor pools, sauna, and child-care facilities.

INEXPENSIVE

There's very good value at the **Riviera Motel**, 2808 King Street East, Kitchener

N2A 1A5, ((519) 893-6641, which has 46 units, attractively decorated, with air conditioning and TV, looking on to an outdoor swimming pool. There's an excellent **Journey's End Motel** at 2899 Long Street East, Kitchener M2A 1A6, ((519) 894-3500, toll-free (800) 668-4200, with 103 air-conditioned, spacious rooms with private bath and TV.

For a list of **Bed & Breakfast** accommodation and brochure contact B&B Southwestern Ontario Countryside Vacation Association, c/o Mrs. E. Alveretta Henderson, RR1, Millbank N0K 1L0, ((519) 595-4604.

There's a **YMCA** in Kitchener at Queen and Water Streets, ((519) 743-5201, and a **YWCA** at Frederick and Weber Streets, ((519) 744-0120. The University of Waterloo also offers accommodation; information is available from the Conference Manager, P.O. Box 610, Village Two, Waterloo N2J 4C1, ((519) 885-1121. For details of accommodation at Wilfrid Laurier University contact the Conference Co-ordinator, 75 University Avenue West, Waterloo N2L 3C5, ((519) 884-8110 ext 251.

Where to Eat

Among the restaurants that cluster along King Street is the **Charcoal Steak House** at 2980 King Street East, ((519) 893-6570, which has a series of six attractive and cozy rooms, and serves very good steaks at moderate prices. For Swiss-style dining there's the **Swiss Castle Inn** at 1508 King Street East, ((519) 744-2391, where you can sample fondues and other Swiss specialties at inexpensive prices. On King Street at the junction of Water Street, **A la Cape Breton** is a good spot for breakfast and crepes. Just off King Street at 24 Eby Street North, the **Brittany**, ((519) 745-7001, provides three attractive dining areas inside an old townhouse, and serves excellent food at moderate prices. It's a popular spot and reservations are recommended. The inexpensive and delightful **Janet Lynn's Bistro** at 1 Market Village, ((519) 742-2843, offers appetizing food in stylish surroundings. For good and basic budget food, **Marbles** at 8 William Street, ((519) 885-4390, serves burgers, salads and the like.

STRATFORD

Set in farmlands, this attractive town with a population of 26,000 has many things in common with the famous English town of the same name, and these similarities are far from accidental. Back in 1830 proprietor William Sargint called his inn the Shakespeare Inn, which prompted the community to change its name to Stratford and its river was named the Avon. The most important link, however, was forged in 1953, with the inauguration of the world-famous Shakespeare Festival which is held here each summer and attracts a large international audience.

What to See and Do

The **Shakespeare Festival** was the dream of local journalist Tom Patterson, a dream that was realized with the help of Sir Tyrone Guthrie in 1953 when the first festival productions were staged inside a tent. The idea took off, an award-winning theater was built, and the festival has grown in size, popularity, and reputation until it now attracts an audience of around 500,000. The season usually extends from June to October, and while the plays performed are predominantly Shakespearean, other classic and contemporary works also feature. International stars appear in the highly-rated productions. There are three theaters in the town — the Festival Theatre at 55 Queen Street, the Avon Theatre at 99 Downie Street, and the Third Stage on Lakeside Drive. For information on the festival write to or call the Stratford Festival, P.O. Box 520, Stratford N5A 6V2, ℂ (519) 273-1600. Tickets go on sale in early March.

The center of the Festival is the **Festival Theatre**, which was built in the late 1950s, innovatively designed along the lines of the Elizabethan stage and reminiscent of the tent in which the plays were originally performed. The nearby **Queen's Park** provides a beautiful setting, with lawns stretching

The Shakespeare Garden in Queen's Park, Stratford, features a bust of the bard.

down to the riverside. Around here the river is dammed to form Victoria Lake, which with its swans and ducks furthers the resemblance to England's Stratford. There are many pleasant walks and spots for picnicking. Footpaths lead you beyond the dam through an old-fashioned gate into the delightful **Shakespeare Garden**, an English-style garden complete with a bust of the bard.

In an old building close by Confederation Park is **The Gallery** at 54 Romeo Street North, ℂ (519) 271-5271, where there are often temporary exhibitions of international modern painting and sculpture, plus lectures and films. There are three galleries, so there's always a choice of exhibitions. It's open daily in the summer and closed on Mondays during the rest of the year.

Where to Stay

MID-RANGE

One of the oldest hotels in Stratford is the **Queen's Inn** at 161 Ontario Street, Stratford N5A 3H3, ℂ (519) 271-1400, which is conveniently central and handy for all three theaters. It has 31 attractive, air-conditioned rooms all with private bath, and there are two restaurants. The prices vary from mid-range to expensive. The **Jester Arms Inn** at 107 Ontario Street, Stratford N5A 3H1, ℂ (519) 271-1121, offers 13 very well-equipped and nicely-furnished rooms, each with private bath and kitchen facilities, and prices again vary from mid-range to expensive. The **Albert Place** at 23 Albert Street, Stratford N5A 3K2, ℂ (519) 273-5800, has 39 spacious modern rooms with TV and air conditioning, and some mini-suites are available. A short drive away from the town, the **Festival Inn**, P.O. Box 811, 1144 Ontario Street, Stratford N5A 6W1, ℂ (519) 273-1150, has a mock-Tudor look throughout and offers 151 comfortable motel accommodations of various kinds, all with private bath. It is set in attractive grounds and guests have the use of tennis courts, an indoor pool, and a dining room.

INEXPENSIVE

A short drive away from the town, **Majer's Hotel** on RR4, Stratford N5A 6S5, ℂ (519) 271-2010, offers 31 comfortable motel units

set around a swimming pool and lawn area. A little closer to town is the **Noretta Motel** at 691 Ontario Street, Stratford N5A 3J6, ((519) 271-6110, which has 15 air-conditioned units.

Among the most interesting **Bed & Breakfast** accommodations in the area is **Brunswick House** at 109 Brunswick Street, Stratford N5A 3L9, ((519) 271-4546, run by two writers, which has six individually and warmly decorated rooms and is filled with books and paintings. Also **Crackers** at 433 Erie Street, Stratford N5A 2N3, ((519) 273-1201, offers five unusual and individually furnished rooms, one of which has a four-poster bed, in a nineteenth-century house just outside downtown. For details and brochures of other B&B accommodation, write or call The Southwestern Ontario Countryside Vacation Association, c/o Mrs. E. Alveretta Henderson, RR1, Millbank NOK 1LO, ((519) 595-4604, and also the Stratford Festival, P.O. Box 520, Stratford N5A 6V2, ((519) 273-1600.

Where to Eat

MODERATE

The place to go has to be the **Church Restaurant**, at 70 Brunswick Street, ((519) 273-3424, but if you're planning to dine here during the festival then reservations really do need to be made at the same time you book your theater tickets, i.e. up to six months in advance. Fine French food is served in this nineteenth-century converted church, which retains its altar, stained glass, and original woodwork. There's also the Belfry grill room and bar for a less expensive menu, snacks and drinks. The restaurant is open daily except Mondays, unless there's a special event. Prices range from moderate to expensive.

Rundles at 9 Coburg Street, ((519) 271-6442, is another excellent restaurant, which is beautifully located by Victoria Lake. Its interior is very modern and adorned with contemporary paintings and sculptures, the food is mouth-watering and imaginative, and the three-course table d'hote is

recommended. They also prepare delicious packed lunches for festival-goers. The restaurant's opening hours adapt to the theater program, but usually it is open for lunch and dinner Wednesday to Saturday, for lunch only on Sunday, and is closed during the winter. Prices vary from moderate to expensive. Local produce features largely on the menu at **The Old Prune**, located in an older building at 151 Albert Street, ((519) 271-5052. The food is light, fresh, and delicious; for dinner there is a *prix-fixe* menu but there is quite a wide choice.

INEXPENSIVE

Bentley's Pub and Restaurant at 99 Ontario Street, ((519) 271-1121, is an 1856 building furnished to look like an English country pub. The dining room serves good food which includes beef, fish, pasta, and freshly baked pastries, and there's a bar at the front. At **Wolfy's**, 127 Downie Street, ((519) 271-2991, there's a relatively small but interesting menu of flavorsome dishes served in what used to be an old fish-and-chip shop, and prices range from inexpensive to moderate. A great spot for breakfast is **Let Them Eat Cake** at 82 Wellington Street, ((519) 273-4774, which also has some good soups and snacks at lunchtime.

LONDON

Situated at the fork of the River Thames, this is the area's industrial center. However, this is not immediately obvious thanks to the town's attractive old houses, tree-lined streets and squares, and exceptional amount of greenery as a result of an extensive tree-planting scheme that started a hundred years ago and is still in progress.

What to See and Do

Overlooking the river is the **Art Gallery**, 421 Ridout Street, ((519) 672-4580, a striking modern building designed by Raymond Moriyama. This unusual structure is a series of interlocking barrel vaults which form large and airy galleries with domed skylights providing natural lighting. The gallery holds changing exhibitions of national and international work, and has

PRECEDING PAGES: Swans on the River Avon glide past Queen's Park in Stratford.

its own large collection of Canadian art. It is open Tuesday to Sunday and admission is free. For a different kind of cultural entertainment, comedies, musicals and drama are performed at the **Grand Theatre**, 471 Richmond Street, ((519) 672-8800, a splendidly restored turn-of-the-century building.

Children have a wonderful time at the **London Regional Children's Museum** at 21 Wharncliffe Road South, ((519) 434-5726, where they are encouraged to explore, participate and play. They can dress up in cos-

tumes or uniforms and "be" a fireman, a doctor, or a builder in the gallery called "The Street Where You Live". They can see what life was like in the past, or explore the Computer Hall, or look into outer space. The museum is open Monday to Saturday and Sunday afternoons.

For a glimpse of what life was like before the settlers arrived in southwestern Ontario, visit the **Museum of Indian Archaeology** and **Lawson Prehistoric Indian Village** at 1600 Attawandaron Road, ((519) 473-1360, where there are displays on the area's prehistory as well as a reconstructed Attawandaron Village. It is open daily April to November. About 32 km (20 miles) southwest of the city is the **Ska-Nah-Doht In-**

dian **Village**, a recreation of a prehistoric Iroquoian village with exhibits and audio-visual presentations that show all aspects of everyday life. It's in the Longwoods Road Conservation area off Route 2 and is open daily.

Life in a pioneer community is re-created at the **Fanshawe Pioneer Village** in Fanshawe Park, ((519) 451-2800, 14 km (9 miles) northeast of the city. This reconstructed village consists of 24 buildings, where you can watch demonstrations of pioneer crafts and take a ride in a wagon. Open daily from early May to Labor Day. The park itself covers 600 hectares or 1,500 acres of land, with a large lake and a pool where you can swim, fish, canoe, windsurf, and sail. It's open all year except for winter weekends.

Where to Stay

MID-RANGE

The best accommodation is probably the **Idlewyld Inn** at 36 Grand Avenue, London N6C 1K8, ((519) 433-2891, a splendid 1878 mansion with tall windows, ornate woodwork, and a grand central staircase. It has 25 guest rooms, each uniquely decorated and with a happy combination of antique furnishings and modern facilities. The **Sheraton Armouries Hotel** at 325 Dundas Street, London N6B 1T9, ((519) 679-6111, provides quite luxurious accommodation in an unusual setting. A thick walled and turreted armory forms the main floor of the building, above which rises a glass tower. There are 250 rooms attractively furnished and all with private bath and TV. There's an indoor swimming pool, fitness facilities, a lounge where you can enjoy musical entertainment, and two restaurants, one offering Japanese food and the other regional cooking. There's the usual good value at the conveniently located **Best Western Lamplighter Inn**, 591 Wellington Road South, London N6C 4R3, ((519) 681-7151, which has 125 rooms with private baths, and there are some mini-suites available.

A demonstration in the Fanshawe Pioneer Village.

Situated near the airport, the **Motor Court Motel** at 1883 Dundas Street East, London N5W 3G3, ((519) 451-2610, has 25 accommodations with some honeymoon and family suites available, and facilities include sauna and whirlpool. There's very good value at the **Golden Pheasant**, RR5, London N6A 4B9, ((519) 473-4551, which offers 41 air-conditioned rooms and an outdoor swimming pool, with children's play area. Details of **university accommodation** are available from King's College,

Where to Eat

For first-rate seafood go to **Anthony's** at 433 Richmond Street, ((519) 679-0960, where the atmosphere is warm and friendly, the food is beautifully presented, and the desserts are homemade. It's open for lunch from Monday to Friday, for dinner Monday to Thursday, and prices range from moderate to inexpensive.

For continental cuisine there's the **Wonderland Riverview Dining Room** at 284 Wonderland Road South, ((519) 471-4662, which is a popular spot with an

Conference Co-ordinator, 266 Epworth Avenue, London N6A 3K7, ((519) 433-3491, and for lists of **Bed & Breakfast** accommodations contact the London Area B&B Association, 72 Headley Drive, London N6H 3V6, ((519) 471-6228.

Fanshawe Park Conservation Area, located 14 km (9 miles) northeast of the city, ((519) 475-4471, offers over 600 well-equipped **campsites** with good facilities and pleasant surroundings where there's a beach, a large lake, and woodland.

outdoor terrace and a dance floor that overlooks the river. Open all day every day and prices again range from moderate to inexpensive. Similarly priced is **Maestro's** at 352 Dundas Street, ((519) 439-8983, where the menu features dishes from all around the world, and particularly good breakfasts are served.

There's an amazing range of wines to be sampled at **Le Taste Vin**, 171 Queen's Avenue, Richmond, ((519) 432-WINE, and light and tasty dishes are served at lunchtime or dinnertime at inexpensive prices. Traditional Canadian food is served in a pleasant, peaceful atmosphere at the **Friar's Cellar II**, 267 Bathurst Street, and there's good home cooking at **Mr. Abnathy's**,

One of the many colorful floats in Windsor's International Freedom Festival Parade.

299 King Street. All three are inexpensively priced.

WINDSOR

Situated on the Detroit River, across from Detroit, Windsor's geographical location has given it great importance in terms of the area's commerce and economy since the early 1700s when it was a major center of the French fur trade. It is now closely linked with Detroit through its large car manufacturing industry, and it is a major entry point into Canada via both bridge and tunnel.

What to See and Do

Between June 19th and July 5th each year, Detroit and Windsor jointly celebrate America's Independence Day and Canada's national holiday with the **International Freedom Festival**. There are bands, parades, concerts, dances, sporting events, and it all ends with a huge fireworks display. Windsor also holds an **Oktoberfest** over two weekends each October. For further information ring (519) 966-3815.

For a little cultural diversion visit the pleasant **Art Gallery of Windsor** at 445 Riverside Drive West, ((519) 258-7111, which is located in a renovated waterfront building and houses a permanent collection of Canadian paintings and sculpture. There's also a children's gallery where pioneer toys are on show. Open daily except Mondays and holidays.

There's top-class **harness racing** at the Windsor Raceway, ((519) 969-8311, which is located about 10 km (six miles) to the south of the city on Route 18. Seating areas are enclosed and there's racing Wednesday to Sunday evenings from mid-October to April, and sometimes on Saturday afternoons.

Where to Stay

Overlooking the river, the **Holiday Inn** at 480 Riverside Drive West, ((519) 253-4411, toll-free (800) HOLIDAY, offers motel accommodation at moderate prices with good facilities, including an outdoor pool, restaurant, and coffee shop. The **Relax Plaza Hotel** at 33 Riverside Drive East,

Windsor N9A 2S4, ((519) 258-7774, has 150 rooms at mid-range prices, an indoor pool, and dining room. It is popular with families. Set in pleasant grounds, the **Ivy Rose Motel** at 2885 Howard Avenue, Windsor N8X 3Y4, ((519) 966-1700, offers 91 spacious accommodations and a good range of facilities which include an outdoor pool, children's play area, and a restaurant. Prices range from inexpensive to expensive. There's a **Journey's End Motel** at 2955 Dougall Avenue, Windsor N9E 1S1, ((519) 966-7800, toll-free (800) 668-4200, which offers its usual high quality and good range of amenities.

The inexpensively priced **Best Western Continental Inn** at 3345 Huron Church Road, Windsor N9E 4H5, ((519) 966-5541, toll-free (800) 528-1234, has 71 air-conditioned rooms and an outdoor swimming pool. The **Cadillac Motel** at 2498 Dougall Avenue, ((519) 969-9340, has very good facilities including water beds, a swimming pool, and babysitting service. Of its 47 units, some are bridal suites, and all are inexpensive. For details of **university accommodation** contact the University of Windsor, Office of Conference Services, Windsor N9B 3P4, ((519) 253-4232 ext 3276.

The Windsor South KOA, ((519) 726-5200, has 150 **campsites**, some with electricity and water, and there are laundry facilities and a restaurant.

Where to Eat

The **Maison-Girardot Alan Manor** at 411 Mill Street, ((519) 253-9212, is a grand nineteenth-century manor house with six lovely dining rooms furnished with antiques, oriental rugs, and chandeliers. The menu is varied and inexpensively priced. It is open daily except Mondays for lunch and dinner. Reservations are recommended at weekends. For Italian food there's the **Casa Bianca** at 345 Victoria Street, ((519) 253-5218. Dedicated carnivores should try **Sir William's Steakhouse** at 650 Ouellette Avenue, ((519) 254-5119.

HOW TO GET THERE

Route 401 between Toronto and Windsor is the concrete spine of the peninsula.

Driving along it, Kitchener is about an hour from Toronto, London is about an hour and a half from Kitchener, and Windsor is about two hours from London. If you are coming from the U.S., Detroit and Windsor are connected by both a bridge and a tunnel. There is also a daily Amtrak train from Chicago and Detroit that calls at Windsor and London on its way to Toronto and Montreal. Canadian Airlines International ($\mathbb{C}$ 519/455-8385) flies into both Windsor and London.

NORTHERN ONTARIO

Northern Ontario is generally considered to be everything north and west of Lake Nipissing, which lies between the Quebec border and the northern tip of Georgian Bay. In other words, it is almost all of Ontario in terms of size — but very little of it in terms of interest to visitors. Thickly forested and thinly populated, this vast wilderness has no towns of any size except near rich mineral deposits and along the shores of Lake Huron and Lake Superior.

On the other hand, its many lakes and rivers and its forests teeming with wildlife make it ideal for the sportsman who really wants to get away from it all.

GENERAL INFORMATION

Visitors to Sudbury should get in touch with the Rainbow Country Travel Assocation, which maintains a Welcome Centre on Route 69 South at Whippoorwill Road, RR3, Site 14, P.O. Box 29, Sudbury P3E 4N1, $\mathbb{C}$ (705) 522-0104. There is also a tourist office in Sudbury at Civic Square, West Tower, on Brady Street, $\mathbb{C}$ (705) 673-4161.

Visitors to Sault Ste. Marie should contact the Algoma Kinniwabi Travel Association, Suite 203, 616 Queen Street East, Sault Ste. Marie P6A 2A4, $\mathbb{C}$ (705) 254-4293. There is also a Tourist Information Centre at 120 Huron Street by the International Bridge, $\mathbb{C}$ (705) 253-1103.

In Thunder Bay there are two tourist offices: one is in Paterson Park at the corner of May Street and Northern Avenue, $\mathbb{C}$ (705) 623-7577, and the other is at the corner of

Red River Road and Water Street, $\mathbb{C}$ (705) 625-2149.

For information about the huge spaces between and beyond these points contact Ontario Travel, Queen's Park, Toronto M7A 2R9, $\mathbb{C}$ (416) 965-4008, toll-free (800) ONTARIO.

SUDBURY

The town of Sudbury sits in the vast Sudbury Basin, a mineral-rich geological formation 37 km (59 miles) long and 27 km (17 miles) wide which is the world's largest single source of nickel. Sudbury is one of Canada's major mining towns with the biggest nickel mining plant in the world, and the resulting pollution has contributed to the bleakness that afflicts parts of the landscape. However, this is compensated for by the surrounding Canadian Shield countryside, wild and wonderful with its forests, rocks, and lakes, offering the outdoor enthusiast all kinds of possibilities.

Of Sudbury's population of around 149,000, about a quarter are Francophone. Laurentian University, which is situated on the shores of Lake Ramsey, is bilingual, and French culture thrives here.

What to See and Do

The major attraction here is probably **Science North**, an impressive science center which stands at the edge of Lake Ramsey. This dramatic building was designed by architect Raymond Moriyama and consists of two snowflake-shaped buildings set over a cavern in the rock. The smaller hexagonal structure is the reception area; it is linked to the larger "snowflake", containing the exhibition halls, by a tunnel through the rock. In the darkness of the cavern you can see a 3-D film of the Northern Ontario landscape before ascending to exhibition areas where a hands-on experience of science awaits you. You can test to find your ideal body weight, measure your fitness, visit a weather station, or find out what the local pollution levels are and how they test for them at the Atmosphere Laboratory. Computers encourage involvement in the center's wide range of displays which cover subjects such as insects, animals, communications, and outer space. The center offers dining facilities, a lounge bar, and a bookshop. Science North is situated one-and-a-half kilometer (one mile) south of the Trans-Canada Highway on Ramsey Lake Road (℡ 705/522-3700) and is open daily from mid-May to mid-October, Tuesday through Sunday the rest of year, and is closed throughout January.

To the west of the town stands Sudbury's famous landmark, the nine-meter (30-ft) high **Big Nickel**, which stands

For a glimpse of how the early settlers lived, visit the **Copper Cliff Museum** on Balsam Street in Copper Cliff, a pioneer log cabin which houses period antiques and tools. Also, there's the **Flour Mill Heritage Museum** at 514 Notre Dame Avenue, ℡ (705) 675-7621, another pioneer house where nineteenth-century artifacts and furniture are on display. Open Monday to Friday and Sunday afternoons from mid-June to Labor Day.

Lovers of the Great Outdoors will enjoy an excursion to the **Killarney Provincial**

among four other huge replicas of coins, and below lies the **Big Nickel Mine**, a hard-rock mine run by Science North and open to the public. You go down in a cage to the tunnels where the mining process is demonstrated. Open daily mid-May to mid-October, ℡ (705) 673-5659.

From the Big Nickel you can take **The Path of Discovery**, a two-and-a-half hour bus tour of the Sudbury Basin, also organized by Science North, which gives the visitor a glimpse of the massive mining, refining, and smelting operations here and includes a visit to the **Inco Refinery**. Tours operate three times daily from late June to Labor Day, ℡ (705) 522-3700 for details.

Park, which lies about 80 km (50 miles) southwest of Sudbury. It covers 363 sq km (140 sq miles) of rugged Canadian Shield wilderness at its most beautiful, against a backdrop of the snow-capped **La Cloche Mountains**. Apart from some campgrounds, there are few facilities here, and you make your way on foot, by canoe, or on ski. For fishing and whitewater canoeing the place to go is **French River**, which is south of Sudbury and runs between Lake Nipissing and Georgian Bay. Also to the north and all around Sudbury the countryside offers

Sudbury's famous Big Nickel which stands above the entrance to the Big Nickel Mine.

endless opportunities for outdoor recreation, and there are plenty of lodges, camps, and organized trips to ease the way.

Where to Stay

Most guest accommodation in Sudbury is to be found in motels located on the outskirts of town. There's a reliable **Journey's End Motel** close to Science North at 2171 Regent Street South, Sudbury P3E 1B1, toll-free (800) 668-4200, which offers the usual high standard of comfort and has 80 accommodations at inexpensive prices. There are the reliable **Holiday Inn** at 85 St Ann Road, P.O. Box 1033, Sudbury P3E 4S4, ((705) 675-1123, with 145 rooms, an indoor swimming pool and sauna, and the **Senator Motor Hotel** at 390 Elgin Street, Sudbury P3B 1B1, ((705) 675-1273, offering similarly good facilities. Prices at both these hotels fall within the mid-range.

For a completely different kind of accommodation, **Pinecrest Farm**, a dairy farm located in a quiet valley about 100 km (62 miles) west of Sudbury, offers bed and breakfast accommodation throughout the year at inexpensive prices. For details write to Mack & Beth Emiry, RR2, Massey P0P 1P0.

For **university accommodation** Laurentian University offers pleasant accommodation southeast of the city; details are available from the Director of Services, Ramsey Lake Road, Sudbury P3E 2C6, ((705) 673-6597. There's also accommodation at Cambrian College, which can be arranged through the Co-ordinator of Residence, 885 Regent Street South, Sudbury P3E 5M4, ((705) 566-8101 ext 7209.

The **Sudbury International Hostel** is at 302 Cedar Street, Sudbury P3B 1M7, ((705) 674-0104.

Where to Eat

Many of Sudbury's eateries are outside the downtown area. Along Regent Street South you'll find some fast-food places and among the best of the rest is the inexpensive **Ponderosa Steak House**, part of a restaurant chain where a help-yourself salad bar provides the accompaniment to your steak, and **Marconi's**, which specializes in Italian dishes, inexpensively. At 302 Notre Dame Avenue the **Continental Cafe** serves European food with quite a few German specialties, and for trusty deli fare there's **Frank's** on Durham Street.

SAULT STE. MARIE

Known as the "Soo", Sault Ste. Marie is separated from its twin town in the U.S. by the rapids of the St. Mary's River which links Lake Superior and Lake Huron. Long before the explorers came, the rapids were a meeting place for Indians who came there to catch whitefish. Established by Jesuit missionaries in 1668, Sault Ste. Marie has grown into an industrial town with a population of over 80,000. It has a large steelworks, pulp and lumber mills, and is also a very important shipping center. A series of locks on the St. Mary's River enable huge ships to pass between Lakes Huron and Superior, bypassing the rapids and making the canal the busiest section of the St. Lawrence Seaway with 90 million metric tonnes (100 million tons) of cargo passing through annually.

The Soo is also linked to its Michigan twin by road and railway bridges, and it's therefore a popular stopping place for travellers. To the north lies the unspoiled and untamed Algoma wilderness; the excursion that runs from the town to the Agawa Canyon is a famous attraction.

What to See and Do

At the bottom of Huron Street you can see the **Soo Locks** that connect the Lakes, and watch the continuous stream of ships passing through from a viewing platform or down by the locks, around which you'll find pleasant walking trails. There are four American locks and one Canadian lock which dates from 1895 and is the oldest of the system. This Canadian lock, now operated by Parks Canada, is used only by pleasure craft now and has some lovely spots for picnicking. **Boat trips** run from Norgoma Dock, off Foster Drive, and operate between late-May and mid-October, ((705) 253-9850. The trips take you through all the locks and last about two hours.

The *MS Norgoma* was the last passenger cruise ship built for use on the Great Lakes, and it is now permanently moored at the bottom of Elgin Street where it has been turned into a marine museum. Guided tours operate daily during June to September. To find out about the area's history, you can visit the small but well-designed **Sault Ste. Marie Museum** housed in a heritage building at the junction of Queen and East Streets. Displays trace 10,000 years of just about every aspect of the area's development and there are hands-on exhibits in the museum's Discovery Gallery. Open Monday to Saturday and Sunday afternoons.

The **Ermatinger Old Stone House** at 831 Queen Street East, ((705) 949-1488, is a lovely Georgian building dating from 1814 and is the oldest surviving dwelling in Northern Ontario. It was built by Charles Oakes Ermatinger, a wealthy fur trader, for his wife, who was an Objiwa princess, and it provided a resting place for many explorers. One floor has been restored and furnished in the style of the early nineteenth century and the other floor houses a museum. Open daily June to September.

The main attraction here is the spectacular excursion north of the city into the beautiful **Agawa Canyon** aboard the Algoma Central Railway. This nine-hour trip starts from the town to Hearst, plunging deep into the unspoiled wilderness, through forests, over rivers and gorges, along trestle bridges, on mountain ledges and around lakes. The trip allows two hours for exploring, fishing, climbing, and camera clicking, and there are trips that allow you to stay over in Hearst. The railway is the only means of access to this area. Trips run daily from mid-June to mid-October and early reservations are recommended. During late December to mid-March the Algoma Central Snow Train runs on weekends and reservations are necessary. The Algoma Central Railway Station is at 129 Bay Street, ((705) 254-4331.

To appreciate more of the area's natural beauty, take the Trans-Canada Highway (Route 17) north of the town to Wawa, a journey of 230 km (143 miles) known as the **Lake Superior Drive** which runs through rugged Canadian Shield country. The route takes you by **Batchawana Bay**, a huge bay on the shore of Lake Superior with miles of

sandy beaches and beautiful views. You'll find plenty of accommodation of all kinds here. Continuing along the TCH beyond the lovely **Alona Bay**, the road takes you through **Lake Superior Provincial Park**, a majestic wilderness of cliffs and forests. Here, rising from the lake, is **Agawa Rock**, on which a series of Indian pictographs are painted telling stories that were the inspiration of Longfellow's epic poem, *Hiawatha*.

For a spectacular view of the lake and St. Mary's River, go 26 km (16 miles) west of the town along Route 550 to the ridge known as **Gros Cap**, where there's a marked trail along the edge.

Sports

Lake Superior Provincial Park is a beautiful setting for **boating** and **canoeing**, and also offers **fishing**. At Batchawana Bay the rivers offer good inland fishing and there are more opporunities during the two-hour stop on the Agawa Canyon trip. For **swimming** Batchawana Bay has some lovely beaches although the waters are cool, and in the Kinsmen–Crystal Creek Conservation Area, also known as Hiawatha Park, a short drive northwest of town, there's a swimming pond and waterfalls.

For **cross-country skiing** the Algoma Central Railway runs a Snow Train on winter weekends. Call (705) 946-7300 for information and reservations. In the town itself there are numerous world-class cross-country trails, a lighted trail and there's **downhill skiing** at Ski Searchmont, located 48 km (30 miles) north on Route 556. There are also hundreds of miles of **snowmobile** trails.

Where to Stay

MID-RANGE

Close to the Algoma Central train station there's a **Holiday Inn** at 208 St. Mary's Drive, Sault Ste. Marie P6A 5V4, ((705) 949-0611, with an indoor pool, sauna, restaurant, and 195 rooms. Ideally situated for shopping is the **Ramada Inn**, 229 Great Northern Road, Sault Ste. Marie, ((705) 942-2500, which has an excellent range of facilities and additional features such as an indoor miniature golf course. The **Bay Front Quality Inn** at 180 Bay Street, Sault Ste. Marie P6A 6S2, ((705) 945-9264, is a 110-room hotel with just about everything you need, and the **Water Tower Inn**, Route 17B, Sault Ste. Marie, ((705) 253-9751, is a Best Western hotel with large, pleasantly furnished rooms, a fitness center, indoor and outdoor swimming pools, and restaurants.

INEXPENSIVE

The **Empire** at 320 Bay Street, Sault Ste. Marie, ((705) 759-8200, is conveniently situated in downtown opposite the Algoma Central station, has 120 well-equipped rooms, a sauna, and indoor swimming pool. It's a good choice. To the north of downtown, the **Journey's End Motel** at 333 Great Northern Road, Sault Ste. Marie P6B 4Z8, ((705) 759-8000, offers the usual value one expects from this chain.

If the idea of **farm accommodation** appeals, the Rainbow Ridge Farm on St. Joseph Island, 61 km (38 miles) east of the town, offers Bed & Breakfast in a late nineteenth-century farmhouse. For details contact M.Clement & N.Powis-Clement, RR1, Richards Landing, St. Joseph Island P0R 1J0, ((705) 246-2683. There are two **youth hostels** in town: one is in an old house at 452 Bay Street, ((705) 256-7233, and the other, L'Auberge de Sault Ste. Marie, is at 8 Queen Street East, ((705) 946-0104.

There's quite a choice of **campgrounds** with good facilities near the town, including a KOA campground about eight kilometers (five miles) north on Route 17, Bar X at Allen's Side Road, near Route 17N, ((705) 253-9751, and campgrounds at Lake Superior Provincial Park, ((705) 856-2284.

Where to Eat

There's good home-style cooking at **A Thymely Manner**, 531 Albert Street East, ((705) 759-3262, in attractive and peaceful surroundings. It's open throughout the year for lunch and dinner Tuesday to Friday, and prices are moderate. Two older houses have been combined to house **Cesira's Italian Cuisine** at 133–137 Spring Street, ((705) 949-0600, where there's good authentic Italian cooking, along with steaks and seafood, at moderate prices. **Barsanti Small Frye** at 23 Trunk Road serves good basic fare at budget prices, open daily, and you can taste the local whitefish and trout as well as other dishes at **Vavalas**, which is

at the junction of Queen and Dennis Streets, and inexpensively priced.

THUNDER BAY

The port of Thunder Bay stands on the shores of Lake Superior, virtually at the exact center of Canada. Situated at the western end of the St. Lawrence Seaway, it is the terminus for freighters and is a pivotal point in the transportation of grain, forest products, and other materials. Thirteen huge grain elevators dominate the skyline, but in recent years reduced grain shipments have meant a reduction in grain traffic through the Lakehead. However, the city's economy remains typically Canadian, being largely dependent on grain, forest products, and mineral resources.

Jobs in shipping attracted many immigrants to Thunder Bay, so there is a rich ethnic mix — which includes a large Finnish community and some 10,000 Indians. With the forest and mountains to the north, the wilderness is never far away and it's not uncommon to see moose and bear wandering about the town. In fact someone swears she once saw a moose running around a high school track.

In the days before the St. Lawrence Seaway, Fort William, as it was then known, was an important fur-trading center. Indians and trappers came here to the mouth of the Kaministikwa with their furs for their meeting — known as the Great Rendezvous — with the buyers who brought their European goods up the St. Lawrence. In 1801 the British built Fort William here, where it served as the headquarters of the North West Company, and each summer more than 2,000 voyageurs met there for the Great Rendezvous, a time of discussion and celebration — and no insignificant amount of drinking — that lasted six weeks. Fort William remained a fur trading post until the late nineteenth century. In 1970 Fort William merged with the communitiy of Port Arthur to form the city of Thunder Bay.

What to See and Do

The largest of the gigantic grain elevators, the **Saskatchewan Wheat Pool Elevator**, is also one of the world's largest and is open to tourists. Tickets are available from the Tourist Office, ✆ (807) 623-7577. If you're interested in seeing how the cargo is handled you could take a tour of the **Keefer Terminal**, on the waterfront at Main Street just off Fort William Road, ✆ (807) 345-6812.

Outside downtown, **Fort William** has been reconstructed along with 50 village buildings. At the Fort you can see trappers, voyageurs, Indians and traders going about their business. To get to the Fort you go 16 km (10 miles) along Broadway Avenue or take a boat from Port Arthur marina. It's open daily from mid-May to early October, ✆ (807) 344-2512.

Among the arts facilities the city has to offer, the pride and joy is the **Thunder Bay Auditorium** which was completed in 1985. Although its design has proved controversial, its acoustics are excellent and it attracts international entertainers and hit shows. The **Thunder Bay Art Gallery** at Confederation Campus focuses particularly on contemporary Indian art, and has examples of the work of Norval Morrisseau, a well-known Indian artist who was born in Thunder Bay. There are changing exhibitions which include crafts, sculpture, and photography.

At the eastern end of the city, the wooded **Centennial Park** covers a 57-hectare (140-acre) area and has a logging camp, museum, and nature trails. It is open daily throughout the year, while the logging camp is open mid-June to Labor Day.

Further out and to the east of the city is the scenic **Sibley Provincial Park** with trails, cliffs, woods, and shoreline. At one end you'll see the **Sleeping Giant** rock formation stretching out into the lake, attached to which is a legend involving a silver mine, a treacherous Indian, and a Great Spirit. There are several **amethyst mines** 56 to 72 km (35 to 45 miles) to the east of the town on Route 11/17, which are open to the public. You can either pick your own amethyst from the mines or buy them from displays.

Sports

There's good canoeing territory between the Lakehead and Rainy River, and at Centennial Park you'll find canoes and boats for rent. Between Thunder Bay and Kenora

there are many **fishing** lodges, details of which can be obtained from the Tourist Office. At the multi-use athletic Canada Games Complex, 420 Winnipeg Avenue, there's an Olympic **swimming** pool and huge waterslide. Sibley Provincial Park is a good spot for swimming, and there are beaches at Kakabeka Falls, situated 25 km (16 miles) to the west of the town.

The long winters and short summers here have given rise to the local saying that here there's "six months of good **skiing**, six months of poor skiing". Certainly, there is

plenty of it. In the immediate vicinity there are three downhill areas with excellent facilities and snow-making equipment. There are also five cross-country trails close to the city, with plenty of aprés-ski and package deals to be had. The Big Thunder Ski Jump is the world's largest with 90-m (295 ft) and 70-m (230-ft) jumps. It's southwest of the city and is where the national ski-jumping team trains.

Where to Stay
MODERATE
Near the airport the **Airlane Motor Hotel**, 698 West Arthur Street, Thunder Bay P7E

The windmill at Thunder Bay's Friendship Gardens.

5R8, ((807) 577-1181, is one of the best hotels in the area. It has 170 rooms, good service, and a host of amenities such as an indoor pool, a sauna, a good restaurant, and a complimentary limo service to the airport. The **Landmark Inn**, 1010 Dawson Road, Thunder Bay P7B 5J4, ((807) 767-1681, has similarly high standards and amenities. It offers 106 air-conditioned rooms with private bath and TV. The reliable **Best Western Crossroads Motor Inn** at 655 West Arthur Street, Thunder Bay P7E 5R8, ((807) 577-4241, toll-free (800) 528-1234, has 60 air-conditioned accommodations with private bath and TV.

INEXPENSIVE

The centrally situated **Shoreline Motor Hotel**, P.O. Box 3105, 61 North Cumberland Street, Thunder Bay P7A 4L7, ((807) 344-9661, has 69 rooms with private bath and TV, and there's a trusty **Journey's End Motel** at 660 Arthur Street West, Thunder Bay P7E 5R8, ((807) 475-3155. For some out-of-town tranquility the **Unicorn Inn and Restaurant** located 36 km (22 miles) south of Thunder Bay Airport at RR1, South Gillies, Thunder Bay P0T 2V0, ((807) 475-4200, nestles in a secluded valley in rural surroundings and offers three guest rooms and a cottage. The house was built at the turn of the century by a Finnish family and features a warm wooden interior.

The **Longhouse Village Hostel** on Lakeshore Drive, 22 km (14 miles) east of town, ((807) 983-2042, offers good accommodation and is open throughout the year, while **Lakehead University** also offers rooms, details of which are available from the Director of Residence & Conference Services, 953 Oliver Road, Thunder Bay P7B 5E1, ((807) 343-8612.

South of the town, off Route 61, Chippewa Park is one of the area's popular **camping spots**, and there are a few places to the east of Port Arthur which include a KOA campground.

Where to Eat

The **Circle Inn**, 686 Memorial Park, ((807) 344-5744, serves good food at moderate prices, and for meat lovers there's the **Prospector**, at the junction of Cumberland and

Park Avenue, where locally produced steaks and beef feature, again moderately priced. Out of town, the delightful **Unicorn Inn and Restaurant** mentioned above offers excellent cuisine in a peaceful and lovely valley setting, which can be appreciated through the dining room's large bay windows. The large and homey **Hoito Restaurant** at 314 Bay Street, ((807) 345-6323, is something of an institution, a gathering place for Thunder Bay's large population of Finnish Canadians. Finnish food is served and they offer a smorgasbord and hearty traditional breakfasts, all inexpensively priced. **Chan's** at 130 May Street North, ((807) 622-2601, is one of the best Chinese restaurants, and the **Bombay Bistro Club**, 219 Brodie Street, is quite a fashionable

little spot which offers food with an Indian influence.

HOW TO GET THERE

Sudbury, Sault Ste. Marie, and Thunder Bay are all served by Air Canada. Nordair also flies in to Sault Ste. Marie and Thunder Bay, while Norontair flies to Sudbury and some of the more northern towns of the province.

There is no train service to Sault Ste. Marie, but there is a daily VIA Rail train eastbound from Vancouver and Winnipeg that stops at Thunder Bay and Sudbury on its way to Ottawa and Montreal, and one westbound daily along the same route. There is also daily train service between Sudbury and Toronto.

Greyhound has frequent buses from major Canadian cities to Sudbury, Sault Ste. Marie, and Thunder Bay, as well as daily buses to Sault Ste. Marie from Detroit and Chicago.

If you are coming by car, the Trans-Canada Highway (Route 17) links Sudbury, Sault Ste. Marie, and Thunder Bay with each other as well as with eastern and western Canada. Approaching from the south, Sudbury can be reached by Route 69 from Toronto; Sault Ste. Marie can be reached by I-75 from Detroit; and Thunder Bay can be reached by I-35 from Minneapolis/St Paul and Duluth, which becomes Route 61 when it crosses the border.

Kakabeka Falls, a few miles west of Thunder Bay.

Travelers' Tips

I'VE SAID IT BEFORE and I'll say it again: the best tip I can offer any traveler is to get yourself a good travel agent. There is no substitute — not even this sparkling chapter — for the information and helpful advice that a travel agent has at his/her command. In a world where fares, schedules, even routes are changing hourly, only someone with access to the very latest information can give you the sort of guidance necessary to ensure a hassle-free holiday. I should also point out that, with the exception of the weather summaries in the WHEN TO GO

section, the information in this chapter covers all of Canada — not just the eastern (or Western) half. This is because, firstly, the laws, customs, and general characteristics of the nation don't suddenly change at the Ontario/Manitoba (or Manitoba/Ontario) border. Secondly, such is the appeal of this lovely country, the visitor may well not want to restrict his or her visit to just one side of that border.

GETTING THERE

BY AIR

All the major international airlines fly to Canada, but Air Canada (toll-free 800/4-CANADA) has more flights to more Canadian cities than any other airline. This is true not only of flights from other continents

but also flights from the U.S. This is worth bearing in mind whatever your place of departure, because often it is cheaper to fly from Europe or elsewhere to the U.S. first and then on to Canada. Also, as you would expect, Air Canada has an extensive connector network of domestic airlines linking cities within Canada.

Another point in Air Canada's favor, from my point of view at least, is that it is a smoke-free airline. Smoking is prohibited on all its European, North American, and transatlantic routes. Even smokers agree that it makes for a distinctly more pleasant environment in which to travel.

One further, general tip regarding air travel to Canada — or anywhere else for that matter — is to get to the airport early. This, I know, is a contentious issue among frequent flyers, some of whom like to arrive at the airport just as the pilot is starting up the engines. But for me there are three compelling arguments in favor of heading for the airport ahead of time. One is that it gives you a safety margin in case you encounter a problem — a traffic jam, a flat tire, a detour — on the way. You would be surprised how many people miss planes because they didn't leave themselves time to absorb unexpected delays. Secondly, by getting to the airport early you have a much better seat selection for your flight — and the longer the flight, the more important it is to have the seat you want. (If you are flying on a British Airways jumbo jet, for example, you can often get a seat upstairs, where it is more comfortable and the service is more attentive.) Thirdly, early arrivals at the airport avoid the long queues to check in, which means that the time that would otherwise be spent standing around shepherding one's luggage slowly forward can be spent reading, shopping, having drinks, having a meal — in a word, relaxing.

BY RAIL

Amtrak has two trains daily from New York City to Montreal, one going through upstate New York and the other, an overnight train which begins in Washington, D.C., going through Vermont. There is also daily service from New York to Toronto, via Niagara

All aboard! A railway station, though it may be small, is never far away.

Falls, and from Chicago to Toronto via Detroit. For details write to Amtrak, 400 North Capitol Street, N.W., Washington D.C. 20001 or call, toll-free, (800) 872-7245.

BY BUS

Greyhound is the only company operating a cross-border service, but it has such a huge route system that you should have no difficulty in getting to virtually any point in Canada from anywhere in the U.S. It also has a hugely complicated system of fares, discount fares, seasonal rates, unlimited-travel passes, and so on. Information is available from any Greyhound office or from Greyhound Line, Inc., Greyhound Tower, Phoenix, Arizona 85077; alternatively, you can call (212) 971-6363 for information about Greyhound's service to eastern Canada and (213) 620-1200 for details of the service in the west.

BY CAR

There are 13 principal border crossing points where the American highway system connects directly with the Canadian. The crossing is usually a quick, simple matter, although in peak season you might want to avoid the busier crossing points such as Detroit-Windsor and Niagara Falls. Once in Canada, no matter where you've crossed, you are only a short drive from the Trans-Canada Highway.

TOURIST INFORMATION

Canada — or I should say the visitor to Canada — is blessed with a whole galaxy of helpful agencies designed to provide information on every subject of potential concern to tourists. In the "General Information" sections of the preceding chapters I have already listed the local and provincial agencies, and in the following pages I will give the addresses and telephone numbers of the specific-interest agencies set up to deal with enquiries relating to the various topics discussed in this chapter. Here, then, are the people who speak for the country as a whole.

IN CANADA
Tourism Canada, 235 Queen Street, Ottawa, Ontario K1A 0H6. ((613) 954-3854 or 954-3980.

IN UNITED STATES.
Canadian Consulates General:
New York 16th Floor, 1251 Avenue of the Americas, New York NY 10020. ((212) 586-2400.
Chicago 12th Floor, 310 South Michigan Avenue, Chicago IL 60604. ((312) 992-0637.
San Francisco Suite 2100, 50 Freemont Street, San Francisco CA 94105. ((415) 495-6021.

IN EUROPE
London Canadian Government Office of Tourism, Canada House, Trafalgar Square, London SW1Y 5BJ. England. ((071) 629-9492 or 930-8540.
Paris Office du Tourisme du Canada, 37 Avenue Monta, Paris 75008, France.
Frankfurt Kanadisches Fremdenverkehrsamt, Immermannstraße 65D, 4000 Düsseldorf 1, ((0211) 360334 oder 360335.

IN AUSTRALIA
Sydney Canadian Government Office of Tourism, 8th Floor, AMP Centre, 50 Bridge Street, Sydney NSW 2000. ((02) 231-6522.

EMBASSIES AND CONSULATES

American Embassy: 100 Wellington Street, Ottawa K1P 5T1. ((613) 238-5335
American Consulates: 360 University Avenue, Toronto M5G 1S4, ((416) 595-1700; Suite 1122, South Tower, Place Desjardins, Montreal H5B 1G1, ((514) 281-1886; 1 Avenue Sainte-Genevieve, Quebec City G1R 4A7, ((418) 692-2095; Suite 910, Scotia Square, Halifax B3J 3K1, ((902) 429-2480; Room 100, 6 Donald Street, Winnipeg R3L 0K7, ((204) 475-3344; Room 1050, 615 Macleod Trail SE, Calgary T2G 4T8, ((403) 266-8962; Columbia Centre IV, 1199 West Hastings Street, Vancouver V6E 2Y4, ((604) 685-4311.
Australian High Commisson: Suite 710, 55 O'Connor Street, Ottawa K1P 6L2, ((613) 238-0844.

Australian Consulate: 22nd Floor, Commerce Court North, King and Bay Streets, Toronto M5L 1B9, ((416) 367-0783.
British High Commission: 80 Elgin Street, Ottawa K1P 5K7, ((613) 237-1530.
British Consulates: Suite 1910, 777 Bay Street, Toronto M5G 2G2, ((416) 593-1290; Suite 901, 1155 University Street, Montreal H3B 3A7, ((514) 866-5863; Suite 501, Purdy's Wharf, Lower Water Street, Halifax B3J 2X1, ((902) 429-4330.
Irish Embassy: 170 Metcalfe Street, Ottawa, ((613) 233-6281.

TRAVEL DOCUMENTS

U.S. citizens require only proof of American citizenship to enter Canada (passport, birth certificate, voter registration card, or naturalization certifcate); U.S. residents who are not citizens must show their Alien Registration Card. British and Australian visitors, as well as citizens of most European and Commonwealth countries, need a valid passport but no visa. If in doubt, check with your travel agent or the nearest Canadian embassy, high commission, or consulate.

CUSTOMS

Customs regulations are similar to those in most countries, including the usual restrictions on bringing in meats, plants, and animals. Items intended for personal or professional use do not have to be declared, and you are allowed up to 200 cigarettes or 50 cigars, and 40 ounces of wine or spirits duty-free. You can bring in gifts up to $40 in value. There are no currency restrictions.

Hunting and fishing equipment may be brought in duty-free as well, but all firearms and ammunition must be declared and a written description of each item, including serial numbers of guns, must be provided.

Details of Customs regulations are available from Revenue Canada, Customs and Excise, Connaught Building, Sussex Drive, Ottawa, Ontario K1A 0L5.

WHEN TO GO

Generally speaking, *very* generally speaking, the seasons in Canada's more temperate climes divide up as follows: winter occupies most of the long stretch from November to the end of March, summer occurs in June, July, and August, while the "shoulder" seasons of spring and autumn are largely confined to April to May and September to October.

In Newfoundland and the Maritimes, winter temperatures seldom rise above freezing and can often fall far below, especially in the inland areas. Spring is brief — just time for the countryside to change from its winter to its summer wardrobe. The summer is comfortably mild, with temperatures in the high teens and 20s (60s and 70s Fahrenheit). The autumn is gloriously colorful, particularly in New Brunswick, as trees erupt in a blaze of reds and golds.

In Ontario and Quebec the winters are just as cold — often, in places, colder — and tend to be gray and damp in southern Ontario, snowy bright and chilly elsewhere in the region. Spring is very pleasant and autumn is very lovely, as in the Maritimes, but summer is considerably warmer and more humid, particularly in Toronto.

Obviously, the decision of when to go will depend on what you are going *for*, and by now you should have a pretty good

Autumn leaves in New Brunswick.

idea of what each region has to offer at what time of the year. But just to make your planning a little more precise, here are the average daytime temperatures in degrees Celsius and Fahrenheit for each month of the year in five principal cities of eastern Canada:

ST JOHN'S
Jan: 4°C/39°F Feb: 4°C/39°F Mar: 3°C/37°F
Apr: 3°C/37°F May: 6°C/43°F Jun: 11°C/52°F
July:15°C/59°F Aug:16°C/61°F Sept:12°C/54°F
Oct: 8°C/46°F Nov: 4°C/39°F Dec : -5°C/24°F

TORONTO
Jan: -5°C/23°F Feb: 4°C/25°F Mar: 1°C/34°F
Apr: 8°C/46°F May: 11°C/52°F Jun: 19°C/66°F
July: 22°C/72°F Aug: 21°C/70°F Sept: 17°C/63°F
Oct:11°C/52°F Nov: 5°C/41°F Dec: -2°C/29°F

WHAT TO TAKE

All seasoned travelers, including this one, will urge you to travel light. That is to say we agree that you should not take more than you think you will need; where we disagree

HALIFAX
Jan: -4°C/25°F Feb: -6°C/22°F Mar: -1°C/30°F
Apr: 5°C/41°F May: 9°C/48°F Jun: 14°C/57°F
July:18°C/64°F Aug:18°C/64°F Sept:15°C/59°F
Oct:10°C/50°F Nov: 5°C/41°F Dec: -1°C/30°F

QUEBEC CITY
Jan:-12°C/10°F Feb:-11°C/12°F Mar: -5°C/23°F
Apr: 3°C/37°F May:10°C/50°F Jun : 16°C/62°F
July:19°C/67°F Aug: 18°C/65°F Sept: 13°C/56°F
Oct: 7°C/44°F Nov: -1°C/30°F Dec -11°C/12°F

MONTREAL
Jan: -9°C/16°F Feb: -9°C/16°F Mar:-2°C/28°F
Apr: 6°C/43°F May:14°C/57°F Jun: 20°C/68°F
July:22°C/72°F Aug:21°C/70°F Sept: 16°C/61°F
Oct:10°C/50°F Nov: 3°C/37°F Dec: -7°C/20°F

is in helping you decide exactly what you do need. For my part, I think the criterion should be not the desirability of having a particular article with you at any given time, but the undesirability of not having a particular article with you when you really need it. On that principle, here is my list of things you should never leave home without.

At the top of the list, by a wide margin, is a Swiss Army knife (or, to put it another way, two knives, two screwdrivers, a bottle opener, a can opener, a corkscrew, a toothpick, tweezers, nail file, and scissors). I would

Snow sculptures adorn Quebec City's Winter Carnival.

also throw in a miniature flashlight and a small travel alarm clock (or clock radio). And of course you will need an adaptor and/or transformer if you plan to take any electrical appliances that don't run on 110 volts or don't have an American-type plug.

Because even the most minor physical irritations or afflictions can ruin a trip if they strike at the wrong time (which is the only time they strike), I would be sure to carry eye drops, an inhaler or nose drops, a lip balm for chapped lips, aspirin or codeine,

anti-diarrhoea tablets, antiseptic ointment, a few bandages and a few packets of tissues (which can also serve as toilet paper in an emergency).

Because looking good can sometimes matter as much as feeling good, I would take along a tube of concentrated detergent, a stain remover, sachets of towelettes or "wet wipes", sachets of shoe polishers, and — please note — a compact, telescoped umbrella. Always take an umbrella, whatever your destination.

Optional near-essentials would include things like a couple of plastic cups, a coil for heating water, coffee and tea bags, a few bouillon cubes, some salt and pepper packets, and artificial sweeteners.

By the way, everything I have mentioned so far, with the exception of the umbrella, will fit easily into a medium-sized plastic freezer bag. Ah, that's another thing! Resealable, ziplock plastic bags come in very handy when traveling — not least when you want to separate items that you want to keep apart, or segregate items that are damp or dirty or might be inclined to leak.

Speaking of separating items, if you are planning to travel by air and you want to take a Swiss Army knife, or anything else that might conceivably be considered a "weapon", be sure to pack it in the luggage you intend to check. You don't want to be mistaken for an armed passenger. On the other hand, if you are taking any battery-powered gadgets — shavers, cassette players, etc. — carry them with you on the airplane or take the batteries out before packing them, Airline security personnel get understandably jumpy when unidentified objects with batteries in them show up on their X-ray screen.

Now we come to those things that you don't need to be told to take with you — passport, tickets, driver's license, health insurance card, travelers' checks, credit cards, cash — because you would be lost without them. But suppose you do suddenly find yourself without them? Then what? Hassle, that's what. But there are ways of minimizing the hassle, and indeed of reducing the risk of incurring it at all, before you go.

First of all, be sure to take with you lists of the numbers of all travel documents, cards, and checks you will be carrying, along with any telephone numbers included on them. This will greatly facilitate their quick replacement if lost. (I also take photocopies of my passport and any travel tickets: duplicates are issued more speedily if people can see a copy of the original — much more speedily in the case of tickets or refunds.) It is a good idea, too, to get an international driver's license, obtainable from your automobile club, so that you can keep your home driver's license tucked away in a safe place. And speaking of safe places, always leave your inessential credit cards behind when you go on a trip, and of those you take with you carry only a couple in your wallet: any others should be tucked away in the same safe place as your passport, driver's license, extra travelers' checks, etc. It's just another way of ensuring that any loss causes only a temporary inconvenience.

I realize that all this may seem like carrying prudence to somewhat extreme lengths, but I can assure you that if you have the misfortune while traveling to lose your wallet, by whatever means, you will be very grateful to have a "shadow wallet" safely in reserve.

When it comes to clothing, toiletries, jewelry, and gadgetry, it's up to you to decide what and how much you want to take. Canadians are very casual in their dress, so there is no need to take formal or semi-formal wear beyond what your taste and your expected engagements require. There is, however, a need to take some warm clothing — a sweater or two perhaps, the odd woollen or corduroy garment, a windbreaker — because even in summer, even in the hottest spots, it can turn quite cool in the evenings, especially if you happen to be on or near the water.

I will leave the last word on what to take with you to my Canadian colleague Wallace Immen, who writes on travel for *The Globe and Mail* in Toronto. He says that while you should always dress comfortably for long flights, you should also dress respectably. After all, he reasons, rather depressingly, if your luggage is lost, you could be dressed like that for quite a while.

BASICS

TIME

Canada is divided into six time zones, including Newfoundland's own, typically quirky time zone, which is only a half-hour ahead of Atlantic Standard Time in the Maritime Provinces. The other four time zones correspond to, and are continuations of, the four U.S. time zones: Eastern Standard Time, Central Standard Time, Mountain Standard Time, and Pacific Standard Time.

Atlantic Time is four hours behind Greenwich Mean Time, so when it is 8 pm

in London, it is 4 pm in the Maritimes (4:30 pm in Newfoundland). Quebec and all of Ontario to the east of Thunder Bay are on Eastern Time, five hours behind GMT. Manitoba and the eastern half of Saskatchewan are on Central Time; the rest of Saskatchewan, Alberta and northeast British Columbia are on Mountain Time. All of British Columbia west of the Rockies is on Pacific Time, eight hours behind GMT.

All of Canada — with the mysterious exception of eastern Saskatchewan —

observes Daylight Savings Time from the first Sunday in April, when the clocks are put forward one hour, until the last Sunday in October.

ELECTRICITY

The electric current is 110–120 volts AC, the same as in the U.S., and the sockets only take American-type plugs with two flat prongs.

OPPOSITE: Winter in Quebec is a time for bundling up. ABOVE: The world's first steam-powered clock keeps time in Vancouver's colorful Gastown district.

WEIGHTS AND MEASURES

Canadians, like just about everybody else in the world except their American neighbors and their British cousins, rely almost exclusively on the metric system. Thus, while Canadians are spared the old question, "How much is that in dollars?", they now have to face the new question, "How far is that in miles?" or "What is that in pounds and ounces?"

To save the uninitiated the bother of having to ask such questions, and the Canadians the bother of having to answer them, I have pored over countless conversion tables (they can be found in any dictionary, almanac, or appointments diary) in an effort to decide which one, or which format, would be the most useful to readers who are, by definition, on the move. In the end I decided that none of them would be of much use — unless you want to have to pick up this book (and a calculator) every time you read a label, or see a road sign, or hear a weather forecast. (Clothing sizes are a different matter, and are dealt with in the "Shopping" section of this chapter.) Therefore, to make life easier for those not yet numerate in metrics, I have devised my own rough-and-ready (and of course approximate) system for making instant conversions on the spot. It is not only simple, but easy to memorize, so long as you remember that the colloquial term "a bit" here represents one-tenth of whatever it is next to. Thus:

One meter = a yard and a bit; One kilometer = a half-mile and a bit; One kilogram = two pounds and a bit (500g = 1 lb & a bit); One liter = a bit more than an American quart and a bit less than a British quart

For converting to degrees Fahrenheit, simply double the figure you are given in Celsius and add 30, topping it up by a couple of degrees when you get above 20°C. The temperature you come up with won't be precisely accurate, but it will be close enough.

HEALTH

You really haven't much to worry about, because health hazards are few and the

health care is excellent. It can be expensive, though, so American visitors should check to make sure that their health insurance provides coverage in Canada, and overseas visitors should arrange short-term medical coverage for the period they expect to be there. An excellent medical emergency policy, which also includes personal travel insurance, is available from Europ Assistance Ltd., 252 High Street, Croydon, Surrey CR0 1NF, England. ((081) 680-1234. A similar policy, similarly priced, is offered by Wexas International, 45-49 Brompton Road, London SW3 1DE, England. ((071) 589-3315.

Another wise precaution is to carry a card in your wallet giving your blood type and listing any allergies or chronic conditions (including the wearing of contact lenses) that might affect treatment in an emergency.

Beyond that, it's always a good idea to have insect repellent with you, because in summer Canada has plenty of insects to repel, especally black flies and mosquitoes. A sunscreen lotion is also advisable, as the Canadian sun has a burning power out of all proportion to its heating power.

MONEY

Canadian currency resembles American currency in every important respect except value: the coins are in the same denominations and go by the same names (penny, nickel, dime, etc.), the paper notes are all the same size (but in different colors according to value). There is, however, a gold-colored $1 coin nicknamed the "loonie" after the bird that appears on it.

American dollars are widely accepted, at their greater value, but using them introduces an unnecessary complication into a transaction, as well as an unnecessary discourtesy.

As in all countries with hard currencies, the banks offer the best exchange rates — much better than hotels, for example. Banking hours are 10 am to 3 pm weekdays, though most banks stay open later on Fridays. All major credit cards are accepted anywhere you are likely to go; consequently you are advised to carry a minimum of cash.

If you prefer using non-plastic money, take it in the form of dollar travelers' checks. They can be cashed everywhere, with proper identification (e.g. passport, driver's license), although the larger denominations will not always be welcome in places like restaurants that don't like being used as banks.

In general, however, I would recommend floating through Canada on little rafts of plastic. Provided that you pay your credit card bills promptly when they come in, you will not only benefit from the detailed accounting they supply but you will have saved the cash deposits often required by hotels, for example, while borrowing the money for your travel expenses interest-free.

CRIME

Crime? What crime? Canada may well be the most law-abiding of the world's industrialized nations. Violent crime isn't exactly unheard of, but it's not heard of very often. The streets of Canada's cities are as safe at night as they are in the daytime.

All this law-and-orderliness notwithstanding, one should still take the same basic precautions here that a sensible person would take anywhere: leaving valuables in the hotel safe, locking your hotel room and car, not leaving valuable items visible in your car when unattended, not carrying all your cash and cards with you when you go out, not going for late-night strolls through slum areas. In short, exercise your common sense, secure in the knowledge that Canadians can be counted on to exercise their common decency.

GETTING AROUND

BY AIR

The country's two major carriers, Air Canada and Canadian Airlines International, handle the bulk of the middle- and long-distance air traffic, while dozens of local carriers connect the remaining dots on the map. Thus there are very few places in Canada,

even including remote offshore islands, that are not accessible by air.

Air fares in Canada are predictably unpredictable, but it is worth noting that Air Canada offers Flexipass tickets which allow vistors to travel at reduced rates between any of 28 Canadian cities. Both Air Canada and Canadian Airlines International offer a variety of holiday packages, called Canadapass and Canadian Routes respectively, that cater to almost every conceivable holiday requirement at special prices. Ask your travel agent for details, or contact:

Air Canada Place Air Canada, 500 blvd Dorchester Ouest, Montreal, Quebec H2Z 1X5. ((514) 879-7000, toll-free (800) 4-CANADA.

Canadian Airlines International 2800-700 Second Street SW, Calgary, Alberta T2P 2W2. ((403) 235-8100, toll-free (800) 426-7000.

BY RAIL

There are two main railways in Canada, Canadian Pacific (CP) and Canadian National (CN), both of whose passenger services are operated by the government-owned VIA Rail. Sadly, the VIA Rail network is shrinking due to cuts in government funding, but there is still regular service between the major cities, especially in eastern Canada, and it is still possible to make the spectacular transcontinental journey by train in

The ferry across the St. Lawrence to Rivière-du-Loup, at the base of the Gaspé Peninsula.

the comfort of your own rolling bedroom or roomette.

VIA Rail also issues a Canrailpass and a Youth Canrailpass, which make possible substantial savings by allowing unlimited travel over specified areas for varying period of time in both high season and low season. Your travel agent will have all the particulars. Alternatively, you can get in touch with:

VIA Rail 935 La Gauchetière Ouest, Montreal, Quebec H3C 3N3. ((514) 871-1331, toll-free (800) 663-0667.

BY BUS

Where there's a way, there's a willing bus to take you wherever you want to go in Canada. Greyhound has a nationwide route system, and there are five or six large regional companies that reach into the nooks and crannies that Greyhound misses. Moreover, most of the bus lines participate in Greyhound's Ameripass coupon program, which allows unlimited travel at a discounted rate. In addition, there is the Across Canada Ticket and the International Canadian Pass, as well as the Tourpass Voyageur in Quebec and Ontario.

For detailed information contact Greyhound Lines of Canada at 877 Greyhound Way SW, Calgary, Alberta, ((403) 265-9111, or Voyageur Inc., 505 blvd Maisonneuve, Montreal, Quebec, ((514) 843-4231.

BY CAR

Canada, only slightly less than the U.S., is a motorist's dream. The highway system may not be as sprawling as in the U.S., but it doesn't have to be, since most of the places visited by tourists and natives alike are within easy driving distance of the Trans-Canada Hghway. And the gasoline may not be as cheap as in the U.S., but it's a lot cheaper than it is in Europe.

All the major American car-rental firms (Hertz, Avis, Budget) are represented across the country, as is the largest Canadian company, Tilden, which is affiliated with Na-

tional Car Rental in the U.S. and has over 370 offices all over Canada. If you are planning to rent a car in the summer, it would be a good idea to reserve one before you leave home.

BY FERRY

There are both car and passenger ferry services available on most of Canada's major lakes and rivers, as well as between the mainland and the offshore islands. Ferries across the St. Lawrence and to Prince Edward Island and Vancouver Island don't require reservations, but other ferries should be booked in advance — well in advance if you are taking a car with you.

The midnight sun shines on a lonely northern road.

Information is available from your travel agent or from:

Marine Atlantic P.O. Box 250, North Sydney, Nova Scotia B2A 3M3. ((902) 794-7203, toll-free (800) 341-7981.

M.S. Chi-Cheemaun Owen Sound, Ontario N4K 4K8. ((519) 596-2510.

British Columbia Ferry Corporation 818 Broughton Street, Victoria, British Columbia V8W 1E4. ((604) 669-1211.

BY LOCAL TRANSPORT

Taxis can always be found at airports, railway stations, and major hotels. They can also be hailed in the street fairly easily in the larger cities; elsewhere they can be ordered by telephone. Rates are quite reasonable by American or European standards, and a tip of 15 percent or so is normal. In some provinces not all the taxis have meters, making it advisable to agree on the fare before beginning a journey.

In Toronto and Montreal the subway system provides a handy way of getting around. Subway tickets, which can be bought singly or in books, are on sale at newsagents as well as at the subway stations. If you choose to travel by bus, be sure to have the exact fare with you, as bus drivers do not carry change.

DRIVING

You will, of course, be required to have a valid driver's license. I would also strongly recommend — indeed, I have already recommended in the section on "What to Take" — that you get an international driving permit as well. In addition, you will need a non-resident's Interprovincial Motor Vehicle Liability insurance card.

The driving regulations will be familiar to anyone used to driving in the U.S. or on the Continent: you drive on the right and overtake on the left, vehicles approaching from the right have the right of way at intersections, the use of seat belts is compulsory (except in Prince Edward Island and Al-

berta), and driving under the influence of alcohol will incur stiff penalties.

The speed limit on highways is usually 100 kph (60 mph), on smaller roads 80 kph (50 mph), and in towns 80 kph down to 50 kph (30 mph). You must stop if you come upon a school bus with its red lights flashing. You may turn right at a red light (except in Quebec) if you stop first and make sure the road is clear.

Note: It is a very bad idea to commit a traffic offense in Quebec, as the fines are much harsher there than elsewhere in Canada.

There are plenty of 24-hour service stations flanking the major highways, while those in town tend to close around 9 pm (7 pm in small towns, and all day on Sundays). Gasoline (or petrol) is sold by the liter, and is available in all grades. Most stations take credit cards, and most are now self-service.

In the event of an accident, you should get to a telephone and dial the operator ("0") who can connect you with the police and emergency services. In case of a breakdown, members of automobile clubs affiliated with the Canadian Automobile Association can call the CAA toll-free at (800) 336-4357. Non-members can call the CAA at (613) 820-1400 and request towing services for which there will be a charge. For additional information contact:

The Canadian Automobile Association 1775 Courtwood Crescent, Ottawa, Ontario K2C 3J2. ((613) 226-7631.

ACCOMMODATION

There is little point in discussing Canadian guest accommodations in any great detail because they are pretty much what you would expect them to be, and you will usually get pretty much what you pay for. In any case, every provincial tourism office will be more than happy to send you a comprehensive and detailed guide to the full range of accommodations available in their particular province.

If there are any surprises to be encountered on the accommodation front, they are contained in that phrase, "full range": the range is very full indeed. Apart from an unusually varied selection of hotels and motels, there are country inns, efficency apartments, bed & breakfast places, youth hostels, YMCAs and YWCAs, "tourist homes", university and college residences, wilderness lodges, campgrounds, and farms and ranches.

To say that one is spoiled for choice is to put it mildly. Wherever you go in Canada, you will find that there are types of accommodation to appeal to every taste and to suit every budget. If luxury and comfort are your priorities, there are deluxe hotels to rank with any in the world. If convenient locations while motoring are important, you will be pleased to know that there are motels in every price range sprinkled along the nation's main roads and highways. If economy is the paramount consideration, you will be able to get rooms at a YMCA, YWCA, college, university hostel, or tourist home in all but the most remote spots — and sometimes even there. If conversation and "character" count alongside economy, there is bound to be a bed & breakfast house to fit the bill.

If you will be staying in one place for a longish period, particularly with children or in a group, you will get both privacy and savings (on food) in an efficiency apartment in one of Canada's many apartment hotels. If you will be staying in one place for a shortish period, you will get privacy and savings and funny stories later in one of Canada's many campgrounds. If rustic charm is what you're looking for, there are delightful country inns spread across the country. If you want to get into serious rusticity, there is no better way than to stay on one of the hundreds of working farms and ranches that offer accommodation as well as hearty meals and healthy activities. And if you just want to get away from it all and hunt or fish or think about the human condition, there are some wonderful lodges in remote wilderness areas where Nature starts at your front door.

If you are looking for a home away from home, you should consider a holiday home exchange with a Canadian family. I can recomend two companies arranging such exchanges:

Interhome Holidays Canada, Inc. 156 Randall Street, Oakville, Ontario L6J 1P4. ((416) 849-9888.

West World Holiday Exchange, 1707 Platt Crescent, North Vancouver, B.C. V7J 1X9. ((604) 987-3262.

If budgetary considerations are uppermost, you can get further information from:

The Canadian Hostelling Association, 1600 James Naismith Drive, 6th Floor, Suite 608, Gloucester, Ontario K1B 5N4. ((613) 748-5638.

The YMCA National Council 2160 Yonge Street, Toronto, Ontario M4S 2A1.

For YMCA and YWCA residence directories you should phone (416) 485-9557 for the YMCA and (416) 593-9886 for the YWCA.

The only way to appreciate fully the extent of the choices available to you in other types of accommodations is to contact the government tourism offices in the individual provinces. As I said, they will be more than happy to provide you with comprehensive guides to the range of accomodation on offer.

EATING OUT

It must be said that Michelin-star-spangled restaurants are few and far between in Canada. But that is not to say that you can't eat well, wonderfully well, in every part of the country. The secret — if you can call something so obvious a secret — is to concentrate on the special delicacies for which each part of the country is best known.

Thus, in the eastern half of the country, you will want to sample some of the many

cod dishes, and the seal flipper pie, which Newfoundland has made famous. In Nova Scotia, you must try the clam chowder, Digby scallops, Lunenberg sausage, and "Solomon Gundy", a pickled-herring-and-chopped-meat concoction that is much better than it sounds. In Prince Edward Island, the Malpeque oysters and the local cheeses are the star attractions. In New Brunswick, go for the broiled Atlantic salmon and the steamed fiddleheads, which are the new shoots of an edible fern unique to the province. In all of the Maritimes you should treat yourself to the glorious desserts made with

OPPOSITE: Ottawa's renowned Château Laurier. ABOVE: A leisurely lunch in Montreal.

any of the berries with which the area abounds. And in all of these provinces you will find, in my opinion, the finest lobster in the world.

Quebec, once the heart of New France, would be called New Normandy if it were named after its stomach, for its distinctive cuisine still remains based on the French peasant cooking of its early Norman (and, to a lesser extent, Breton) settlers. Not that you can't get classic—or nouvelle—French cooking in Quebec; you can, famously, in both Montreal and Quebec City. But you can get that in New York, or Los Angeles, or Mexico City, or in dozens of other cities around the world. What makes Quebec special is the way provincial Canadian food-stuffs have been used to create provincial French food. A few examples: soupe aux pois, a thick pea soup; tourtires, delicious meat pies (the meat is usually pork, but can be hare or even venison); cretons, pork pâté usually served with rye bread; cipaille, a pastry-layered game-and-potato pie; andouillette aux fines herbes, a spicy pork tripe sausage; trempette, fresh baked bread saturated with maple syrup and covered in whipped cream. Maple syrup, in fact, is a theme running through (or over) almost all of Quebecois cooking — in sauces, in desserts, in curing ham — which is hardly surprising, given that the province literally oozes with maple syrup. What is perhaps surprising is that Montreal rivals New York as a Mecca for worshippers of the great deli sandwich.

Happily, the French influence — and the maple syrup — doesn't stop running when you get to Ontario, although here the culinary emphasis shifts to the province's game birds — you must have the Haliburton pheasant—and its dazzling variety of freshwater fish from Ontario's countless lakes and rivers. There is also, in Toronto, a rapidly growing array of first-rate ethnic restaurants: Greek, Italian, Chinese, Indian, Polish, Hungarian, and even Japanese. One of my favorite sushi bars, in fact, is in the middle of Toronto.

In the western half of the country, you will want to go for the Pacific salmon, shrimp, black cod, and king crab in British Columbia. And for a change from all the wonderful seafood, you should try the lamb from Saltspring Island or the moose steaks from the Yukon. Afterwards, or any other time for that matter, you can enjoy the fresh fruit from the Okanagan Valley.

In Alberta, The Steak is the thing. Even if you are not normally a beefeater, you will be won over by Alberta's beef. Only

in Argentina have I ever tasted steaks to compare with the ones you can get here. In fact, across all the Prairie Provinces the beef is exceptional—as is the freshwater fish from the thousands of lakes and rivers carved into the prairies. In Saskatchewan and Manitoba, I would urge you to order wildfowl — especially the partridge and wild duck — and even the prosaic farm birds, which are tastier here than almost anywhere else because they eat better here. In these provinces, too, you will come across a sort of Borscht Belt, where the large Ukrainian population has left its mark on the menus in the form of spicy sausages, dumplings, and a variety of cabbage dishes.

A quick lunch in Toronto.

On the other hand, if you are just looking for a pit stop where you can refuel quickly, you will find coffee shops, diners, and fast-food places everywhere you go — many of them open 24 hours a day.

As in the U.S., Canadian restaurants generally tend to be informal and welcoming. They also tend to serve meals at earlier hours than Europeans are used to, so if you are counting on having a late lunch or dinner you would be wise to check on kitchen closing times first.

DRINKING

Canadians are funny about drinking (alcohol, I mean). I remember the first time I was ever in Canada I asked a shopkeeper where I might find the nearest liquor store. This simple question caused utter consternation, followed by endless consultations, followed by... blank. The reason, it turned out, was that liquor stores — or just ordinary grocery stores or supermarkets selling liquor — do not exist outside Quebec. To buy liquor by the bottle, except in parts of Quebec, you have to go to an official government outlet — of which there are maddeningly few, maddeningly out of the way, maddeningly closed at night and on Sundays and holidays — and there, but only there, are you allowed to conduct your thirsty transaction. Why this should be the case I cannot say. What I can say is that it interferes with one's budgeting more than with one's drinking, because even the happiest of Happy Hours is not as economical as a couple of self-catered cocktails, and a Rémy in your room is better value than any post-prandial drink in a restaurant.

Even the most convivial imbibing is complicated by local laws, which come in various shades of blue. In some places you can get a drink if you're 18, in other places you have to be 19. In some places the bars close at midnight, in other places they stay open as late as 4 am. In most places you can only buy a drink on Sundays at a restaurant or a hotel dining room, and then only if you buy a meal. In a few places you can't buy a drink — period — whatever day it is. All very strange.

Equally strange, Canadians are not great whiskey drinkers, although they make some excellent whiskies. But they are great beer drinkers, although the beer they make is at best mediocre, at worst comparable to what passes for beer south of the border. The only logical, or easily understandable, element that I have been able to detect in Canadian drinking habits is their reluctance to drink much of the wine they produce.

TIPPING

When buying something you can never be absolutely certain of getting exactly what you pay for, but when tipping you can always make certain that you pay for what you got. That said, I would never tip less than 10 percent except in extreme circumstances. Once upon a time I was given to the retributive tactic of rewarding insultingly bad service with an insultingly low tip, but I soon came to realize that all I accomplished thereby was to add an unpleasant sequel to an unsatisfactory experience. As a rule, then, I would tip more or less 15 percent — more if the service is outstanding, less if it is not so good. I would tip porters $1 a bag, chambermaids $1 a day — rounding off the total upwards in deserving cases, downwards in undeserving ones.

SHOPPING

The same rule applies with shopping as with dining: look for the local specialties. This means that in the Maritime Provinces you may want to check out the hand-knit sweaters, hunting jackets, and fishermen's gear such as oilskins. In Quebec you will be amazed to learn how many things can be made from maple syrup. In Ontario you will want to inspect the Indian basketwork. In the Prairie Provinces, especially Alberta, you will find every item of cowboy attire you could possibly want. And in British Columbia, you should look over the elaborately carved handcrafts of the West Coast Indians.

There is one caveat that should be borne in mind when shopping for Native Canadian arts and crafts. Although these items, when genuine, are among the loveliest things to buy in Canada, they are often swamped by cheap imitations. Be suspicious of any handcrafted article that strikes you as a bargain. To be certain that you are getting the real thing, either buy from a crafts guild or cooperative or from a museum shop.

Shops in Canada are generally open from 9:30 am to 6 pm, Monday to Saturday, except in the big shopping malls and the "underground cities" of Toronto and Montreal, where shops are frequently open late and sometimes even on Sundays.

If you are shopping for clothes, the following table will enable you to convert Canadian sizes to their British and European equivalents. (Canadian and American sizes are the same.)

Men's suits

Canadian	British	European
34	34	44
35	35	46
36	36	48
37	37	49½
38	38	51
39	39	52½
40	40	54
41	41	55½
42	42	57

Women's dresses and blouses

Canadian	British	European
6	8	36
8	10	38
10	12	40
12	14	42
14	16	44
16	18	46
18	20	48

Men's shoes

Canadian	British	European
7	6	39½
8	7	41
9	8	42
10	9	43
11	10	44½
12	11	46
13	12	47

Women's shoes

Canadian	British	European
4½	3	35½
5	3½	36
5½	4	36½
6	4½	37
6½	5	37½
7	5½	38
7½	6	38½
8	6½	39
8½	7	39½
9	7½	40

The following sizes are the same in Canada and Britain:

Men's shirt collars

Canadian	European
14	36
14½	37
15	38
15½	39
16	41
16½	42
17	43

Men's sweaters:

Canadian	European
SMALL	
34	87
MEDIUM	
36	91
38	97
LARGE	
40	102
42	107
EXTRA LARGE	
44	112
46	117

Men's trouser waists

Canadian	European
24	61
26	66
28	71
30	76
32	80
34	87
36	91
38	97

From lush river valleys to vast open prairies, Canada has a landscape to suit every taste.

CAMPING

Canada is a camper's paradise. There are thousands upon thousands of campgrounds throughout the country, campgrounds of every size and description. Many are in the national and provincial parks, some are municipally owned, others are privately run. Most are open from May until late September, with campsites costing from $10 to $15. Facilities usually include toilets, showers, a laundry, picnic tables, campfire sites, and power hook-ups for caravans. The fancier ones will also have a shop and a restaurant. Generally speaking, the privately run campgrounds will have more amenities and will be more expensive, while the public ones in the national and provincial p arks will be more beautifully situated.

As most campgrounds are run on a first-come, first-served basis, during the high season — July and August — it's a good idea to start looking for a site no later than mid-afternoon.

There are however, three nocturnal nuisances that can thoroughly spoil a camping holiday if you come unprepared. The first is that familiar bane, the mosquito. So bring plenty of insect repellent, as well as a tent fitted with a mosquito net. The second nuisance is the scavenging animal — often, in Canada, a bear. These creatures can be discouraged by never keeping food in or near the tent (unless it's in the car), and by always disposing of uneaten food and washing up immediately after meals. No leftovers, no problems. Thirdly, the temperature at night can suddenly drop, leaving you shivering unless you have brought enough warm clothing.

For lists of campgrounds write to the national tourism office or the provincial offices in the provinces you plan to visit. There is also a very informative publication, National Parks, available free from the Canadian Parks Service, Ottawa, Ontario K1A 0H3. ℂ (819) 997-2800.

HUNTING

It's small wonder that great herds of hunters migrate to Canada every year, usually in the autumn: one of Canada's richest natural re-

sources is its superabundance of game. There is big game on the ground — moose, elk caribou, deer, bear — and there is small game in the air — partridge, ducks, and geese.

Each province has its own rules and regulations concerning hunting, in addition to which there are a few federal laws. For example, all guns and ammunition must be declared at Customs, while an export license is required if you want to take skins or hunting trophies out of the country. Hunting is strictly forbidden in the national parks, and foreigners are only permitted to hunt in the forests if accompanied by an official guide. No buffalo, polar bear, mink, or beaver may be hunted, and there are restrictions on the hunting of certain migratory birds. For the specific regulations of each province, as well as license applications, write to the provincial tourist information office or to the Ministry of Natural Resources, Wildlife Branch, Queen's Park, Toronto, Ontario M7A 1W3.

FISHING

The situation regarding fishing in Canada almost exactly mirrors that regarding hunting: there is a superabundance of fish to be caught, and the laws regulating the catching of them vary from province to province. In the Maritimes there is the Atlantic salmon and, offshore, bluefin tuna, cod, mackerel, and halibut. In British Columbia there is the Pacific salmon and, offshore, sea bass. In between there is pike, perch, grayling, whitefish, goldeye, muskie, bass, and every kind of trout known to man.

All non-resident anglers must have a fishing permit, which is available from any tourist office in the province where you intend to fish, as well as from local sporting goods stores and marinas. A separate license is required for fishing in national parks, which is valid for all parks and is available from any park office or from Parks Canada, Ottawa, Ontario K1A 1G2.

SKIING

Not for nothing is Canada referred to colloquially as the "Great White North." It has snow the way Brazil has coffee. Where the snow lies flat, you get wonderful cross-country skiing. Where it lies at an angle, you get wonderful downhill skiing. And where it doesn't lie at all, or not enough of it, there is snowmaking equipment to compensate for Nature's oversight. Wonderful skiing is not hard to find in Canada.

What is perhaps surprising, given the country's size and topography, is that you rarely have to go very far to find good skiing. Even in Newfoundland and the Maritimes, even in Manitoba and Saskatchewan, there are some decent ski runs. And in Ontario there are excellent ski areas near both Toronto and Ottawa. But it is in Quebec and the Rockies that you find ski slopes of a variety and grandeur unsurpassed anywhere in the world. It is no accident that there are over 130 ski areas in Quebec's Laurentian Mountains alone, nor was it a fluke that the 1988 Winter Olympics were held in the mountains outside of Calgary.

If you like skiing, and you plan to go to Canada between November and March, prepare to be made very happy.

PUBLIC HOLIDAYS AND FESTIVALS

NATIONAL HOLIDAYS

NEW YEAR'S DAY: January 1
GOOD FRIDAY
EASTER MONDAY
VICTORIA DAY: Monday nearest May 24
CANADA DAY: July 1
LABOR DAY: First Monday in September
THANKSGIVING DAY: Second Monday in October
REMEMBRANCE DAY: November 11
CHRISTMAS DAY: December 25
BOXING DAY: December 26

PROVINCIAL HOLIDAYS

Epiphany (Quebec): January 6
Ash Wednesday (Quebec): First Wednesday in Lent
St. Patrick's Day (Newfoundland): Monday nearest March 17

St. George's Day (Newfoundland): Monday nearest April 23
Ascension Day (Quebec): Fortieth day after Easter
St. Jean Baptiste Day (Quebec): June 24
Discovery Day (Newfoundland): Monday nearest June 24
Memorial Day (Newfoundland): Monday nearest July 1
Orangeman's Day (Newfoundland): Monday nearest July 12
Civic Holiday (almost everywhere except Quebec): First Monday in August
All Saints Day (Quebec): November 1

FESTIVALS

JANUARY
New Year's Day Polar Bear Swim in Vancouver
Montreal Winter Festival
Toronto International Boat Show
Ice Canoe Race in Toronto

FEBRUARY
Quebec City Winter Carnival
North York (Ontario) Winter Carnival
Vernon (British Columbia) Winter Carnival
Winterlude in Ottawa
Chinese New Year in Vancouver
Toronto International Auto Show

MARCH
Outdoors Show in Montreal
Springtime Craft Show and Sale in Toronto
"Sugaring Off" parties in Eastern Townships (Quebec)

APRIL
National Home Show in Toronto
International Book Fair in Quebec City
Stratford Shakespeare Festival season opens

MAY
Blossom Festival in Niagara Falls
International Mime Festival in Montreal
Festival of Spring in Ottawa
Scotia Festival of Music in Halifax
International Theatre Fortnight in Quebec City
Banff Arts Festival season opens
Shaw Festival season opens in Niagara-on-the-Lake

JUNE

Charlottetown Summer Festival season opens

Molson Grand Prix in Montreal

Midnight Sun Golf Tournament in Yellowknife (Northwest Territories)

All That Jazz Festival in Toronto

Nova Scotia Tattoo in Halifax

Montreal International Jazz Festival

JULY

Quebec International Summer Festival in Quebec City

Just For Laughs Festival in Montreal

Loyalist Days in Saint John (New Brunswick)

Molson Indy auto race in Toronto

The Calgary Stampede

Klondike Days in Edmonton

Nova Scotia International Tattoo in Halifax

Shediac (New Brunswick**) Lobster Festival**

Antigonish (Nova Scotia) **Highland Games**

Caribana, Caribbean music festival in Toronto

National Ukrainian Festival in Dauphin (Manitoba)

AUGUST

Montreal International Film Festival

Gaelic Mod — Scottish Highlands Festival in St. Ann's (Nova Scotia)

Festival By the Sea in St. John (New Brunswick)

Canadian National Exhibition in Toronto

The Americas Cycling Grand Prix in Montreal

Old Home Week in Charlottetown (Prince Edward Island)

Folklorama in Winnipeg

Buffalo Days in Regina

Tyne Valley (Prince Edward Island) **Oyster Festival**

Player's International Tennis Championships in Montreal and Toronto

Expo-Quebec in Quebec City

Acadian Festival in Caraquet (New Brunswick)

Quidi Vidi Lake Regatta in St. John's (Newfoundland)

Canadian Open golf championship in Toronto

SEPTEMBER

Festival of Festivals in Toronto

Niagara Grape and Wine Festival in St. Catharines (Ontario)

The Montreal Marathon

The Molson Export Challenge horse race in Toronto

Montreal International Music Festival

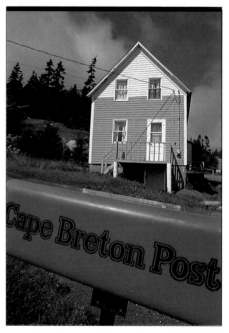

OCTOBER

Oktoberfest in Kitchener (Ontario)

NOVEMBER

Royal Agriculture Winter Fair in Toronto

DECEMBER

Quebec Crafts Show in Quebec City

Christmas Ice Bridge at Niagara Falls

MAIL

Although main post offices in Canada may open as early as 8 am and close as late as 6 pm on weekdays, and some are open on Saturday mornings, you can avoid disap-

From the Atlantic to the Pacific: a house on Cape Breton Island and a telephone booth in Vancouver's Chinatown.

pointment by going between 9 am and 5 pm, Monday-Friday. In fact, you can avoid post offices altogether for most purposes, as stamps can be bought at hotels and vending machines in airports, railway stations, shopping centers, drugstores and many small shops. Letters and postcards can be mailed at most hotels' front desks or at any red mailbox.

If sending mail to a Canadian address, it will speed things up considerably if you use the (admittedly complicated) zip code. Also, I am told by the postal authorities that every

year there are some Americans who think it is just as good to use American stamps as Canadian ones. It's not.

If you want to receive mail in Canada but are unsure of your exact whereabouts at a given time, you can have mail sent to you c/o "General Delivery" at the mail post office in the town or city where you wish to pick it up. But remember that it must be picked up within 15 days or it will be returned to sender. Alternatively, if you have an American Express card, or traveler's checks from American Express or Thomas Cook, you can have mail sent to you at any office of either company. It should be marked "Client Mail," and it will be held for you for as long as a month.

Telegrams are handled by CNCP Telecommunications, while most good hotels now have telex and/or fax facilities available for guests' use.

TELEPHONES

The Canadian telephone system is completely integrated with that of the United States, which means that it is splendidly efficient and economical, and that no international codes are necessary for calls between the U.S. and Canada. As in the U.S., for information on local telephone numbers dial 411; for information on long-distance numbers dial 1-555-1212. For calls requiring operator assistance — such as long-distance personal or collect calls, or for emergency calls — dial 0.

To place a long-distance call within the same area code, dial 1 + the number you are calling. To place a call outside your area code, dial 1 + area code + telephone number. For direct dialing of overseas calls, dial 011 + country code + city code + telephone number.

Calls placed in the evening or on the weekend are less expensive, although any call from a hotel will incur a (usually steep) surcharge. There are public telephones just about everywhere, but they only accept Canadian quarters.

RADIO AND TELEVISION

I am tempted to say that if you are in Canada you shouldn't be indoors, and leave it at that. I am further tempted to say that if you do find yourself indoors in North America, you definitely shouldn't be watching television. You know the reasons; you've probably seen a number of them already, wherever you live. Even so, it's difficult to convey the feeling of dull despair that comes over you when you contemplate a galaxy of up to 40 television channels — not one of which is shining brightly enough to engage your attention for more than a few minutes.

If it's any consolation, though, you are better off watching television in Canada then in the U.S., simply because you have a choice of programs in addition to the American ones (which nonetheless predominate even in areas beyond the reach of American stations). And its precarious finances notwithstanding, the CBC (Canadian Broadcasting Corporation) manages to produce some worthy programming of its own, while the French-language channels serve up the occasional treat. But don't be surprised when you switch channels to escape Teenage Mutant Ninja Turtles only to be confronted with Popeye et son fils.

For rabid sports fans — and that includes the author of these lines — there is one exceedingly bright spot in Canadian TV programming. What's more, it appears at a time in the week when you might reasonably be expected to be otherwise unoccupied. At 9:30 am Eastern Standard Time on Saturday mornings from September until May the cable Sports Network televises live an English First Division soccer match. A good way to start the weekend.

The Canadian radio dial, like the American, features end-to-end music — classical, pop, rock, country, jazz — interspersed with talk-shows, phone-ins, and news.

NEWSPAPERS AND MAGAZINES

Canadian journalism, too, closely resembles its American counterpart. With the exception of the Globe and Mail, which is published in Toronto, the newspapers are all local papers. Certainly, some big-city papers such as the Toronto Star are national, even international, in stature, but their main emphasis remains on coverage of their own communities. This enlightened parochialism benefits the visitor not only by providing a useful introduction to topics of local interest, but also by providing through its listings and advertisements a comprehensive guide to local events and entertainments. As a matter of fact, many of the places to go and things to do that I have recommended in this book were originally suggested to me by articles or reviews I came upon in the local press. So don't neglect this valuable resource whenever you arrive in a new place.

All of the larger news agents in Canada have shelves that are identical to the ones you would expect to find in comparable shops in the U.S. — except that in addition to all the American newspapers and magazines you get the Canadian ones as well. I wish I could say that in my frequent browsings among these shelves I discovered a Canadian periodical of compelling interest. But I didn't. You can't have everything.

Recommended Reading

BROOK, STEPHEN. Maple Leaf Rag. Pan Books, London 1989.

HARDY, ANNE. Where To Eat In Canada. Oberon Press, Ottawa 1990.

MACKAY, CLAIRE. The Toronto Story. Annick Press, Toronto 1990.

MacKAY, DONALD. Flight from Famine: The Coming of the Irish to Canada. McClelland & Stewart, Toronto 1990.

MACLENNAN, HUGH. Papers. University of Calgary Press, Calgary 1986.

MALCOLM, ANDREW H. The Canadians. Times Books, New York 1985.

MCNAUGHT, KENNETH. The Penguin History of Canada. Penguin Books, London 1988.

MORTON, DESMOND. A Peculiar Kind of Politics. University of Toronto Press, Toronto 1982.

MORTON, WILLIAM L. The Canadian Identity. University of Wisconsin Press, Madison 1973.

PATTERSON, FREEMAN. The Last Wilderness: Images of the Canadian Wild. Canadian Geographic Society, Vanier, Ontario 1991.

MUISE, D.A., ed. Reader's Guide to Canadian History, Vol. I. University of Toronto Press, Toronto 1982. Vol. II ed. GRANATSTEIN, À.L. & STEVENS, P. University of Toronto Press, Toronto 1982.

RICHLER, MODECAI. The Apprenticeship of Duddy Kravitz. Penguin Books, London 1991. Broadsides. Vintage Books, London 1991. Papers. University of Calgary Press, Calgary 1987.

WALLACE, DONALD C. & FLETCHER, FREDERICK À. Canadian Politics through Press Reports. Oxford University Press, Toronto 1985.

Quick Reference A–Z Guide to Places and Topics of Interest with Listed Accommodation, Restaurants and Useful Telephone Numbers

W

Y